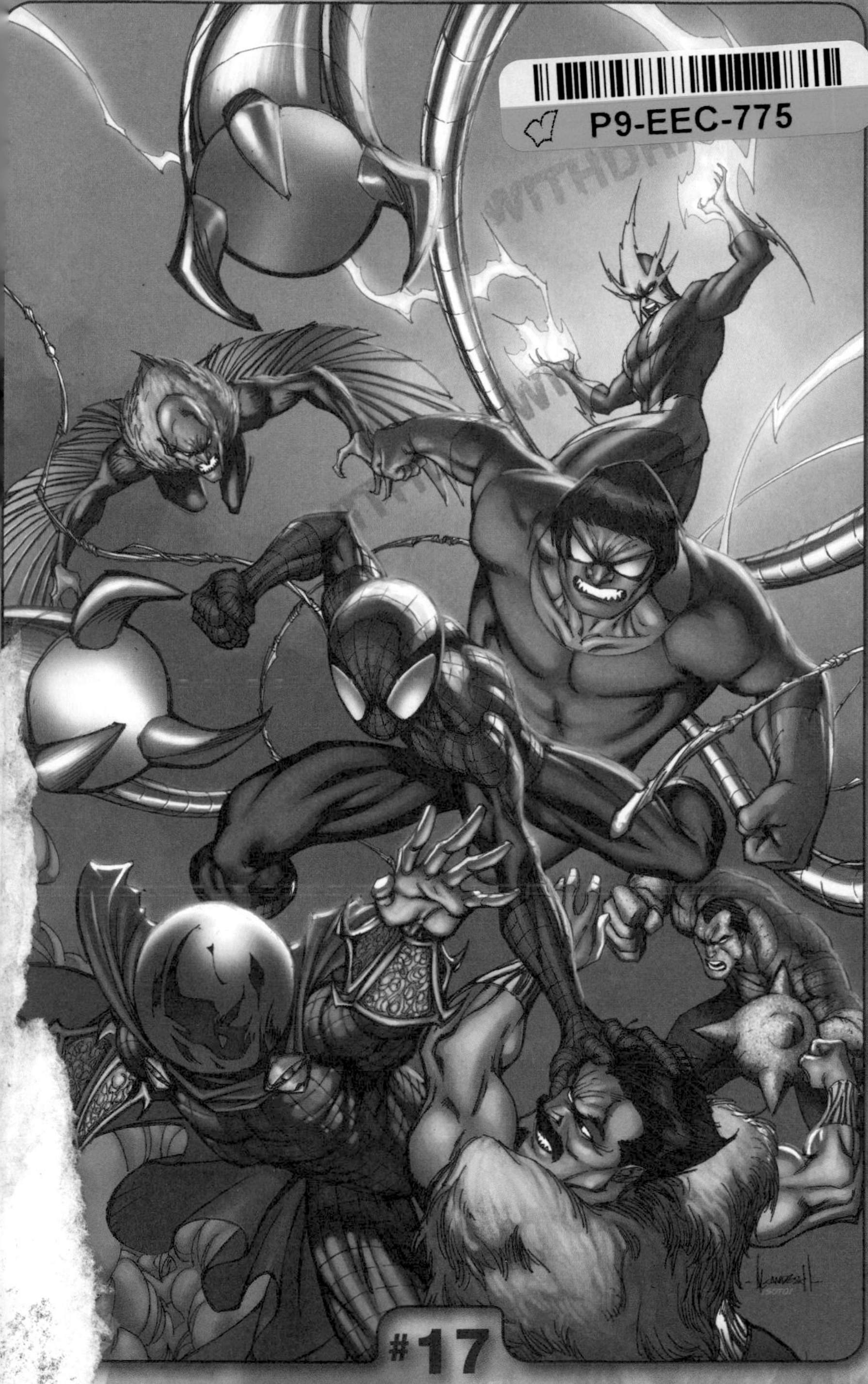
#17

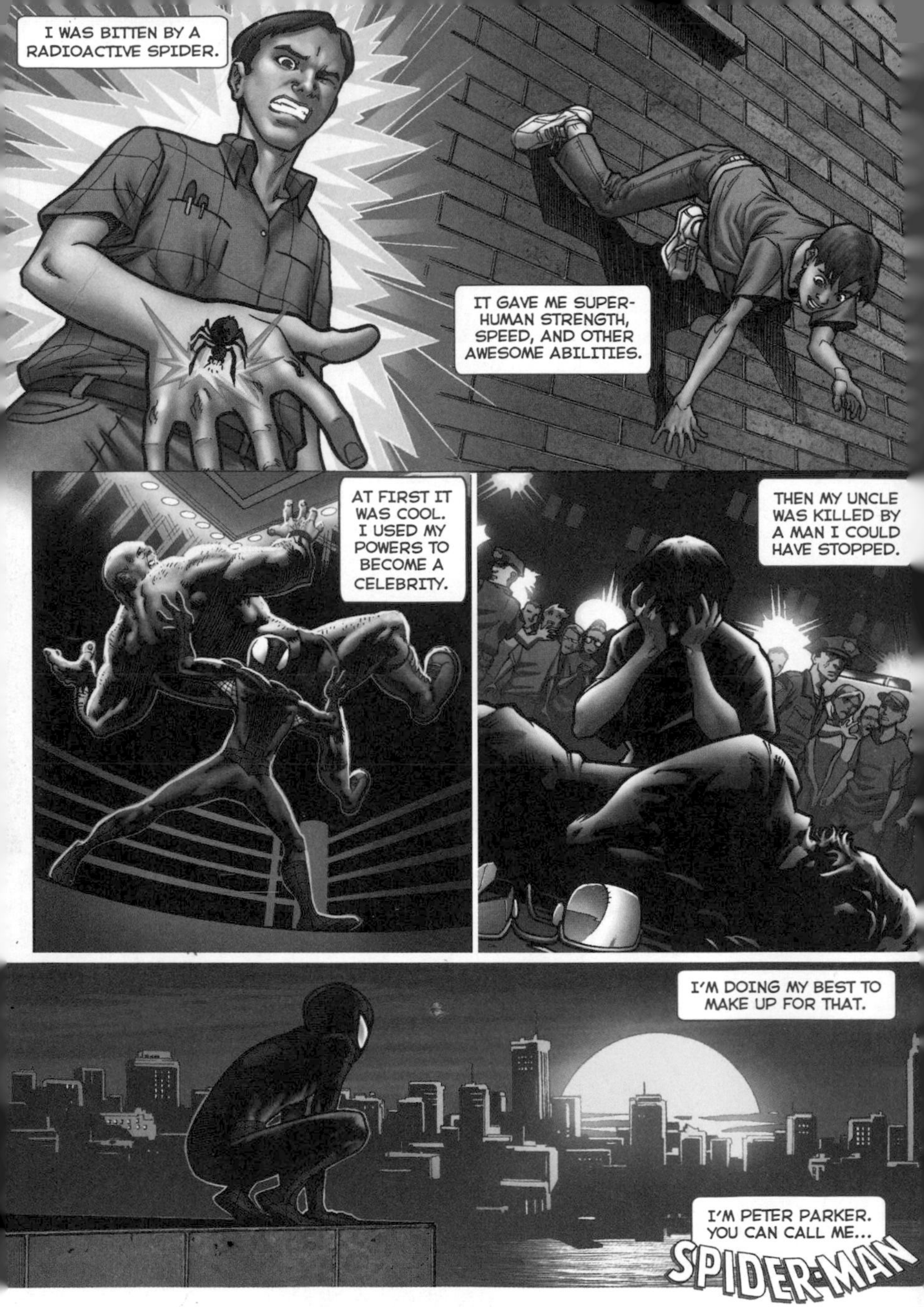
I WAS BITTEN BY A RADIOACTIVE SPIDER.
IT GAVE ME SUPER-HUMAN STRENGTH, SPEED, AND OTHER AWESOME ABILITIES.
AT FIRST IT WAS COOL. I USED MY POWERS TO BECOME A CELEBRITY.
THEN MY UNCLE WAS KILLED BY A MAN I COULD HAVE STOPPED.
I'M DOING MY BEST TO MAKE UP FOR THAT.
I'M PETER PARKER. YOU CAN CALL ME...
SPIDER-MAN

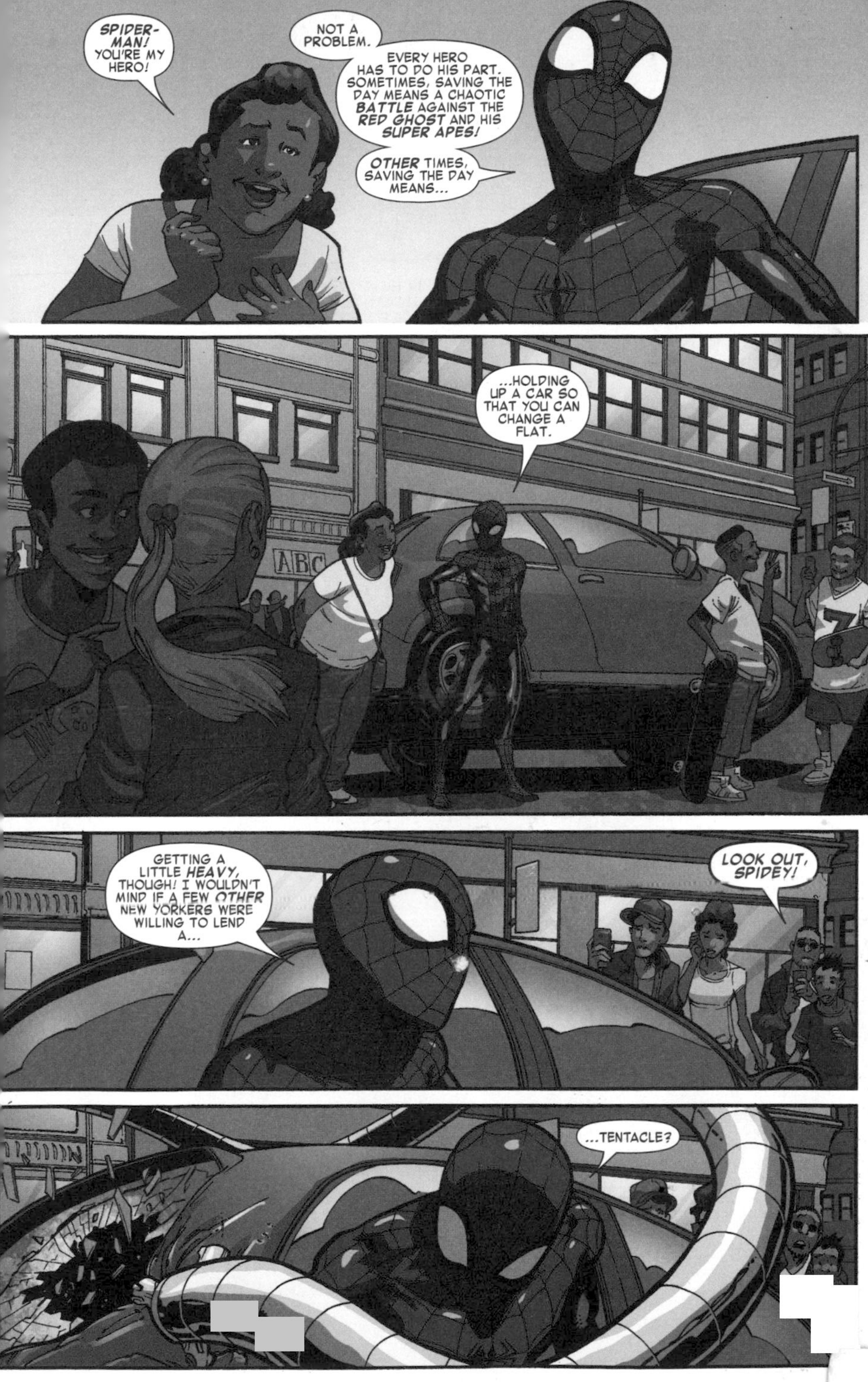
SPIDER-MAN! YOU'RE MY HERO!
NOT A PROBLEM.
EVERY HERO HAS TO DO HIS PART. SOMETIMES, SAVING THE DAY MEANS A CHAOTIC BATTLE AGAINST THE RED GHOST AND HIS SUPER APES!
OTHER TIMES, SAVING THE DAY MEANS...
...HOLDING UP A CAR SO THAT YOU CAN CHANGE A FLAT.
ABC
GETTING A LITTLE HEAVY, THOUGH! I WOULDN'T MIND IF A FEW OTHER NEW YORKERS WERE WILLING TO LEND A...
LOOK OUT, SPIDEY!
...TENTACLE?

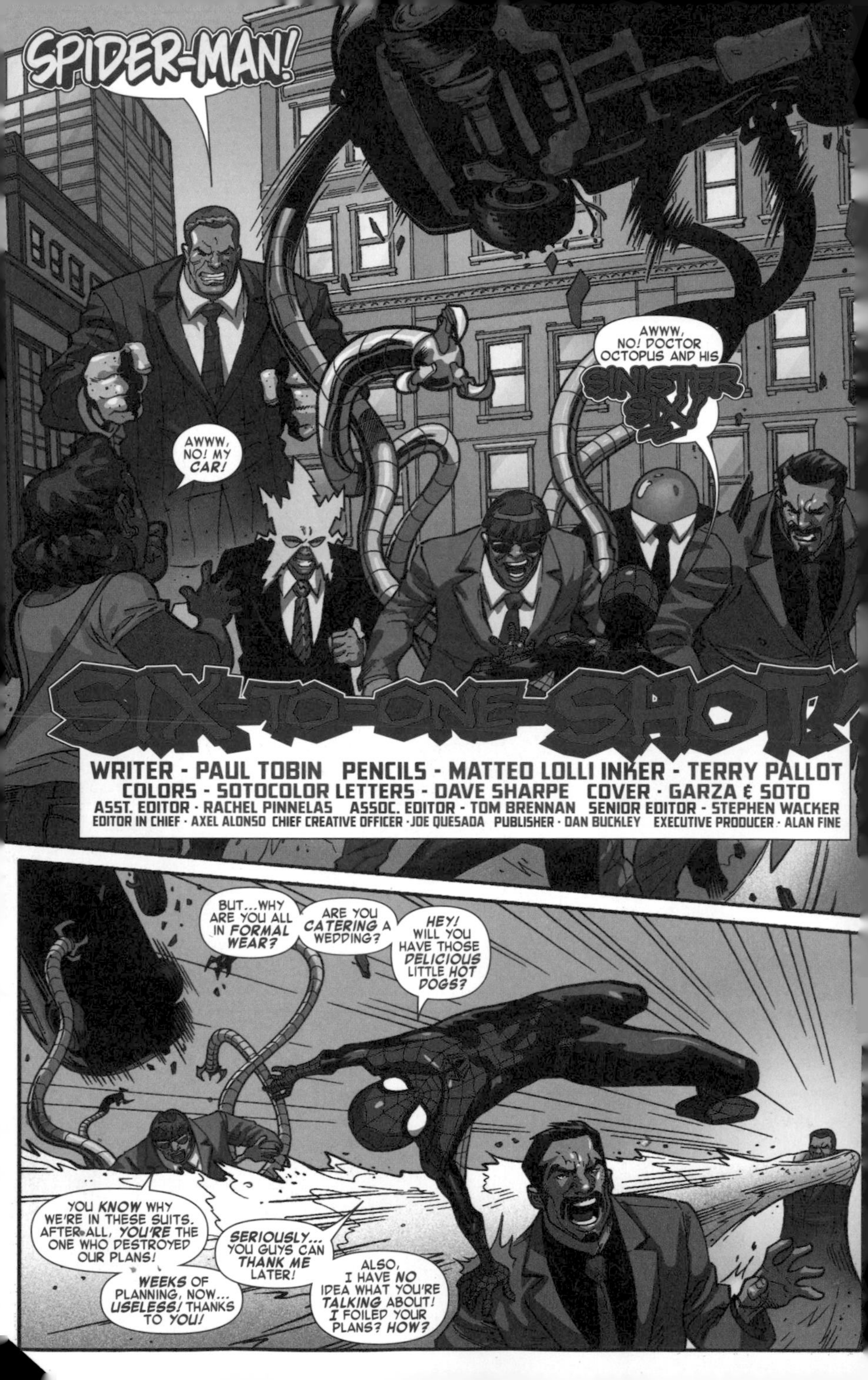
SPIDER-MAN!
AWWW, NO! MY CAR!
AWWW, NO! DOCTOR OCTOPUS AND HIS SINISTER SIX!
SIX-TO-ONE-SHOT
WRITER - PAUL TOBIN PENCILS - MATTEO LOLLI INKER - TERRY PALLOT
COLORS - SOTOCOLOR LETTERS - DAVE SHARPE COVER - GARZA & SOTO
ASST. EDITOR - RACHEL PINNELAS ASSOC. EDITOR - TOM BRENNAN SENIOR EDITOR - STEPHEN WACKER
EDITOR IN CHIEF - AXEL ALONSO CHIEF CREATIVE OFFICER - JOE QUESADA PUBLISHER - DAN BUCKLEY EXECUTIVE PRODUCER - ALAN FINE
BUT...WHY ARE YOU ALL IN FORMAL WEAR?
ARE YOU CATERING A WEDDING?
HEY! WILL YOU HAVE THOSE DELICIOUS LITTLE HOT DOGS?
YOU KNOW WHY WE'RE IN THESE SUITS. AFTER ALL, YOU'RE THE ONE WHO DESTROYED OUR PLANS!
WEEKS OF PLANNING, NOW... USELESS! THANKS TO YOU!
SERIOUSLY... YOU GUYS CAN THANK ME LATER!
ALSO, I HAVE NO IDEA WHAT YOU'RE TALKING ABOUT! I FOILED YOUR PLANS? HOW?

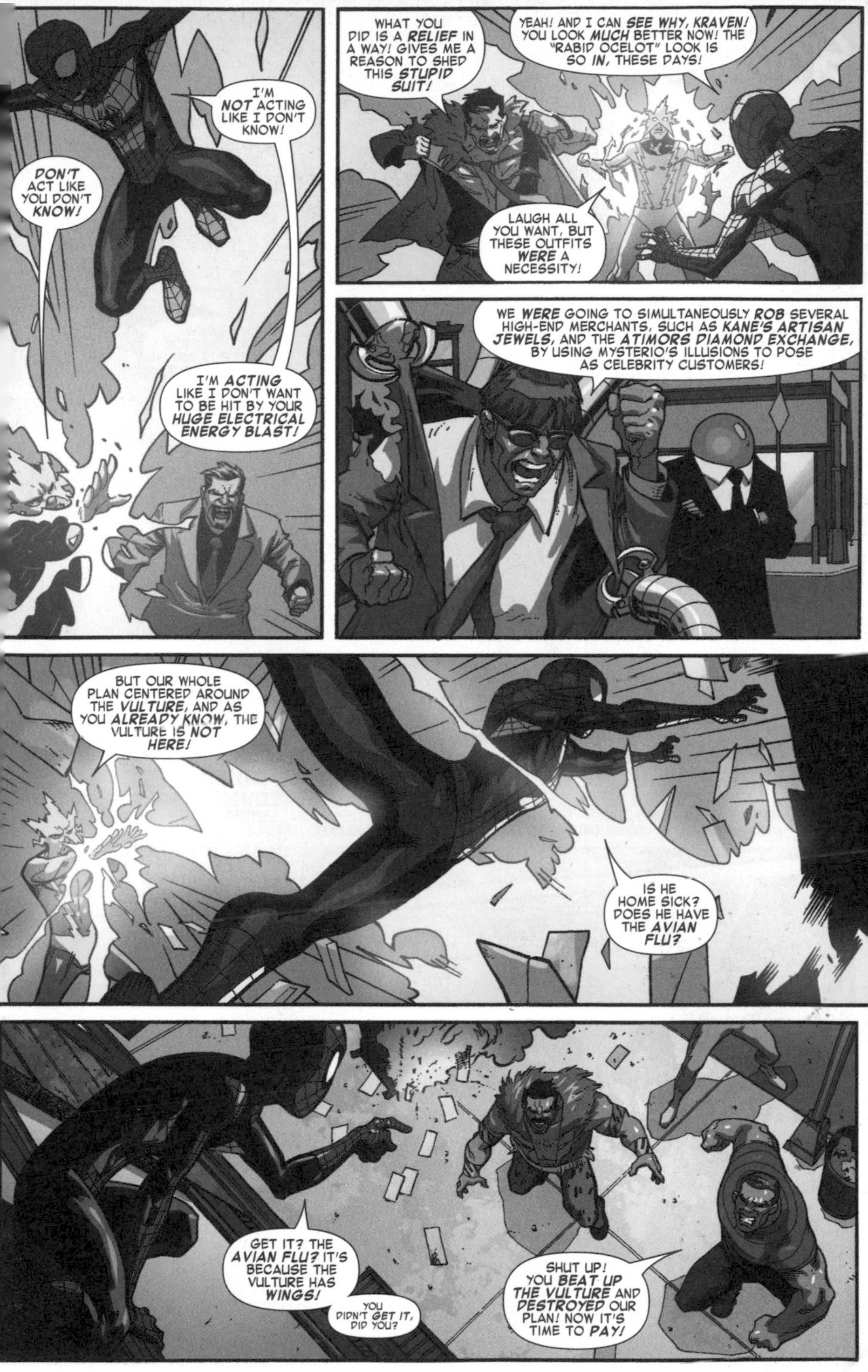
DON'T ACT LIKE YOU DON'T KNOW!
I'M NOT ACTING LIKE I DON'T KNOW!
I'M ACTING LIKE I DON'T WANT TO BE HIT BY YOUR HUGE ELECTRICAL ENERGY BLAST!
WHAT YOU DID IS A RELIEF IN A WAY! GIVES ME A REASON TO SHED THIS STUPID SUIT!
YEAH! AND I CAN SEE WHY, KRAVEN! YOU LOOK MUCH BETTER NOW! THE "RABID OCELOT" LOOK IS SO IN, THESE DAYS!
LAUGH ALL YOU WANT, BUT THESE OUTFITS WERE A NECESSITY!
WE WERE GOING TO SIMULTANEOUSLY ROB SEVERAL HIGH-END MERCHANTS, SUCH AS KANE'S ARTISAN JEWELS, AND THE ATIMORS DIAMOND EXCHANGE, BY USING MYSTERIO'S ILLUSIONS TO POSE AS CELEBRITY CUSTOMERS!
BUT OUR WHOLE PLAN CENTERED AROUND THE VULTURE, AND AS YOU ALREADY KNOW, THE VULTURE IS NOT HERE!
IS HE HOME SICK? DOES HE HAVE THE AVIAN FLU?
GET IT? THE AVIAN FLU? IT'S BECAUSE THE VULTURE HAS WINGS!
YOU DIDN'T GET IT, DID YOU?
SHUT UP! YOU BEAT UP THE VULTURE AND DESTROYED OUR PLAN! NOW IT'S TIME TO PAY!

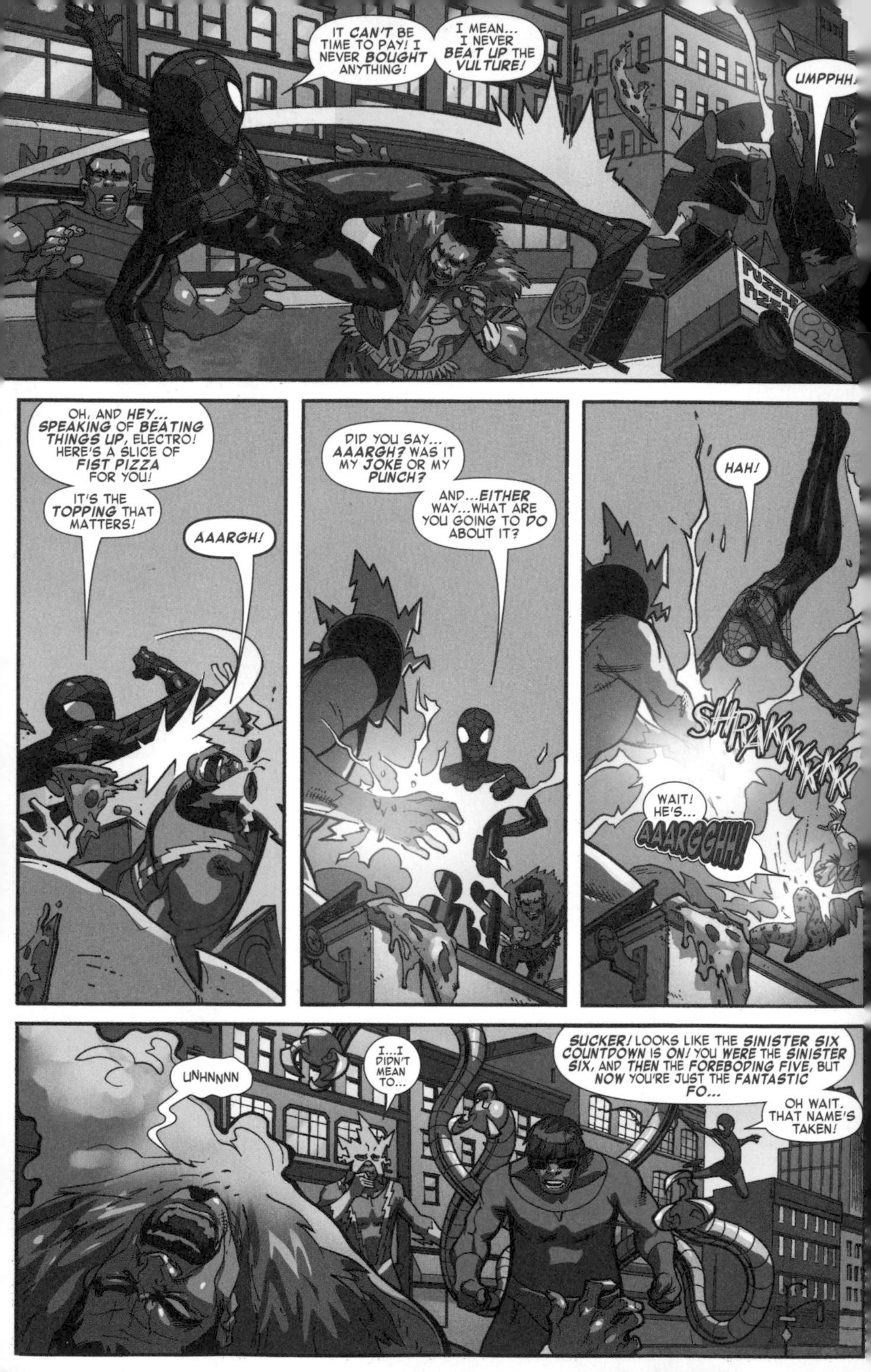

IT CAN'T BE TIME TO PAY! I NEVER BOUGHT ANYTHING!
I MEAN... I NEVER BEAT UP THE VULTURE!
UMPPHH!
PUZZLE PIZZA
OH, AND HEY... SPEAKING OF BEATING THINGS UP, ELECTRO! HERE'S A SLICE OF FIST PIZZA FOR YOU!
IT'S THE TOPPING THAT MATTERS!
AAARGH!
DID YOU SAY... AAARGH? WAS IT MY JOKE OR MY PUNCH?
AND...EITHER WAY...WHAT ARE YOU GOING TO DO ABOUT IT?
HAH!
SHRAKKKKKK
WAIT! HE'S...
AAARGGHH!
UNHNNNN
I...I DIDN'T MEAN TO...
SUCKER! LOOKS LIKE THE SINISTER SIX COUNTDOWN IS ON! YOU WERE THE SINISTER SIX, AND THEN THE FOREBODING FIVE, BUT NOW YOU'RE JUST THE FANTASTIC FO...
OH WAIT. THAT NAME'S TAKEN!

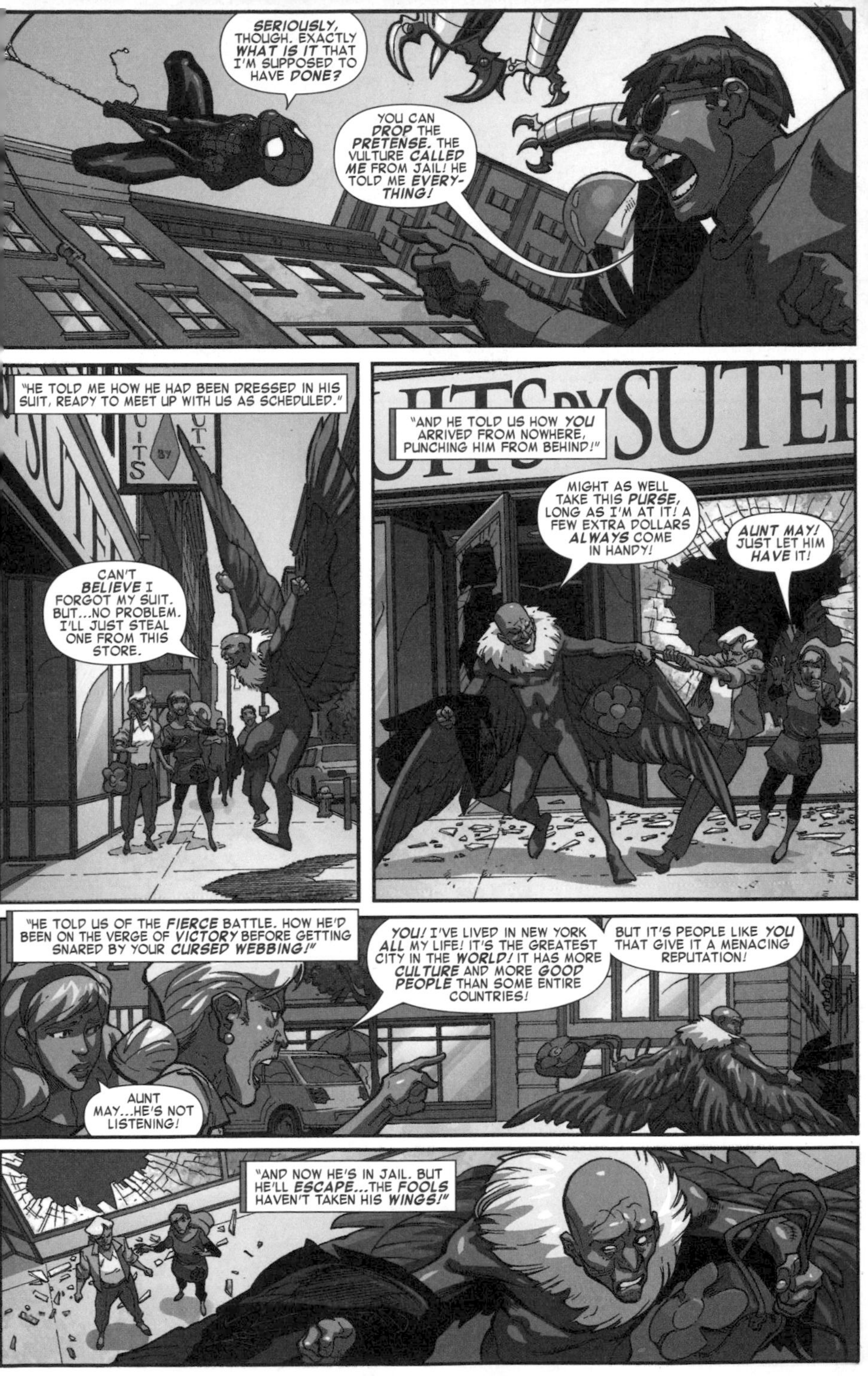

SERIOUSLY, THOUGH. EXACTLY WHAT IS IT THAT I'M SUPPOSED TO HAVE DONE?
YOU CAN DROP THE PRETENSE. THE VULTURE CALLED ME FROM JAIL! HE TOLD ME EVERYTHING!
"HE TOLD ME HOW HE HAD BEEN DRESSED IN HIS SUIT, READY TO MEET UP WITH US AS SCHEDULED."
CAN'T BELIEVE I FORGOT MY SUIT. BUT...NO PROBLEM. I'LL JUST STEAL ONE FROM THIS STORE.
"AND HE TOLD US HOW YOU ARRIVED FROM NOWHERE, PUNCHING HIM FROM BEHIND!"
MIGHT AS WELL TAKE THIS PURSE, LONG AS I'M AT IT! A FEW EXTRA DOLLARS ALWAYS COME IN HANDY!
AUNT MAY! JUST LET HIM HAVE IT!
"HE TOLD US OF THE FIERCE BATTLE. HOW HE'D BEEN ON THE VERGE OF VICTORY BEFORE GETTING SNARED BY YOUR CURSED WEBBING!"
YOU! I'VE LIVED IN NEW YORK ALL MY LIFE! IT'S THE GREATEST CITY IN THE WORLD! IT HAS MORE CULTURE AND MORE GOOD PEOPLE THAN SOME ENTIRE COUNTRIES!
BUT IT'S PEOPLE LIKE YOU THAT GIVE IT A MENACING REPUTATION!
AUNT MAY...HE'S NOT LISTENING!
"AND NOW HE'S IN JAIL. BUT HE'LL ESCAPE...THE FOOLS HAVEN'T TAKEN HIS WINGS!"

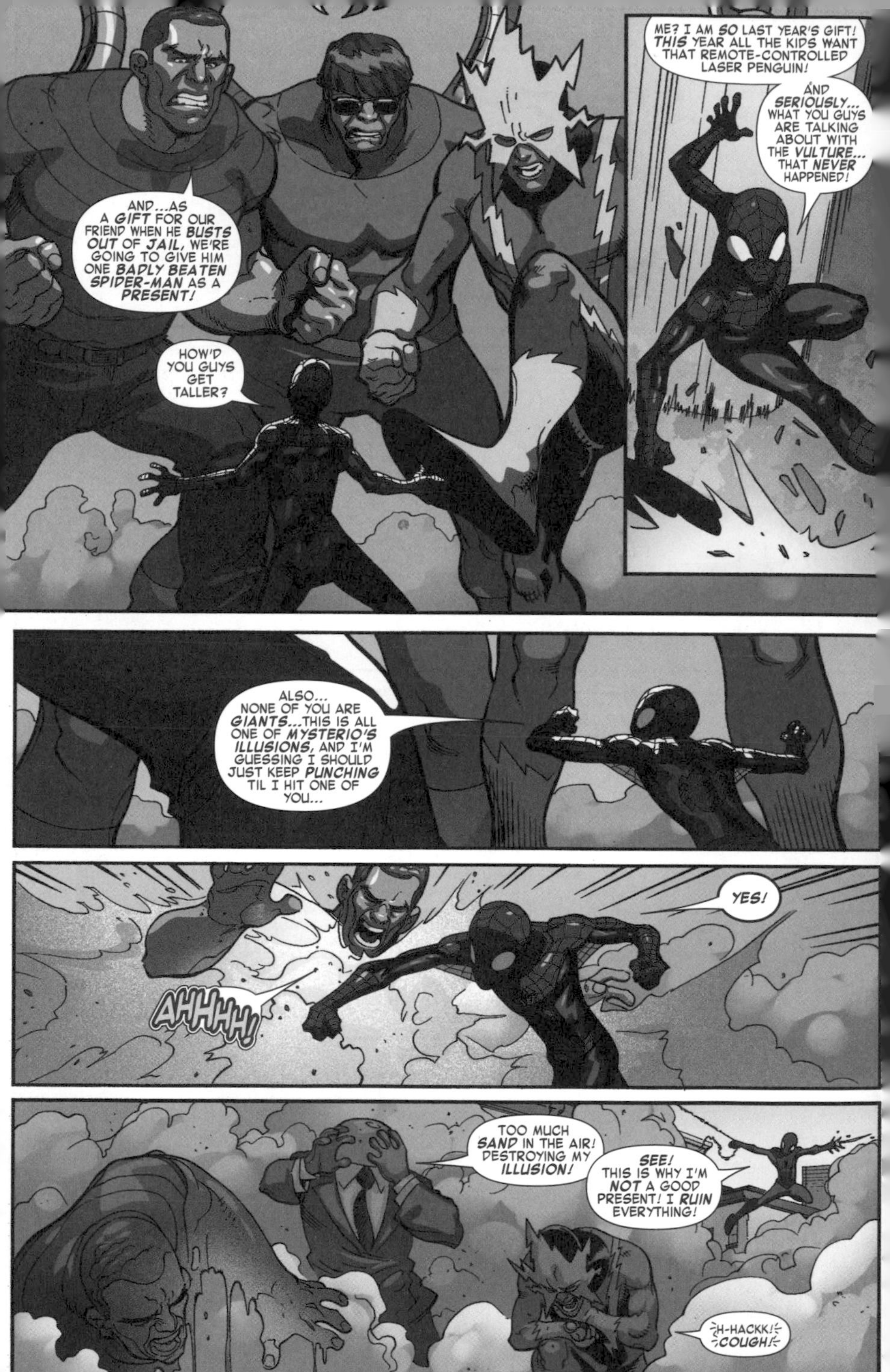
AND...AS A GIFT FOR OUR FRIEND WHEN HE BUSTS OUT OF JAIL, WE'RE GOING TO GIVE HIM ONE BADLY BEATEN SPIDER-MAN AS A PRESENT!
HOW'D YOU GUYS GET TALLER?
ME? I AM SO LAST YEAR'S GIFT! THIS YEAR ALL THE KIDS WANT THAT REMOTE-CONTROLLED LASER PENGUIN!
AND SERIOUSLY... WHAT YOU GUYS ARE TALKING ABOUT WITH THE VULTURE... THAT NEVER HAPPENED!
ALSO... NONE OF YOU ARE GIANTS...THIS IS ALL ONE OF MYSTERIO'S ILLUSIONS, AND I'M GUESSING I SHOULD JUST KEEP PUNCHING TIL I HIT ONE OF YOU...
YES!
AHHHH!
TOO MUCH SAND IN THE AIR! DESTROYING MY ILLUSION!
SEE! THIS IS WHY I'M NOT A GOOD PRESENT! I RUIN EVERYTHING!
H-HACKK! COUGH!

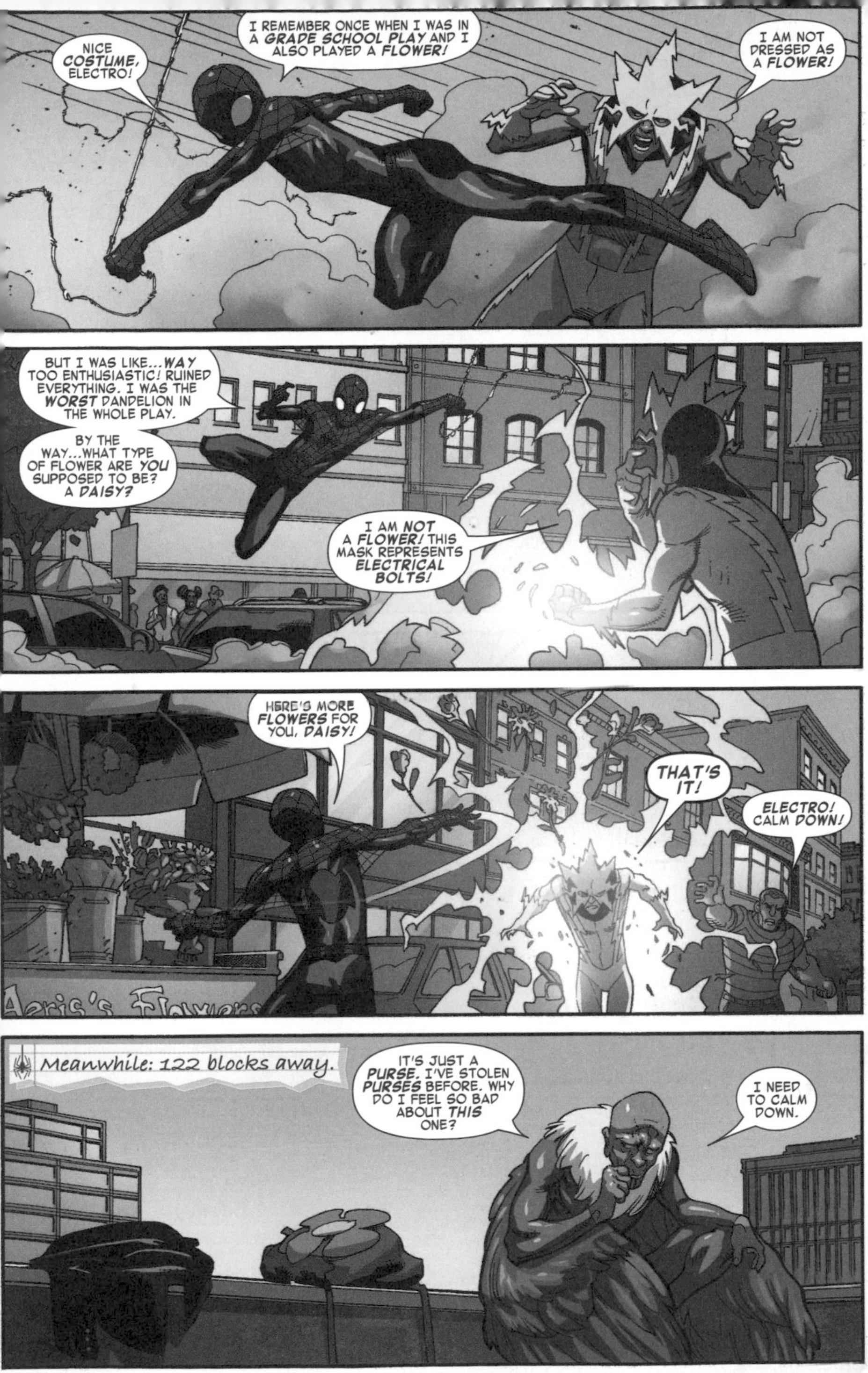
NICE COSTUME, ELECTRO!
I REMEMBER ONCE WHEN I WAS IN A GRADE SCHOOL PLAY AND I ALSO PLAYED A FLOWER!
I AM NOT DRESSED AS A FLOWER!
BUT I WAS LIKE... WAY TOO ENTHUSIASTIC! RUINED EVERYTHING. I WAS THE WORST DANDELION IN THE WHOLE PLAY.
BY THE WAY... WHAT TYPE OF FLOWER ARE YOU SUPPOSED TO BE? A DAISY?
I AM NOT A FLOWER! THIS MASK REPRESENTS ELECTRICAL BOLTS!
HERE'S MORE FLOWERS FOR YOU, DAISY!
THAT'S IT!
ELECTRO! CALM DOWN!
Aeris's Flowers
Meanwhile: 122 blocks away.
IT'S JUST A PURSE. I'VE STOLEN PURSES BEFORE. WHY DO I FEEL SO BAD ABOUT THIS ONE?
I NEED TO CALM DOWN.

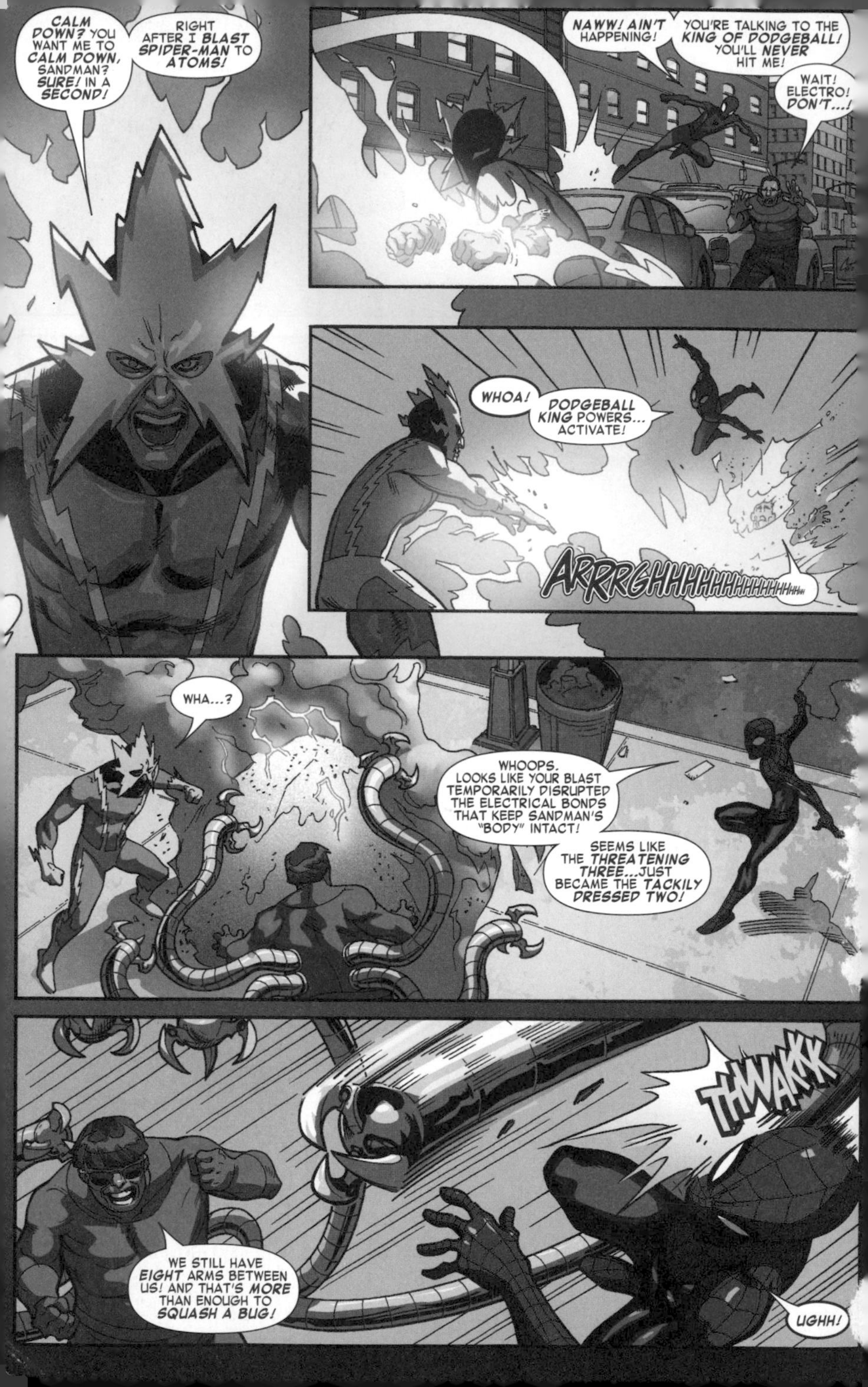
CALM DOWN? YOU WANT ME TO CALM DOWN, SANDMAN? SURE! IN A SECOND!
RIGHT AFTER I BLAST SPIDER-MAN TO ATOMS!
NAWW! AIN'T HAPPENING!
YOU'RE TALKING TO THE KING OF DODGEBALL! YOU'LL NEVER HIT ME!
WAIT! ELECTRO! DON'T...!
WHOA!
DODGEBALL KING POWERS... ACTIVATE!
ARRRGHHHHHHHHHHHHHHH
WHA...?
WHOOPS. LOOKS LIKE YOUR BLAST TEMPORARILY DISRUPTED THE ELECTRICAL BONDS THAT KEEP SANDMAN'S "BODY" INTACT!
SEEMS LIKE THE THREATENING THREE...JUST BECAME THE TACKILY DRESSED TWO!
THWAKKK
WE STILL HAVE EIGHT ARMS BETWEEN US! AND THAT'S MORE THAN ENOUGH TO SQUASH A BUG!
UGHH!

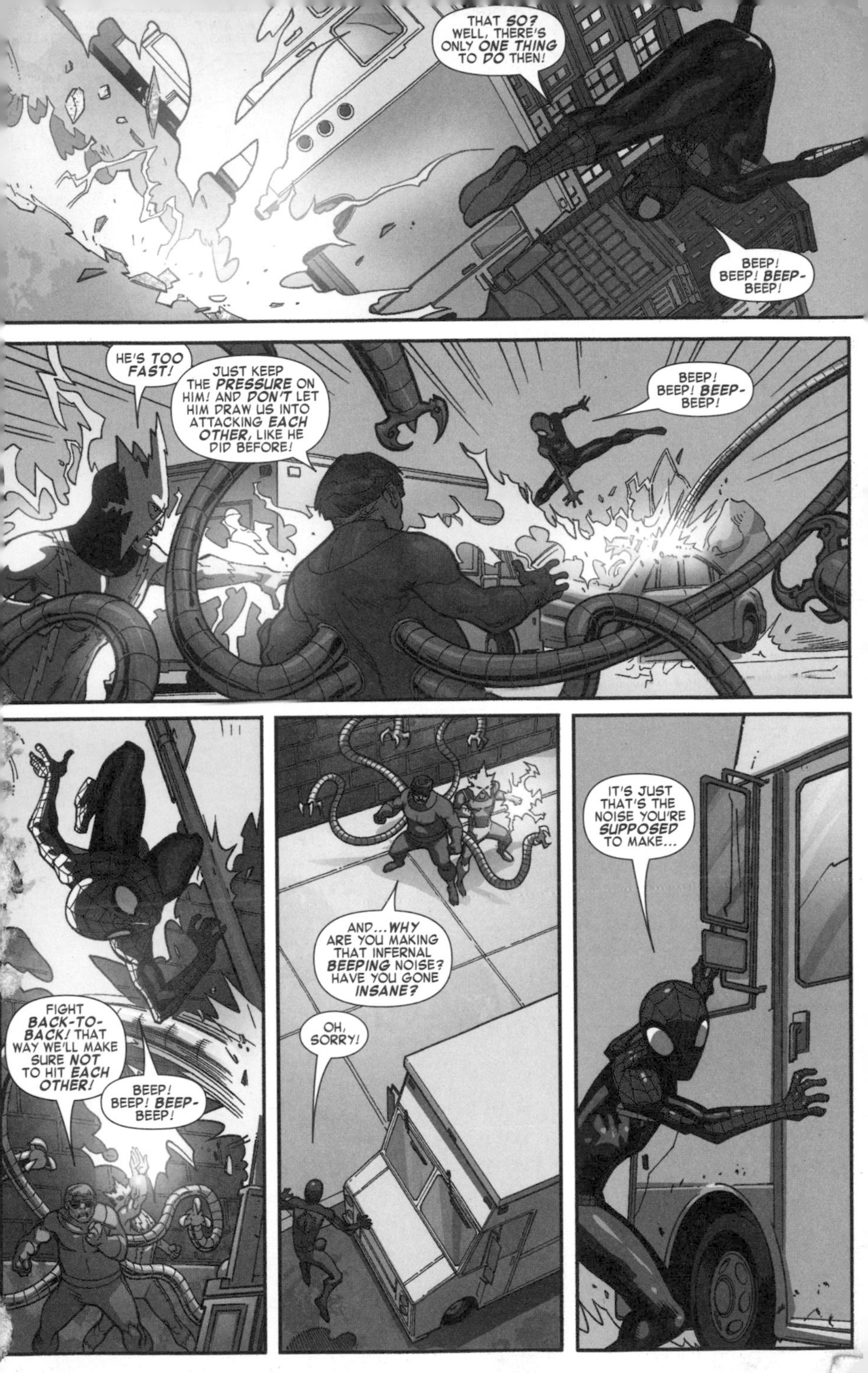
THAT SO? WELL, THERE'S ONLY ONE THING TO DO THEN!
BEEP! BEEP! BEEP-BEEP!
HE'S TOO FAST!
JUST KEEP THE PRESSURE ON HIM! AND DON'T LET HIM DRAW US INTO ATTACKING EACH OTHER, LIKE HE DID BEFORE!
BEEP! BEEP! BEEP-BEEP!
FIGHT BACK-TO-BACK! THAT WAY WE'LL MAKE SURE NOT TO HIT EACH OTHER!
BEEP! BEEP! BEEP-BEEP!
AND...WHY ARE YOU MAKING THAT INFERNAL BEEPING NOISE? HAVE YOU GONE INSANE?
OH, SORRY!
IT'S JUST THAT'S THE NOISE YOU'RE SUPPOSED TO MAKE...

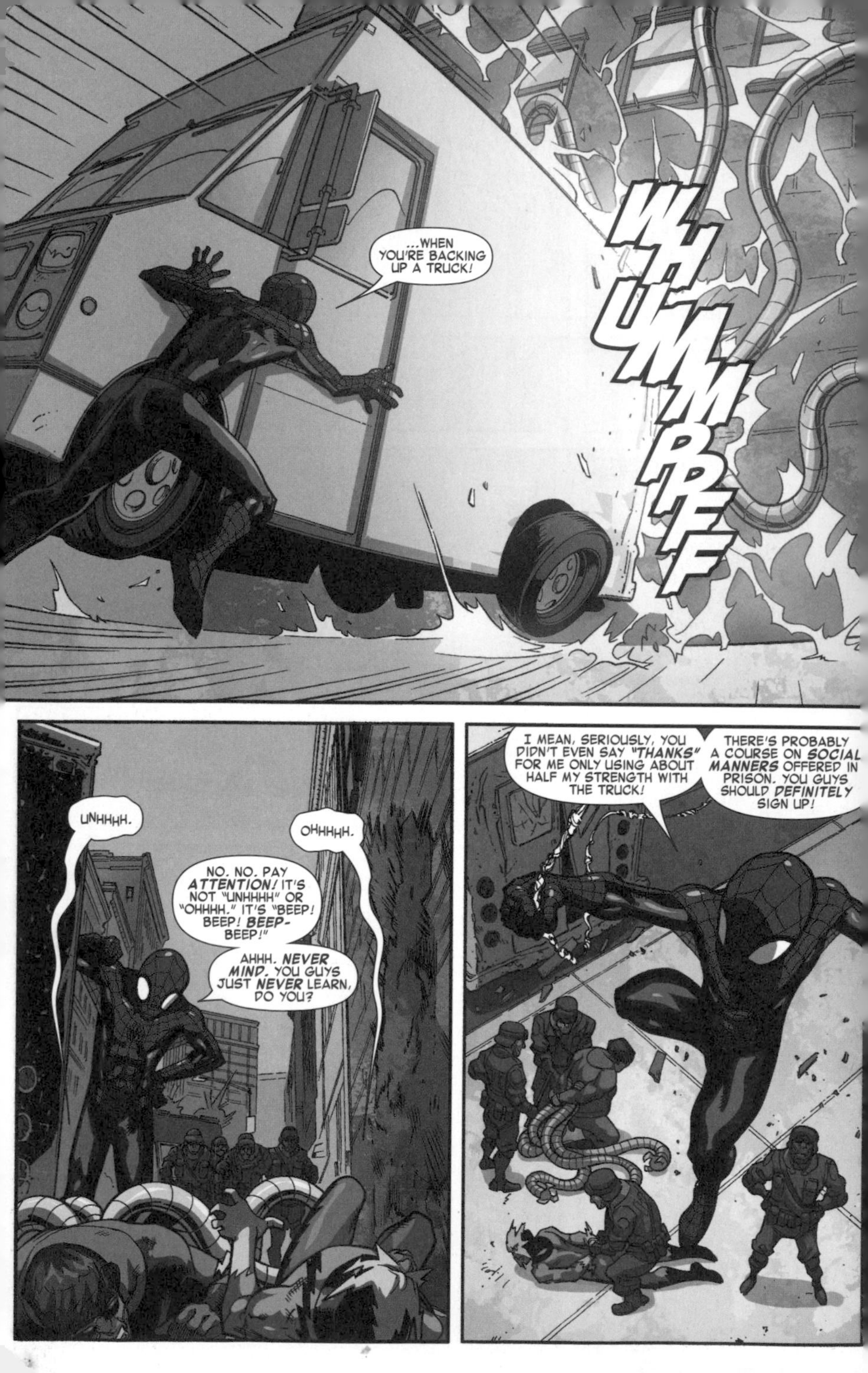
...WHEN YOU'RE BACKING UP A TRUCK!
WHUMMRFF
UNHHHH.
OHHHHH.
NO. NO. PAY ATTENTION! IT'S NOT "UNHHHH" OR "OHHHH." IT'S "BEEP! BEEP! BEEP-BEEP!"
AHHH. NEVER MIND. YOU GUYS JUST NEVER LEARN, DO YOU?
I MEAN, SERIOUSLY, YOU DIDN'T EVEN SAY "THANKS" FOR ME ONLY USING ABOUT HALF MY STRENGTH WITH THE TRUCK!
THERE'S PROBABLY A COURSE ON SOCIAL MANNERS OFFERED IN PRISON. YOU GUYS SHOULD DEFINITELY SIGN UP!

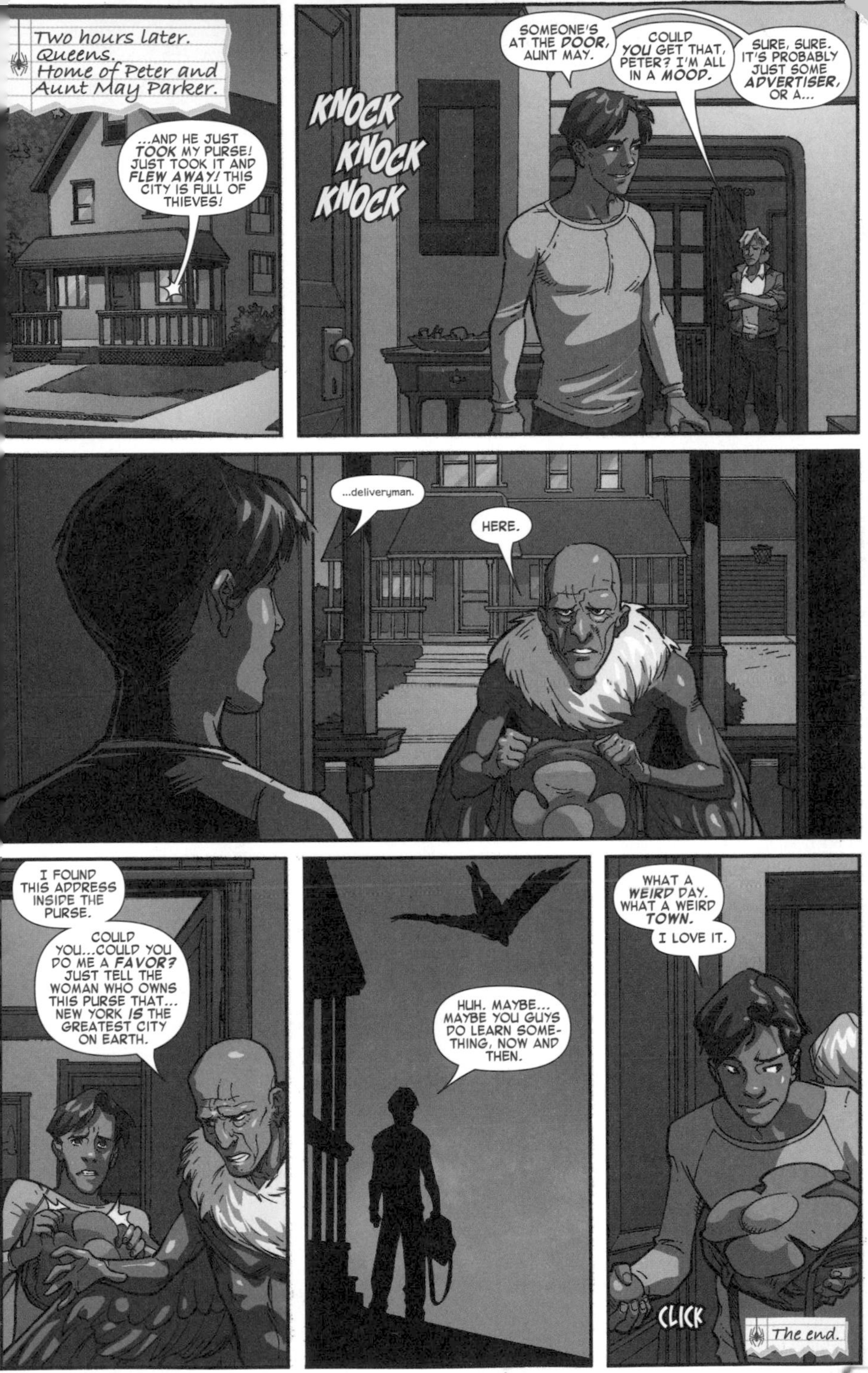
Two hours later. Queens. Home of Peter and Aunt May Parker.
...AND HE JUST TOOK MY PURSE! JUST TOOK IT AND FLEW AWAY! THIS CITY IS FULL OF THIEVES!
KNOCK KNOCK KNOCK
SOMEONE'S AT THE DOOR, AUNT MAY.
COULD YOU GET THAT, PETER? I'M ALL IN A MOOD.
SURE, SURE. IT'S PROBABLY JUST SOME ADVERTISER, OR A...
...deliveryman.
HERE.
I FOUND THIS ADDRESS INSIDE THE PURSE.
COULD YOU...COULD YOU DO ME A FAVOR? JUST TELL THE WOMAN WHO OWNS THIS PURSE THAT... NEW YORK IS THE GREATEST CITY ON EARTH.
HUH. MAYBE... MAYBE YOU GUYS DO LEARN SOME-THING, NOW AND THEN.
WHAT A WEIRD DAY. WHAT A WEIRD TOWN.
I LOVE IT.
CLICK
The end.

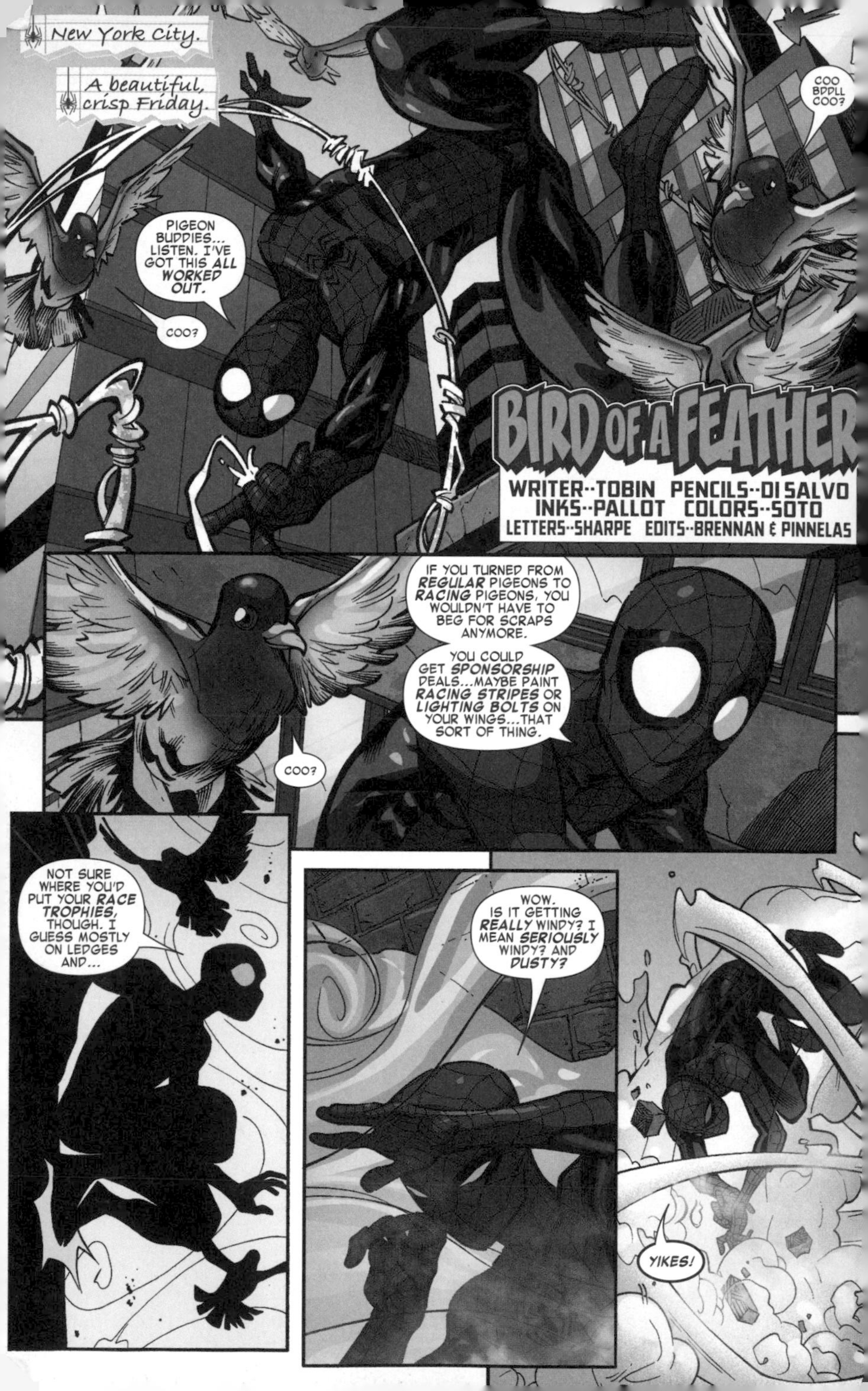
New York City.
A beautiful, crisp Friday.
PIGEON BUDDIES... LISTEN. I'VE GOT THIS ALL WORKED OUT.
COO?
COO BDDLL COO?
BIRD OF A FEATHER
WRITER--TOBIN PENCILS--DI SALVO
INKS--PALLOT COLORS--SOTO
LETTERS--SHARPE EDITS--BRENNAN & PINNELAS
IF YOU TURNED FROM REGULAR PIGEONS TO RACING PIGEONS, YOU WOULDN'T HAVE TO BEG FOR SCRAPS ANYMORE.
YOU COULD GET SPONSORSHIP DEALS...MAYBE PAINT RACING STRIPES OR LIGHTING BOLTS ON YOUR WINGS...THAT SORT OF THING.
COO?
NOT SURE WHERE YOU'D PUT YOUR RACE TROPHIES, THOUGH. I GUESS MOSTLY ON LEDGES AND...
WOW. IS IT GETTING REALLY WINDY? I MEAN SERIOUSLY WINDY? AND DUSTY?
YIKES!

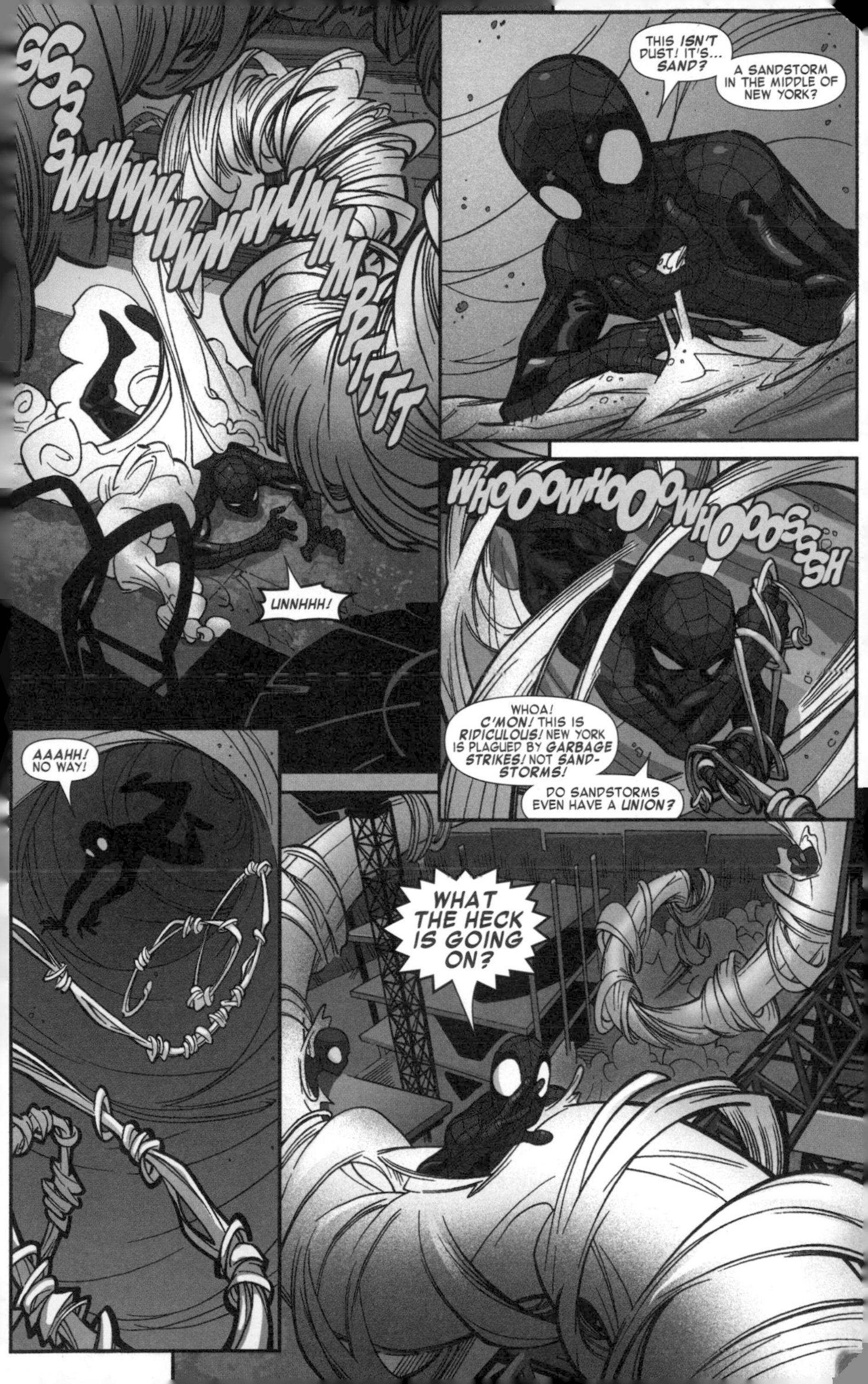
SSSSSWWWWWWWWWWWUMMMRRTTTTT
UNNHHH!
THIS ISN'T DUST! IT'S... SAND?
A SANDSTORM IN THE MIDDLE OF NEW YORK?
WHOOOWHOOOOWHOOOSSSH
WHOA! C'MON! THIS IS RIDICULOUS! NEW YORK IS PLAGUED BY GARBAGE STRIKES! NOT SAND-STORMS!
DO SANDSTORMS EVEN HAVE A UNION?
AAAHH! NO WAY!
WHAT THE HECK IS GOING ON?

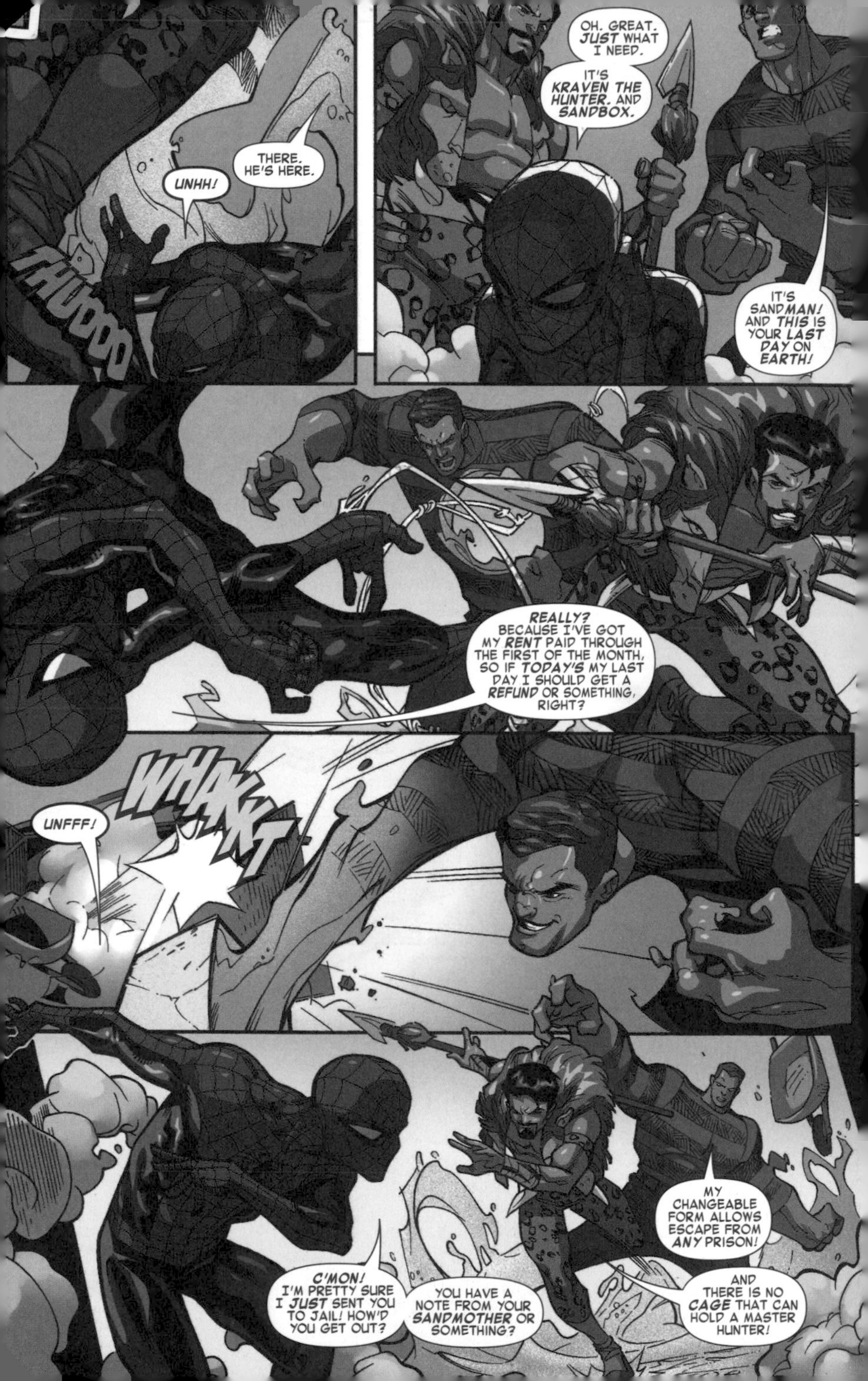
THUDOO
UNHH!
THERE. HE'S HERE.
OH. GREAT. JUST WHAT I NEED.
IT'S KRAVEN THE HUNTER. AND SANDBOX.
IT'S SANDMAN! AND THIS IS YOUR LAST DAY ON EARTH!
REALLY? BECAUSE I'VE GOT MY RENT PAID THROUGH THE FIRST OF THE MONTH, SO IF TODAY'S MY LAST DAY I SHOULD GET A REFUND OR SOMETHING, RIGHT?
WHAKT
UNFFF!
C'MON! I'M PRETTY SURE I JUST SENT YOU TO JAIL! HOW'D YOU GET OUT?
YOU HAVE A NOTE FROM YOUR SANDMOTHER OR SOMETHING?
MY CHANGEABLE FORM ALLOWS ESCAPE FROM ANY PRISON!
AND THERE IS NO CAGE THAT CAN HOLD A MASTER HUNTER!

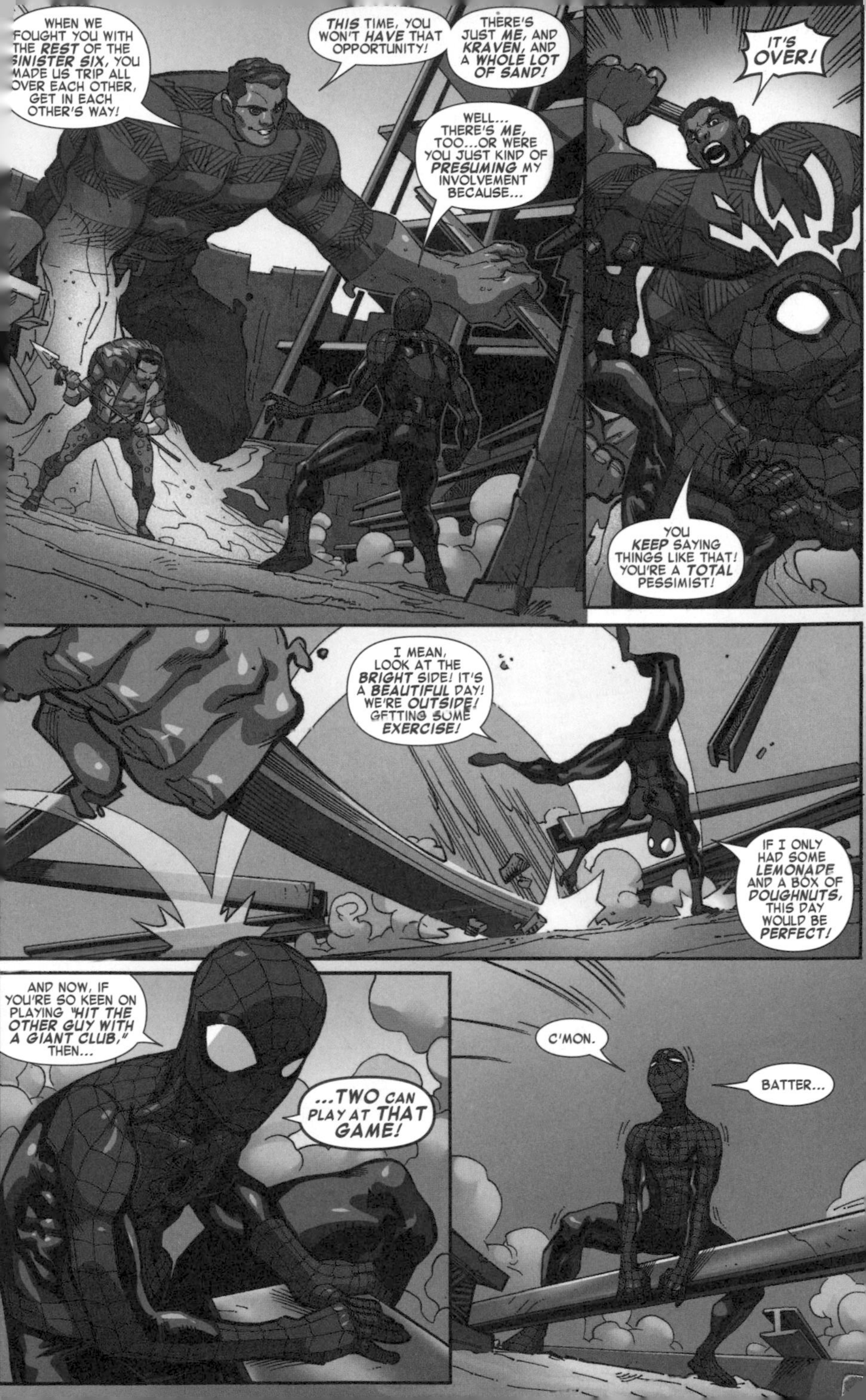
WHEN WE FOUGHT YOU WITH THE REST OF THE SINISTER SIX, YOU MADE US TRIP ALL OVER EACH OTHER, GET IN EACH OTHER'S WAY!
THIS TIME, YOU WON'T HAVE THAT OPPORTUNITY!
THERE'S JUST ME, AND KRAVEN, AND A WHOLE LOT OF SAND!
WELL... THERE'S ME, TOO...OR WERE YOU JUST KIND OF PRESUMING MY INVOLVEMENT BECAUSE...
IT'S OVER!
YOU KEEP SAYING THINGS LIKE THAT! YOU'RE A TOTAL PESSIMIST!
I MEAN, LOOK AT THE BRIGHT SIDE! IT'S A BEAUTIFUL DAY! WE'RE OUTSIDE! GETTING SOME EXERCISE!
IF I ONLY HAD SOME LEMONADE AND A BOX OF DOUGHNUTS, THIS DAY WOULD BE PERFECT!
AND NOW, IF YOU'RE SO KEEN ON PLAYING "HIT THE OTHER GUY WITH A GIANT CLUB," THEN...
...TWO CAN PLAY AT THAT GAME!
C'MON.
BATTER...

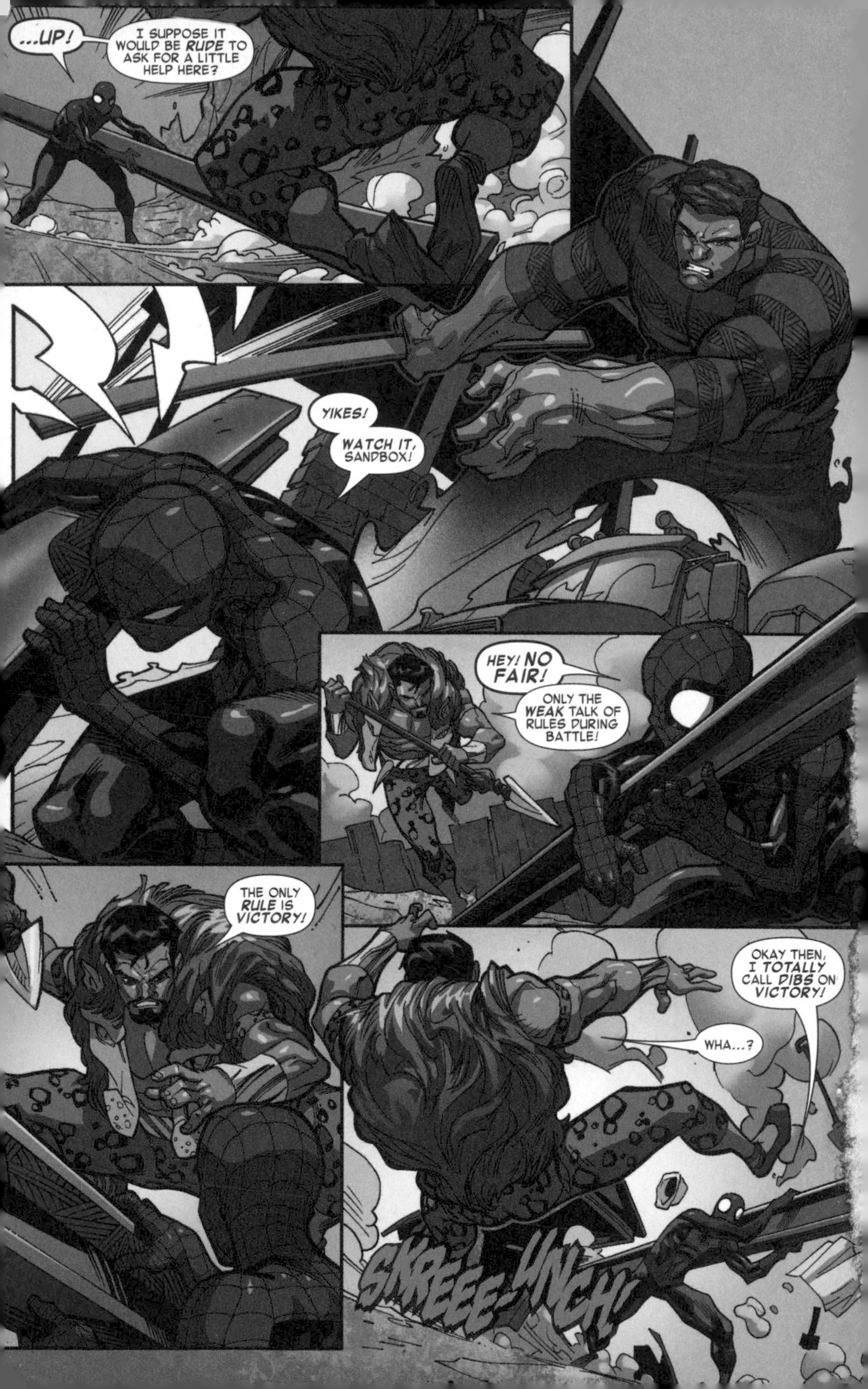

...UP!
I SUPPOSE IT WOULD BE RUDE TO ASK FOR A LITTLE HELP HERE?
YIKES!
WATCH IT, SANDBOX!
HEY! NO FAIR!
ONLY THE WEAK TALK OF RULES DURING BATTLE!
THE ONLY RULE IS VICTORY!
OKAY THEN, I TOTALLY CALL DIBS ON VICTORY!
WHA...?
SKREEE-UNCH!

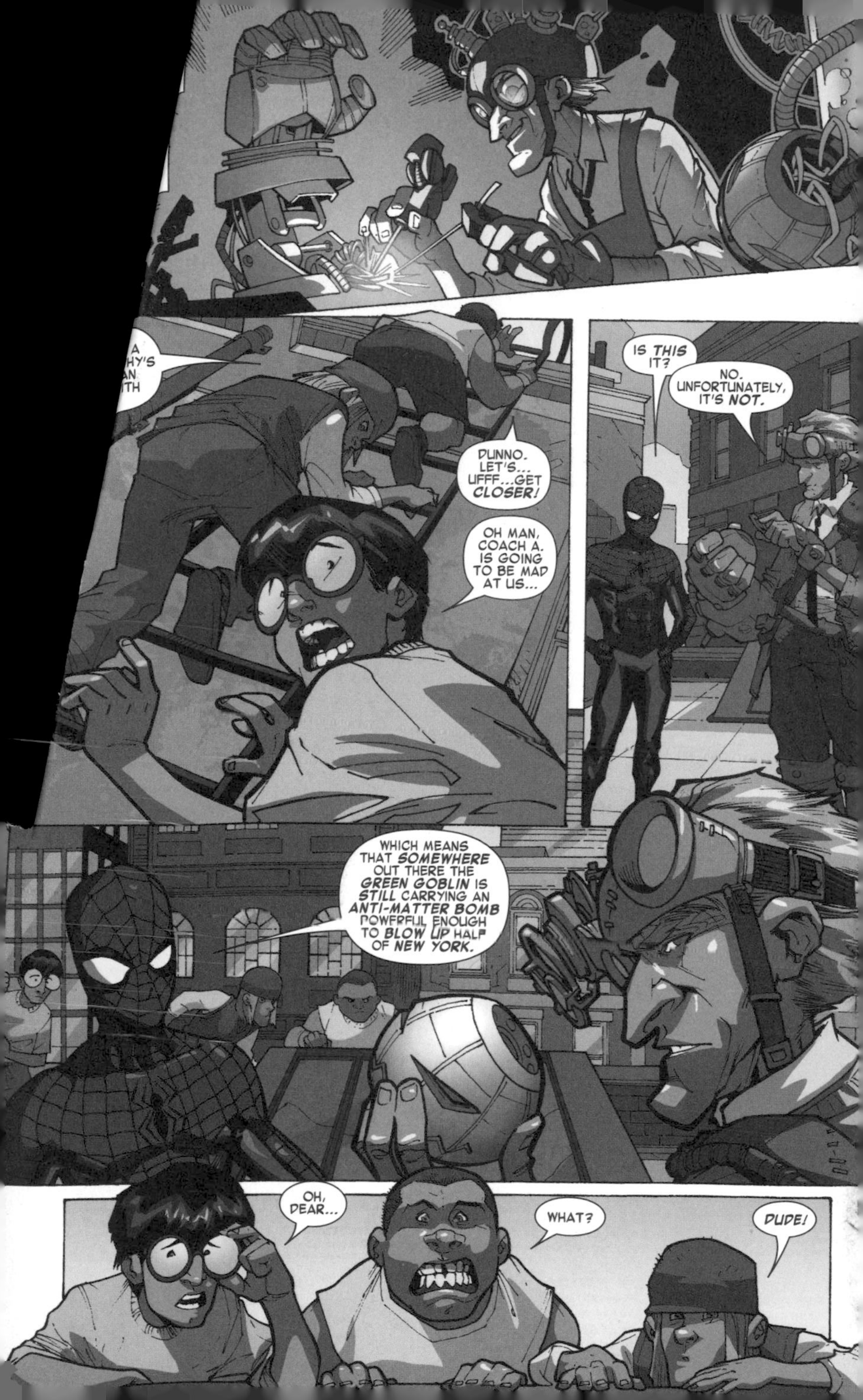
DUNNO. LET'S... UFFF...GET CLOSER!
OH MAN, COACH A. IS GOING TO BE MAD AT US...
IS THIS IT?
NO. UNFORTUNATELY, IT'S NOT.
WHICH MEANS THAT SOMEWHERE OUT THERE THE GREEN GOBLIN IS STILL CARRYING AN ANTI-MATTER BOMB POWERFUL ENOUGH TO BLOW UP HALF OF NEW YORK.
OH, DEAR...
WHAT?
DUDE!

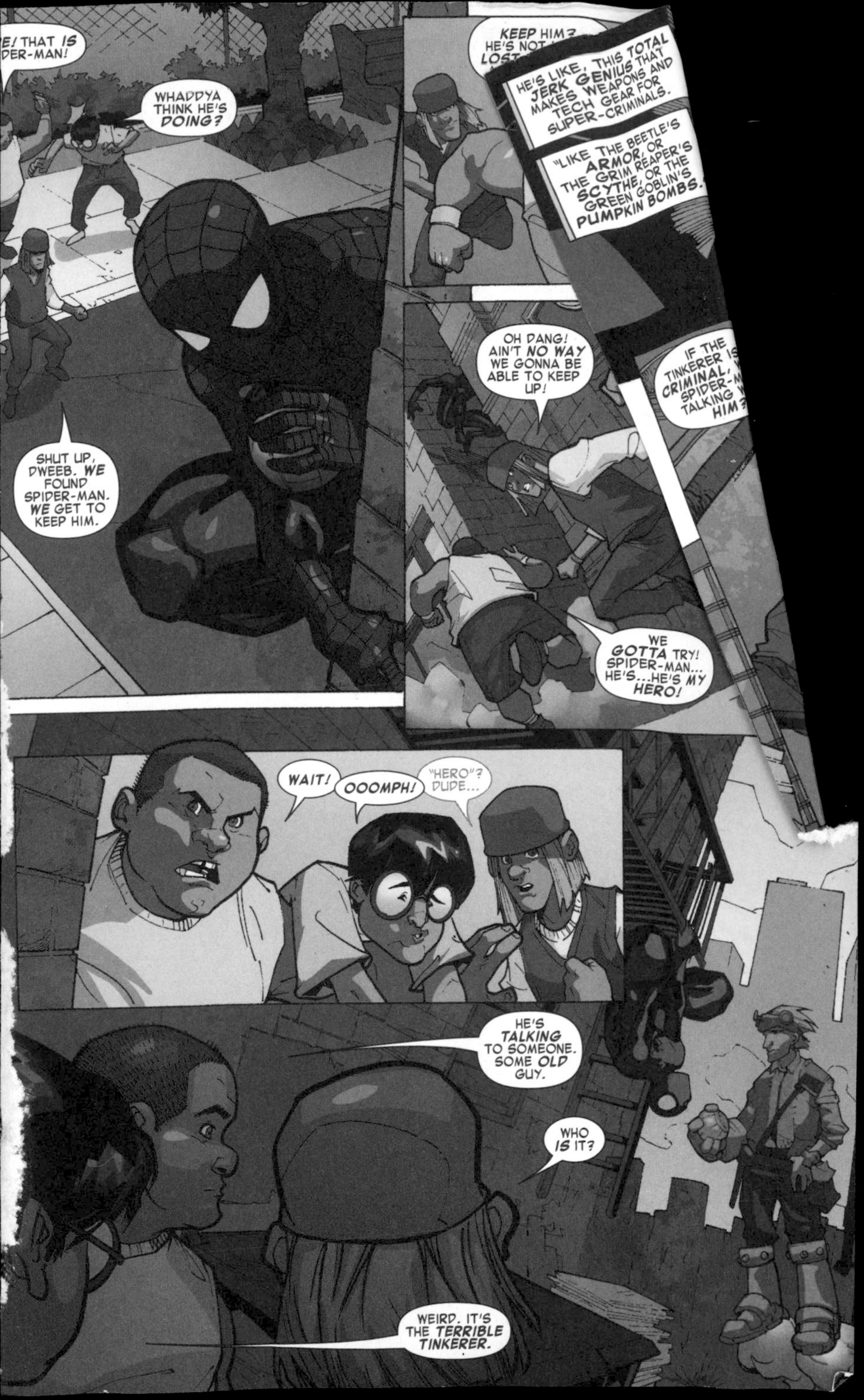

E! THAT IS
DER-MAN!
WHADDYA THINK HE'S DOING?
SHUT UP, DWEEB. WE FOUND SPIDER-MAN. WE GET TO KEEP HIM.
KEEP HIM? HE'S NOT
LOST
HE'S LIKE, THIS TOTAL JERK GENIUS THAT MAKES WEAPONS AND TECH GEAR FOR SUPER-CRIMINALS.
"LIKE THE BEETLE'S ARMOR, OR THE GRIM REAPER'S SCYTHE, OR THE GREEN GOBLIN'S PUMPKIN BOMBS.
OH DANG! AIN'T NO WAY WE GONNA BE ABLE TO KEEP UP!
IF THE TINKERER IS
CRIMINAL,
SPIDER-
TALKING
HIM?
WE GOTTA TRY! SPIDER-MAN... HE'S...HE'S MY HERO!
WAIT!
OOOMPH!
"HERO"? DUDE...
HE'S TALKING TO SOMEONE. SOME OLD GUY.
WHO IS IT?
WEIRD. IT'S THE TERRIBLE TINKERER.

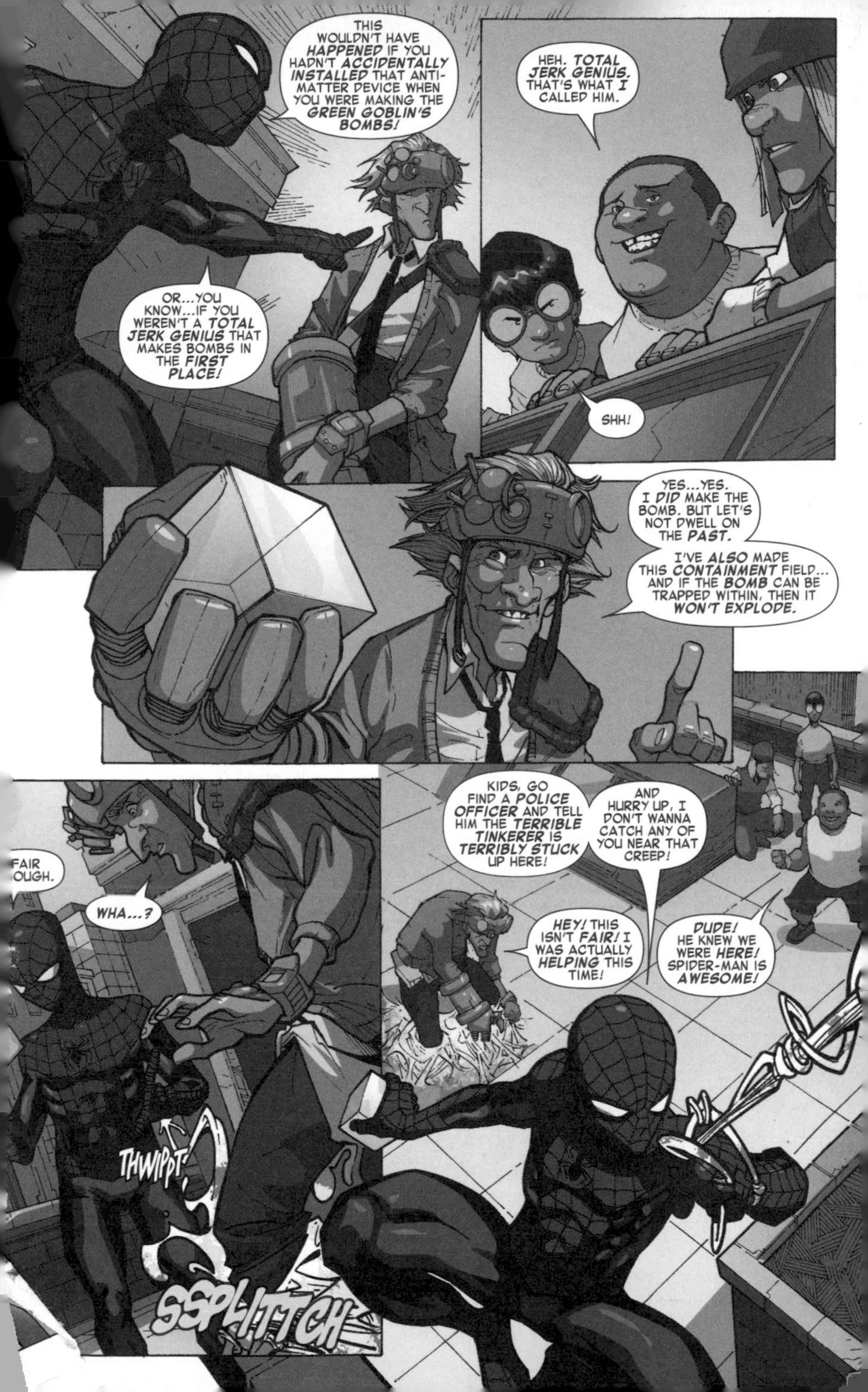
THIS WOULDN'T HAVE HAPPENED IF YOU HADN'T ACCIDENTALLY INSTALLED THAT ANTI-MATTER DEVICE WHEN YOU WERE MAKING THE GREEN GOBLIN'S BOMBS!
OR...YOU KNOW...IF YOU WEREN'T A TOTAL JERK GENIUS THAT MAKES BOMBS IN THE FIRST PLACE!
HEH. TOTAL JERK GENIUS. THAT'S WHAT I CALLED HIM.
SHH!
YES...YES. I DID MAKE THE BOMB. BUT LET'S NOT DWELL ON THE PAST.
I'VE ALSO MADE THIS CONTAINMENT FIELD... AND IF THE BOMB CAN BE TRAPPED WITHIN, THEN IT WON'T EXPLODE.
FAIR OUGH.
WHA...?
THWIPPT!
SSPLITTCH
KIDS, GO FIND A POLICE OFFICER AND TELL HIM THE TERRIBLE TINKERER IS TERRIBLY STUCK UP HERE!
AND HURRY UP, I DON'T WANNA CATCH ANY OF YOU NEAR THAT CREEP!
HEY! THIS ISN'T FAIR! I WAS ACTUALLY HELPING THIS TIME!
DUDE! HE KNEW WE WERE HERE! SPIDER-MAN IS AWESOME!

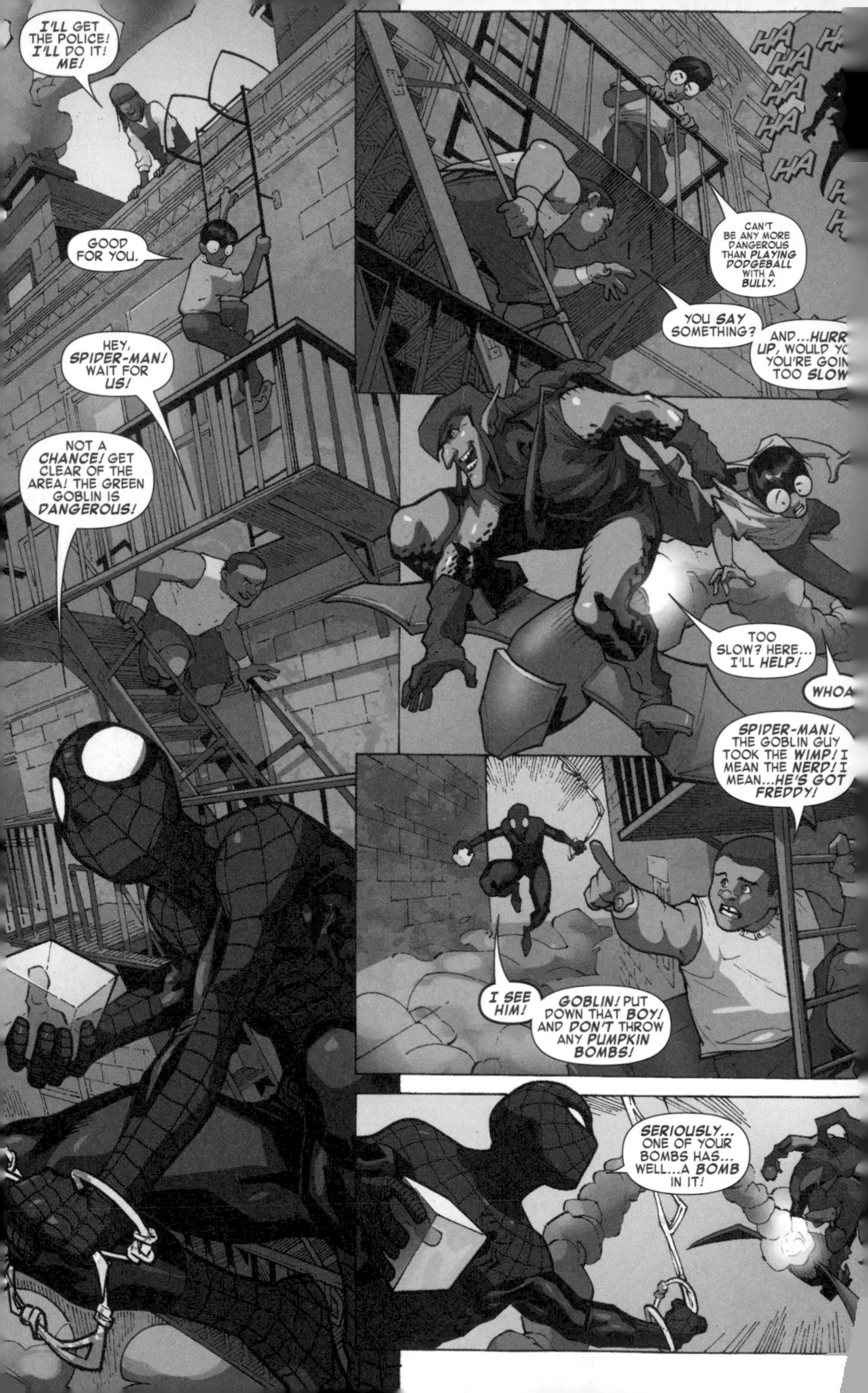
I'LL GET THE POLICE! I'LL DO IT! ME!
GOOD FOR YOU.
HEY, SPIDER-MAN! WAIT FOR US!
NOT A CHANCE! GET CLEAR OF THE AREA! THE GREEN GOBLIN IS DANGEROUS!
CAN'T BE ANY MORE DANGEROUS THAN PLAYING DODGEBALL WITH A BULLY.
YOU SAY SOMETHING?
AND...HURR UP, WOULD YO YOU'RE GOIN TOO SLOW
TOO SLOW? HERE... I'LL HELP!
WHOA
SPIDER-MAN! THE GOBLIN GUY TOOK THE WIMP! I MEAN THE NERD! I MEAN...HE'S GOT FREDDY!
I SEE HIM!
GOBLIN! PUT DOWN THAT BOY! AND DON'T THROW ANY PUMPKIN BOMBS!
SERIOUSLY... ONE OF YOUR BOMBS HAS... WELL...A BOMB IN IT!

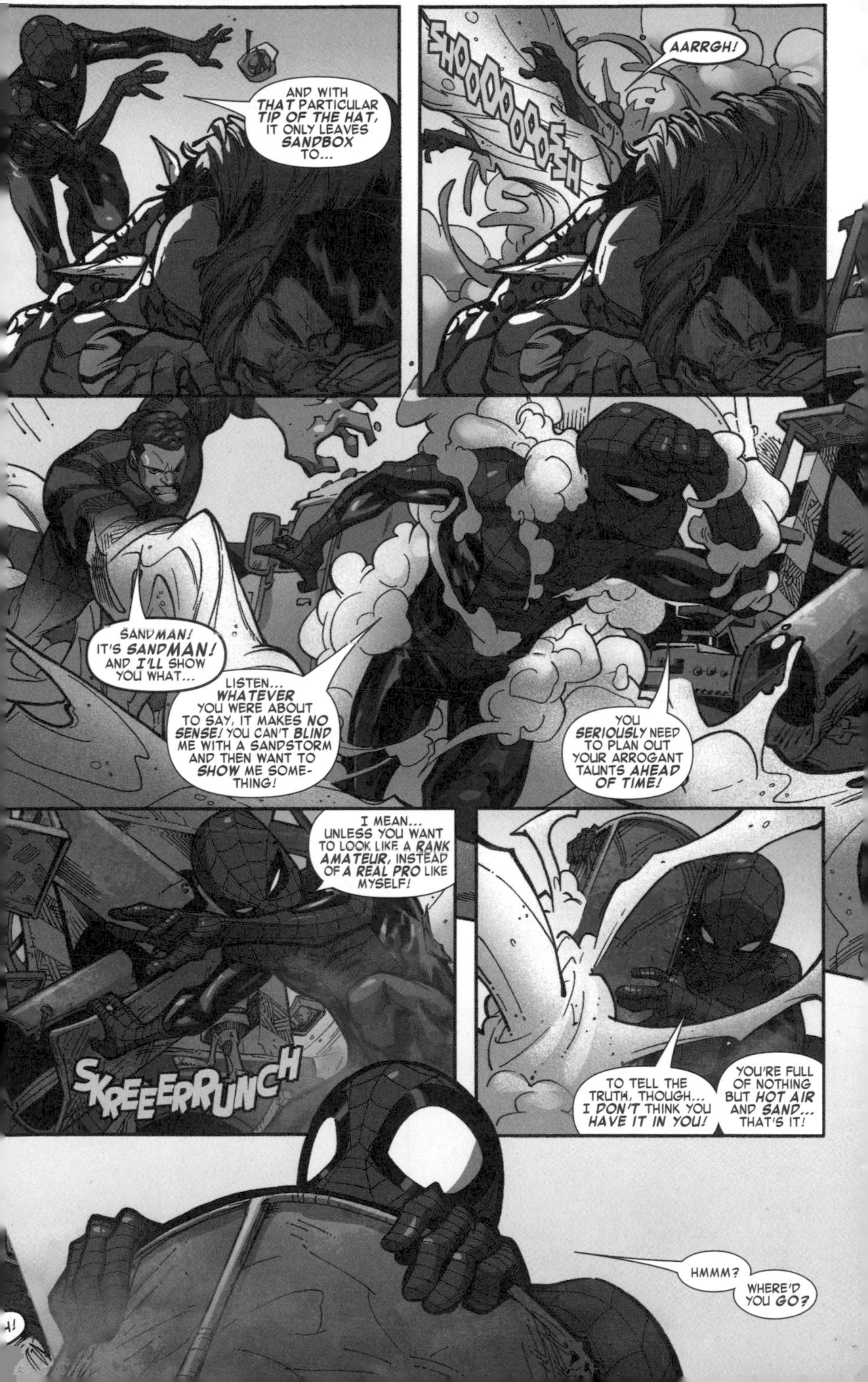

AND WITH THAT PARTICULAR TIP OF THE HAT, IT ONLY LEAVES SANDBOX TO...
SHOOOOOOOSH
AARRGH!
SANDMAN! IT'S SANDMAN! AND I'LL SHOW YOU WHAT...
LISTEN... WHATEVER YOU WERE ABOUT TO SAY, IT MAKES NO SENSE! YOU CAN'T BLIND ME WITH A SANDSTORM AND THEN WANT TO SHOW ME SOME-THING!
YOU SERIOUSLY NEED TO PLAN OUT YOUR ARROGANT TAUNTS AHEAD OF TIME!
I MEAN... UNLESS YOU WANT TO LOOK LIKE A RANK AMATEUR, INSTEAD OF A REAL PRO LIKE MYSELF!
SKREEERRUNCH
TO TELL THE TRUTH, THOUGH... I DON'T THINK YOU HAVE IT IN YOU!
YOU'RE FULL OF NOTHING BUT HOT AIR AND SAND... THAT'S IT!
HMMM?
WHERE'D YOU GO?

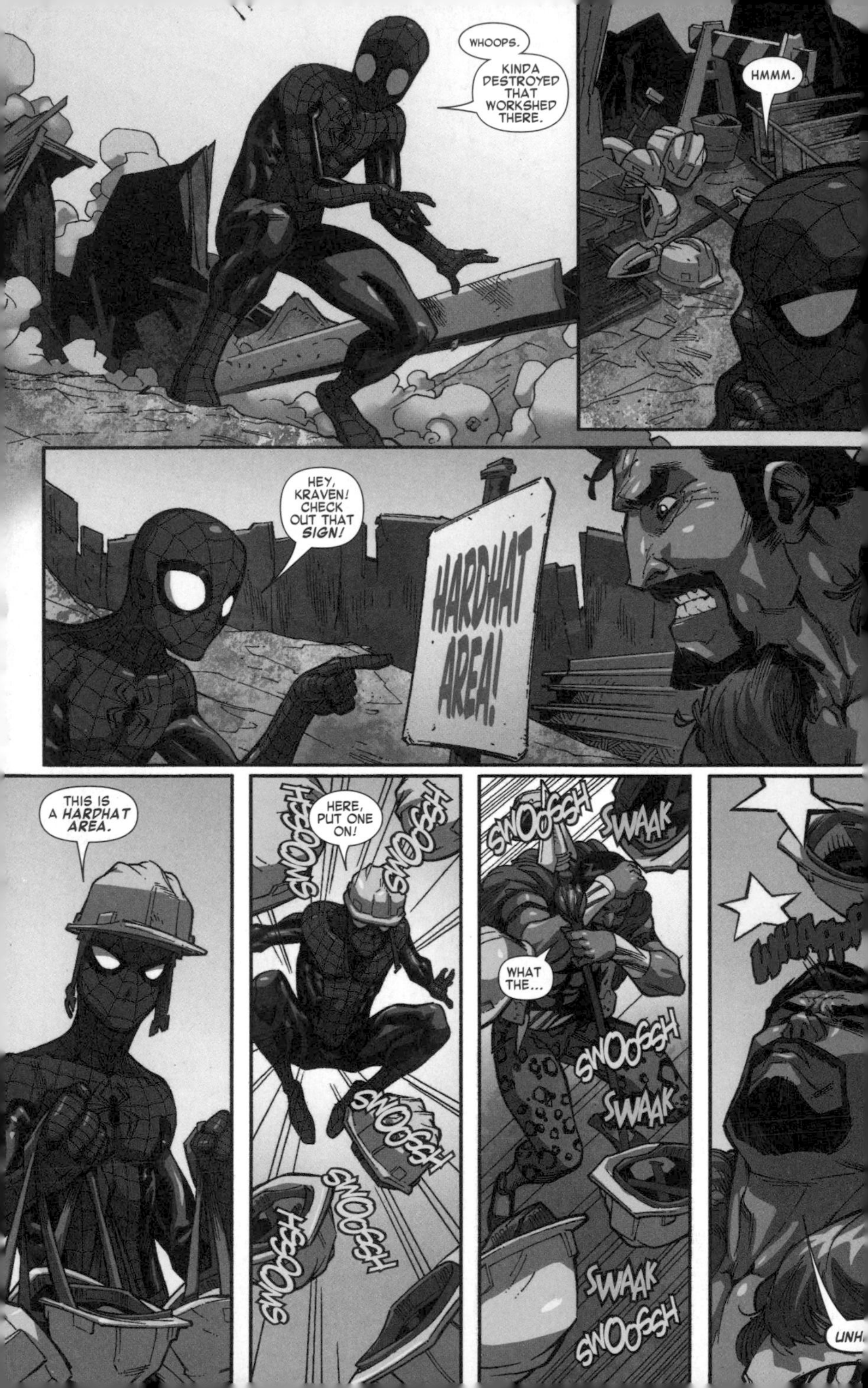
WHOOPS.
KINDA DESTROYED THAT WORKSHED THERE.
HMMM.
HEY, KRAVEN! CHECK OUT THAT *SIGN!*
HARDHAT AREA!
THIS IS A *HARDHAT AREA.*
HERE, PUT ONE ON!
SWOOSSH
SWOOSSH
SWOOSSH
SWOOSSH
SWOOSSH
SWOOSSH
SWAAK
WHAT THE...
SWOOSSH
SWAAK
SWAAK
SWOOSSH
UNH

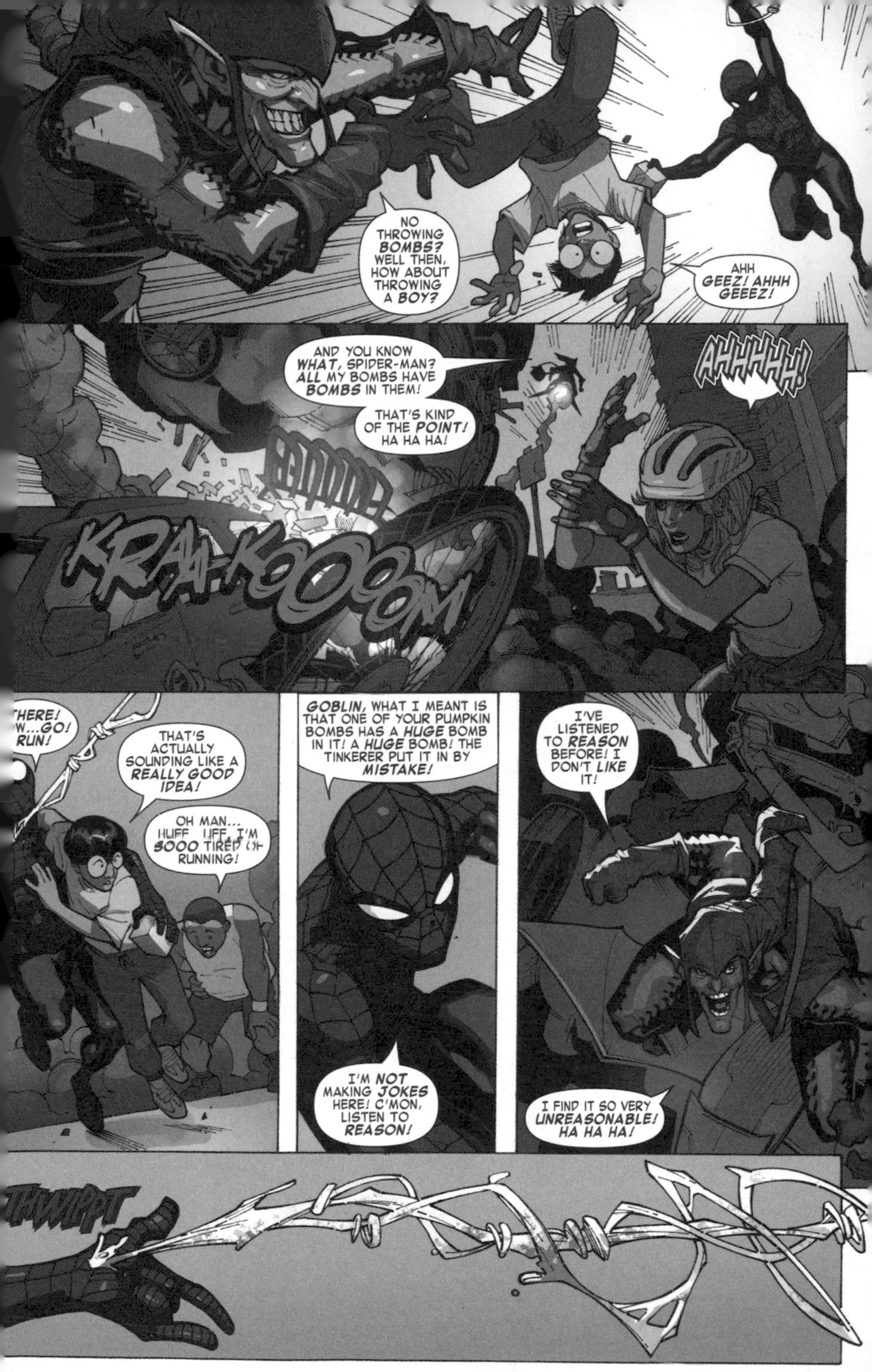
NO THROWING BOMBS? WELL THEN, HOW ABOUT THROWING A BOY?
AHH GEEZ! AHHH GEEEZ!
AND YOU KNOW WHAT, SPIDER-MAN? ALL MY BOMBS HAVE BOMBS IN THEM!
THAT'S KIND OF THE POINT! HA HA HA!
AHHHHH!
KRA-KOOOOM
THERE! ...W...GO! RUN!
THAT'S ACTUALLY SOUNDING LIKE A REALLY GOOD IDEA!
OH MAN... HUFF UFF, I'M SOOO TIRED OF RUNNING!
GOBLIN, WHAT I MEANT IS THAT ONE OF YOUR PUMPKIN BOMBS HAS A HUGE BOMB IN IT! A HUGE BOMB! THE TINKERER PUT IT IN BY MISTAKE!
I'M NOT MAKING JOKES HERE! C'MON, LISTEN TO REASON!
I'VE LISTENED TO REASON BEFORE! I DON'T LIKE IT!
I FIND IT SO VERY UNREASONABLE! HA HA HA!
THWIPPT

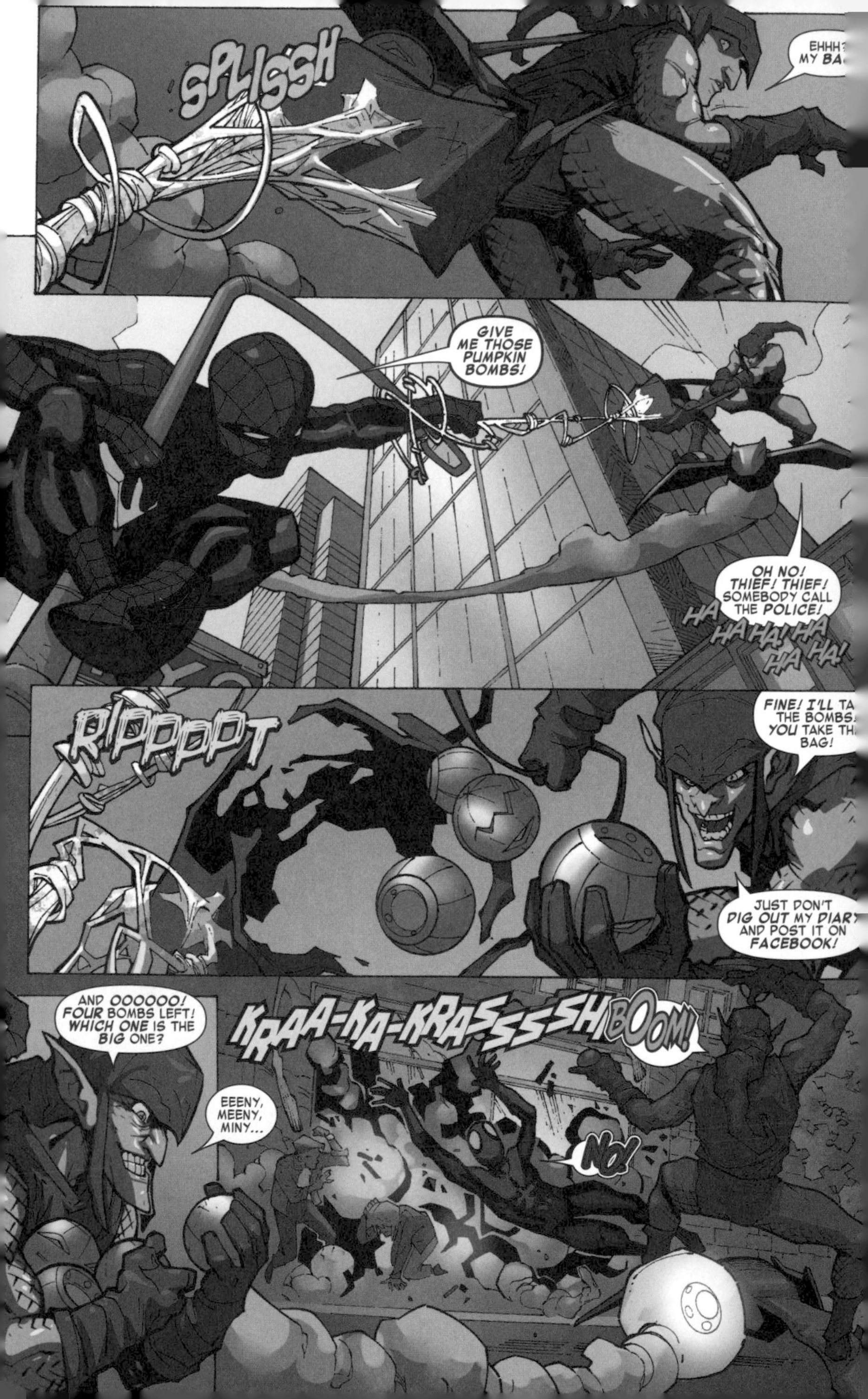
SPLISSH
EHHH? MY BA
GIVE ME THOSE PUMPKIN BOMBS!
OH NO! THIEF! THIEF! SOMEBODY CALL THE POLICE!
HA HA HA! HA HA HA!
RIPPPPT
FINE! I'LL TA THE BOMBS. YOU TAKE TH BAG!
JUST DON'T DIG OUT MY DIAR AND POST IT ON FACEBOOK!
AND OOOOOO! FOUR BOMBS LEFT! WHICH ONE IS THE BIG ONE?
EEENY, MEENY, MINY...
KRAA-KA-KRASSSSSHBOOM!
NO!

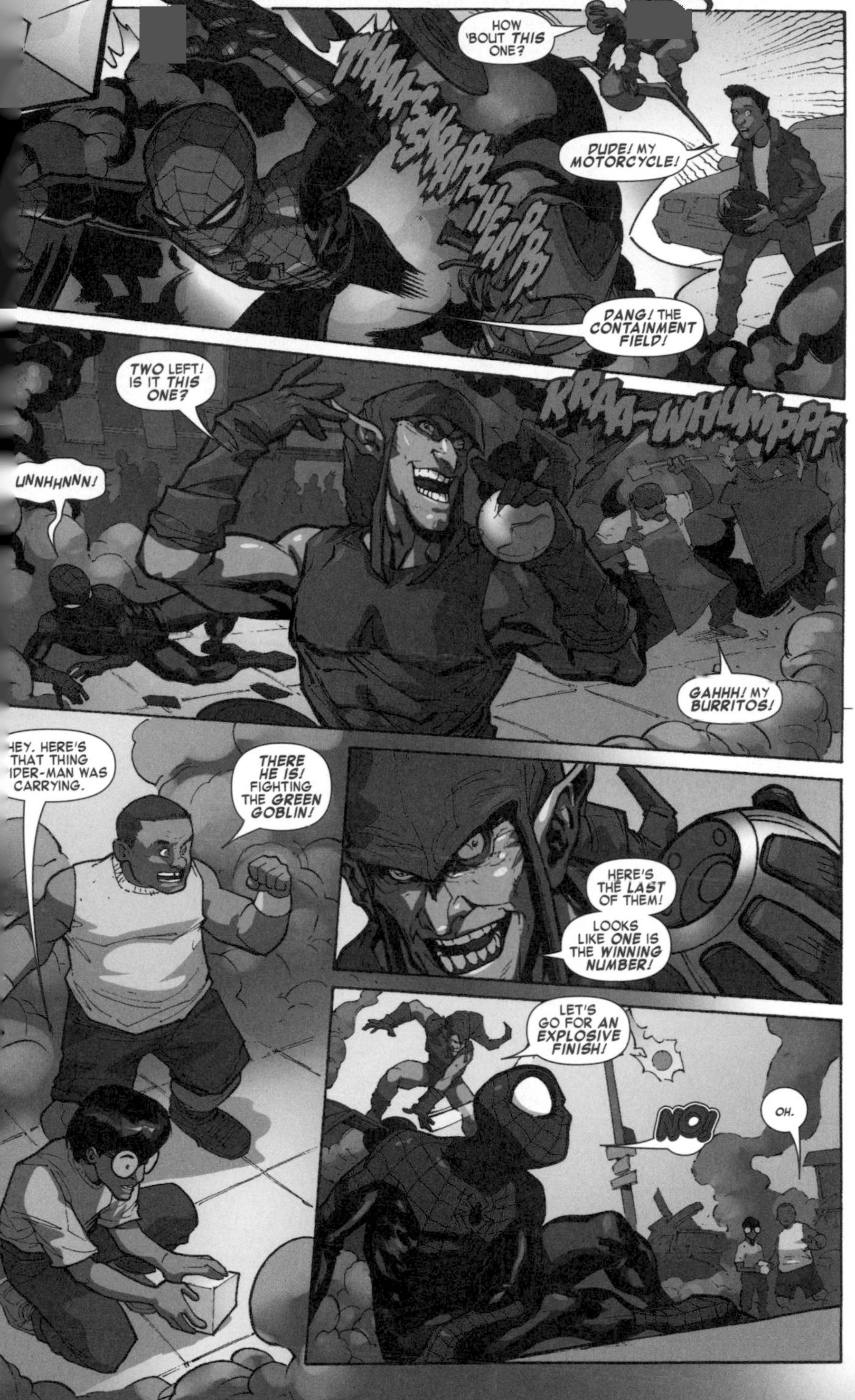

HOW 'BOUT THIS ONE?
THWAK-SNAP-HEARP
DUDE! MY MOTORCYCLE!
DANG! THE CONTAINMENT FIELD!
TWO LEFT! IS IT THIS ONE?
KRAA-WHUMPFF
UNNHHNNN!
GAHHH! MY BURRITOS!
HEY. HERE'S THAT THING IDER-MAN WAS CARRYING.
THERE HE IS! FIGHTING THE GREEN GOBLIN!
HERE'S THE LAST OF THEM!
LOOKS LIKE ONE IS THE WINNING NUMBER!
LET'S GO FOR AN EXPLOSIVE FINISH!
NO!
OH.

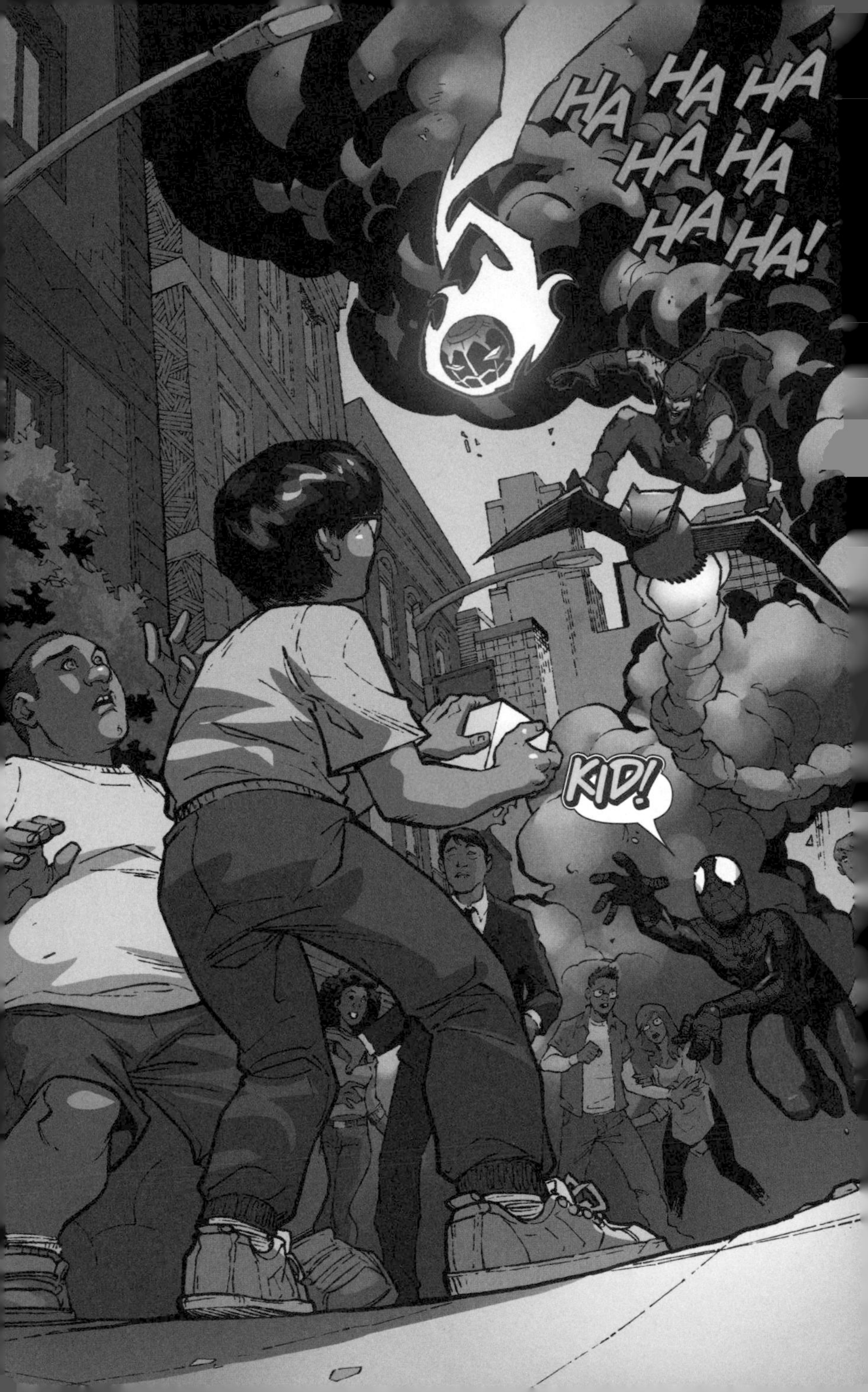
HA HA HA
HA HA HA
HA HA!
KID!

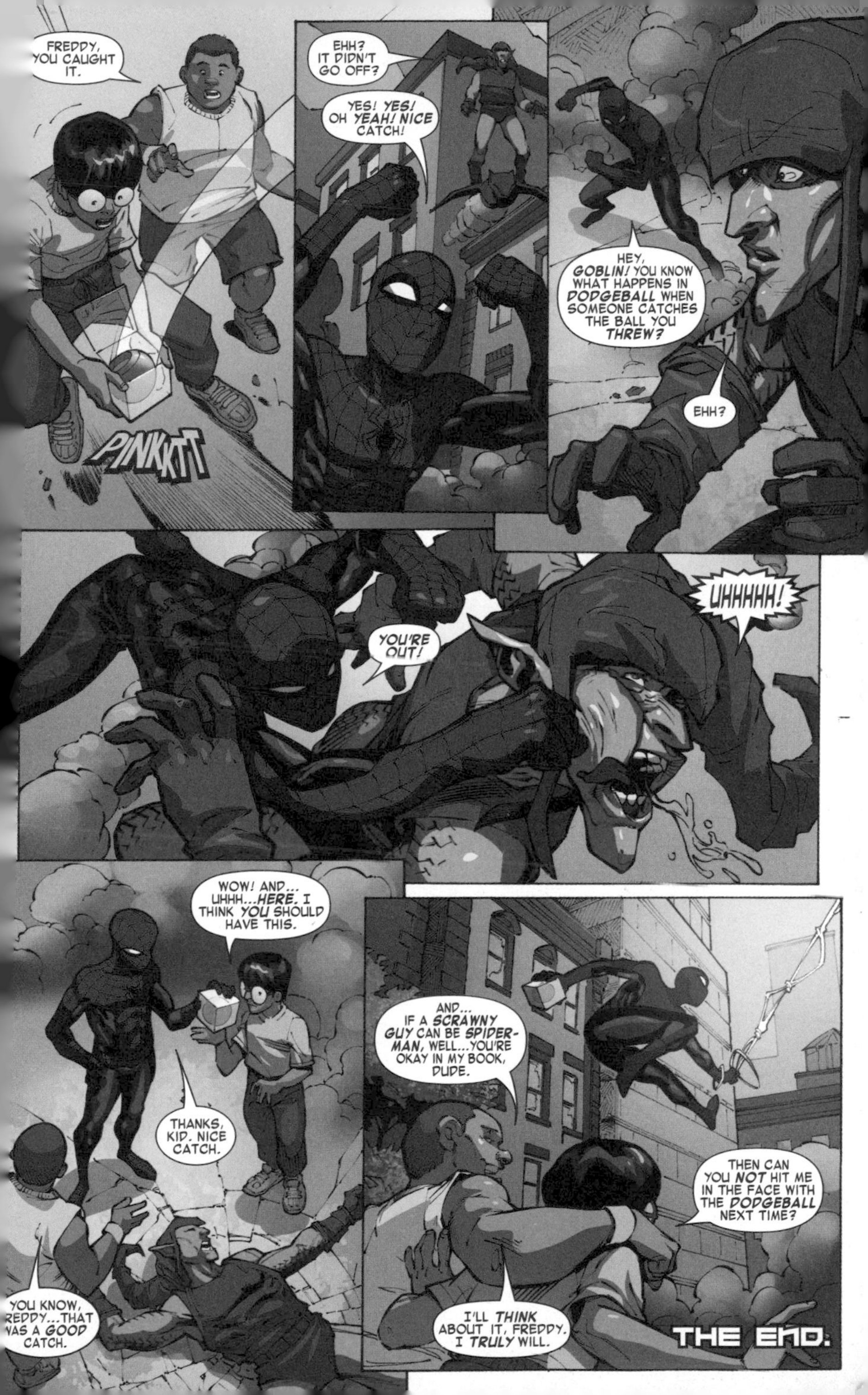
FREDDY, YOU CAUGHT IT.
PINKKTT
EHH? IT DIDN'T GO OFF?
YES! YES! OH YEAH! NICE CATCH!
HEY, GOBLIN! YOU KNOW WHAT HAPPENS IN DODGEBALL WHEN SOMEONE CATCHES THE BALL YOU THREW?
EHH?
YOU'RE OUT!
UHHHHH!
WOW! AND... UHHH...HERE. I THINK YOU SHOULD HAVE THIS.
THANKS, KID. NICE CATCH.
YOU KNOW, FREDDY...THAT WAS A GOOD CATCH.
AND... IF A SCRAWNY GUY CAN BE SPIDER-MAN, WELL...YOU'RE OKAY IN MY BOOK, DUDE.
THEN CAN YOU NOT HIT ME IN THE FACE WITH THE DODGEBALL NEXT TIME?
I'LL THINK ABOUT IT, FREDDY. I TRULY WILL.
THE END.

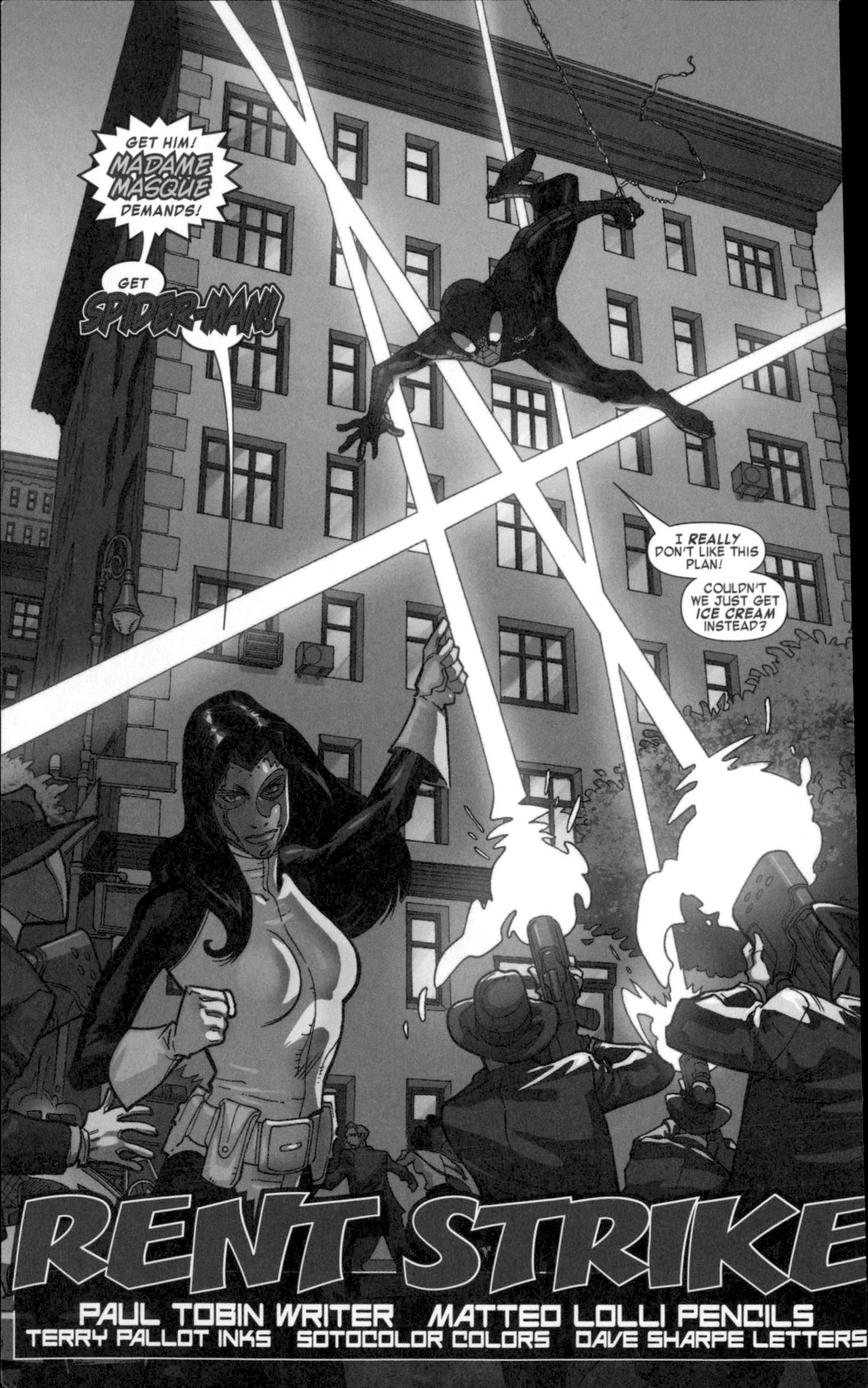
GET HIM! MADAME MASQUE DEMANDS!
GET SPIDER-MAN!!
I REALLY DON'T LIKE THIS PLAN!
COULDN'T WE JUST GET ICE CREAM INSTEAD?
RENT STRIKE
PAUL TOBIN WRITER MATTEO LOLLI PENCILS
TERRY PALLOT INKS SOTOCOLOR COLORS DAVE SHARPE LETTERS

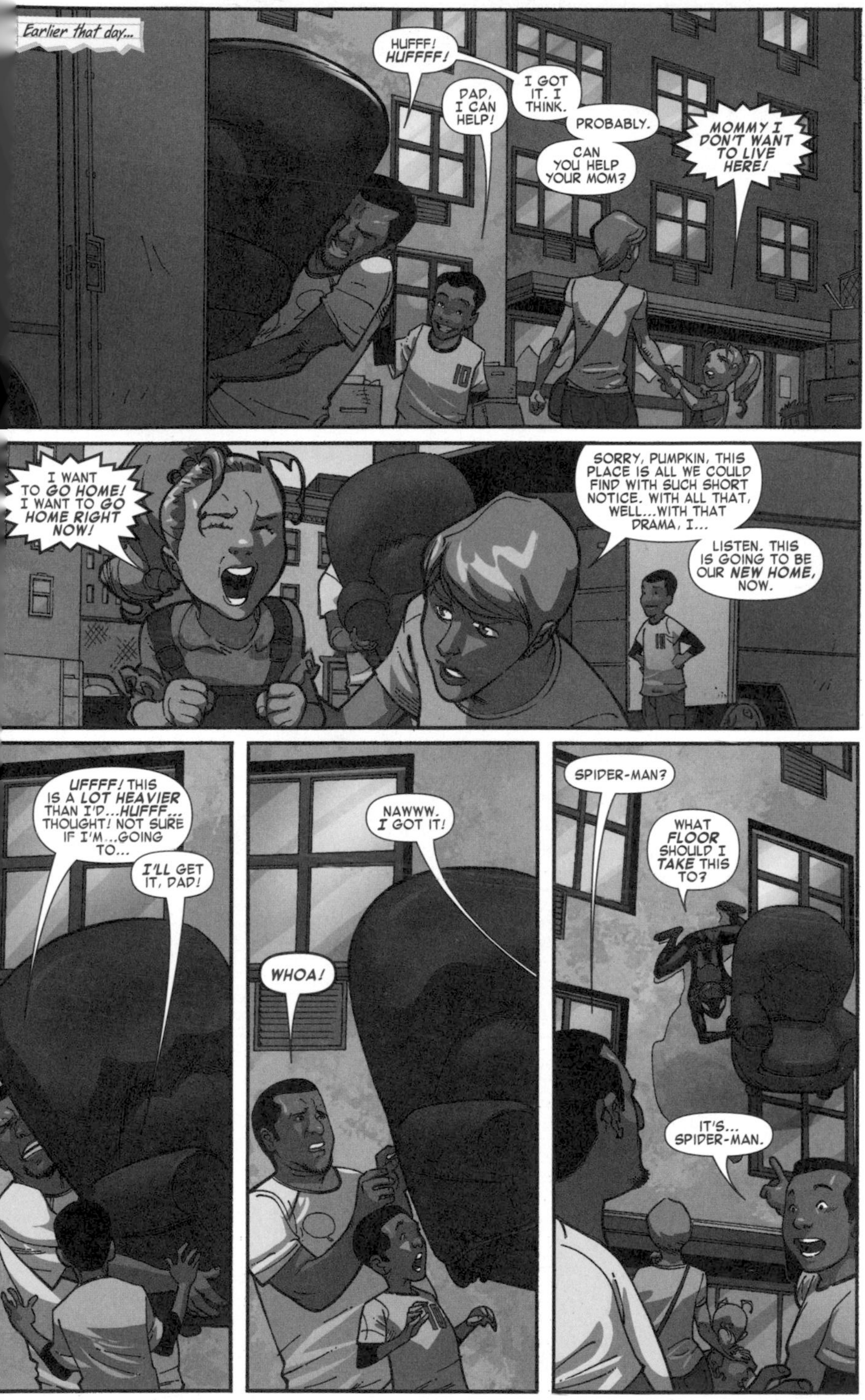

Earlier that day...
HUFFF! HUFFFF!
DAD, I CAN HELP!
I GOT IT. I THINK.
PROBABLY.
CAN YOU HELP YOUR MOM?
MOMMY I DON'T WANT TO LIVE HERE!
I WANT TO GO HOME! I WANT TO GO HOME RIGHT NOW!
SORRY, PUMPKIN, THIS PLACE IS ALL WE COULD FIND WITH SUCH SHORT NOTICE. WITH ALL THAT, WELL...WITH THAT DRAMA, I...
LISTEN. THIS IS GOING TO BE OUR NEW HOME, NOW.
UFFFF! THIS IS A LOT HEAVIER THAN I'D...HUFFF... THOUGHT! NOT SURE IF I'M...GOING TO...
I'LL GET IT, DAD!
NAWWW. I GOT IT!
WHOA!
SPIDER-MAN?
WHAT FLOOR SHOULD I TAKE THIS TO?
IT'S... SPIDER-MAN.

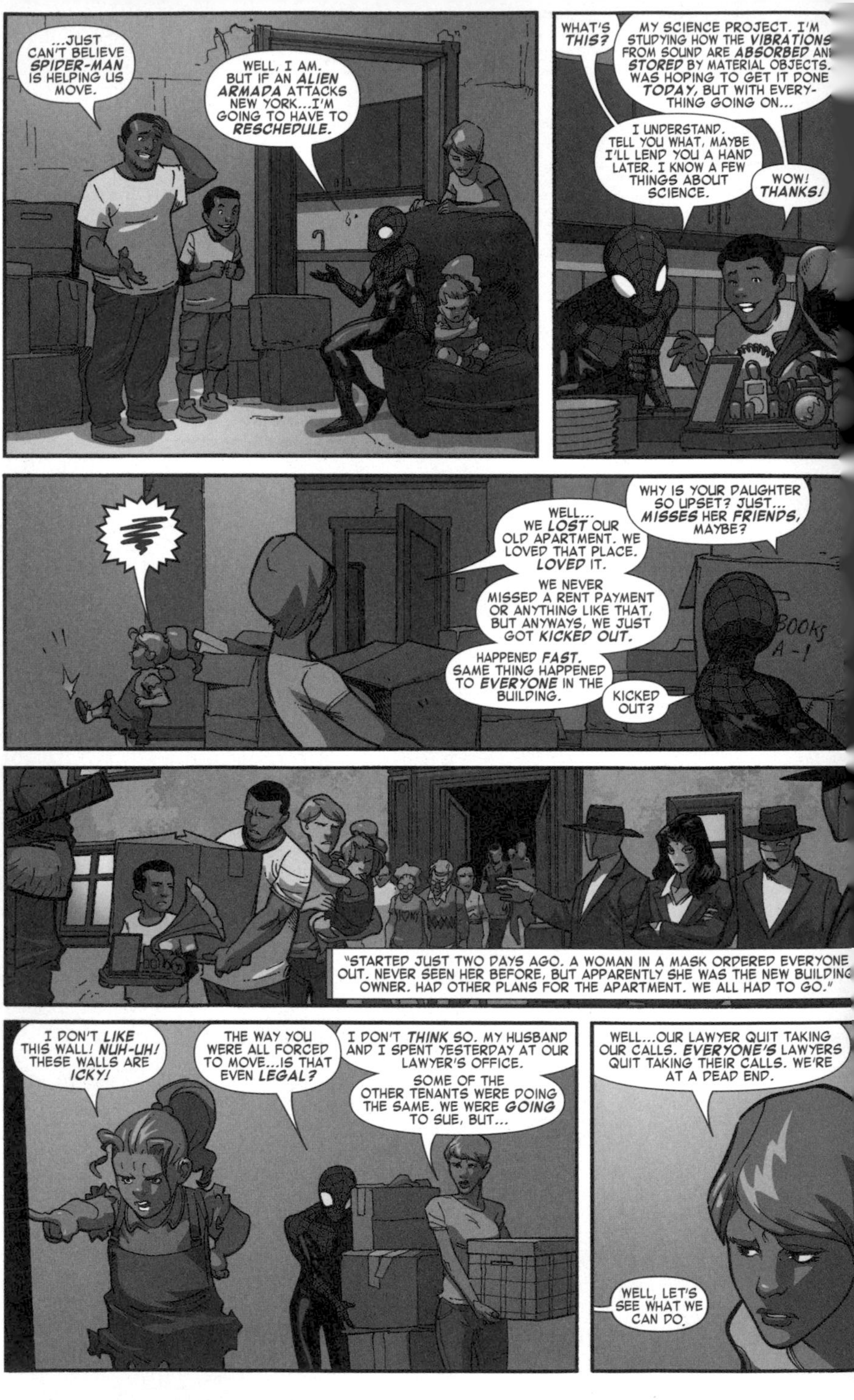
...JUST CAN'T BELIEVE SPIDER-MAN IS HELPING US MOVE.
WELL, I AM. BUT IF AN ALIEN ARMADA ATTACKS NEW YORK...I'M GOING TO HAVE TO RESCHEDULE.
WHAT'S THIS?
MY SCIENCE PROJECT. I'M STUDYING HOW THE VIBRATIONS FROM SOUND ARE ABSORBED AND STORED BY MATERIAL OBJECTS. WAS HOPING TO GET IT DONE TODAY, BUT WITH EVERY-THING GOING ON...
I UNDERSTAND. TELL YOU WHAT, MAYBE I'LL LEND YOU A HAND LATER. I KNOW A FEW THINGS ABOUT SCIENCE.
WOW! THANKS!
WHY IS YOUR DAUGHTER SO UPSET? JUST... MISSES HER FRIENDS, MAYBE?
WELL... WE LOST OUR OLD APARTMENT. WE LOVED THAT PLACE. LOVED IT.
WE NEVER MISSED A RENT PAYMENT OR ANYTHING LIKE THAT, BUT ANYWAYS, WE JUST GOT KICKED OUT.
HAPPENED FAST. SAME THING HAPPENED TO EVERYONE IN THE BUILDING.
KICKED OUT?
BOOKS A-I
"STARTED JUST TWO DAYS AGO. A WOMAN IN A MASK ORDERED EVERYONE OUT. NEVER SEEN HER BEFORE, BUT APPARENTLY SHE WAS THE NEW BUILDING OWNER. HAD OTHER PLANS FOR THE APARTMENT. WE ALL HAD TO GO."
I DON'T LIKE THIS WALL! NUH-UH! THESE WALLS ARE ICKY!
THE WAY YOU WERE ALL FORCED TO MOVE...IS THAT EVEN LEGAL?
I DON'T THINK SO. MY HUSBAND AND I SPENT YESTERDAY AT OUR LAWYER'S OFFICE.
SOME OF THE OTHER TENANTS WERE DOING THE SAME. WE WERE GOING TO SUE, BUT...
WELL...OUR LAWYER QUIT TAKING OUR CALLS. EVERYONE'S LAWYERS QUIT TAKING THEIR CALLS. WE'RE AT A DEAD END.
WELL, LET'S SEE WHAT WE CAN DO.

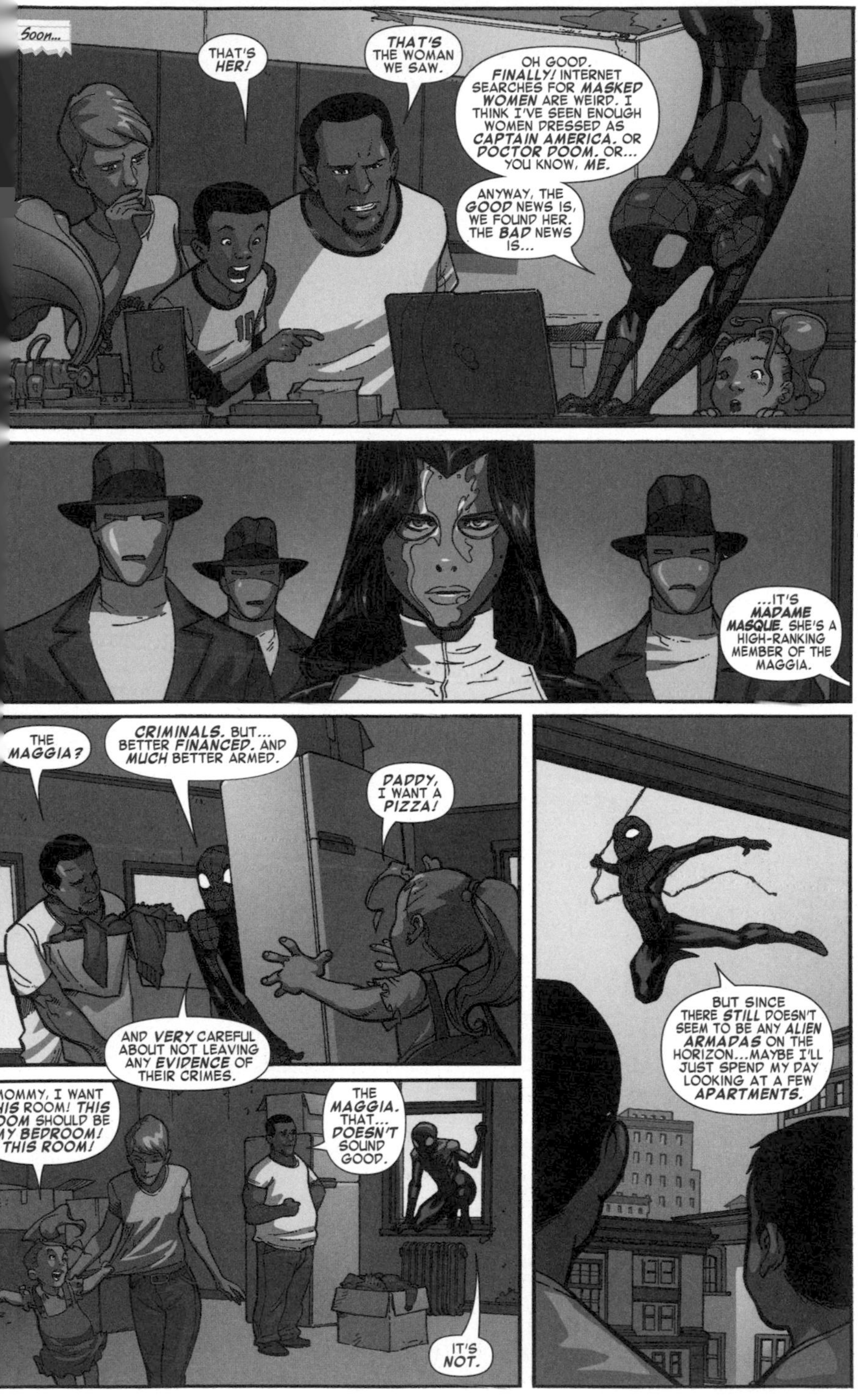
Soon...
THAT'S HER!
THAT'S THE WOMAN WE SAW.
OH GOOD. FINALLY! INTERNET SEARCHES FOR MASKED WOMEN ARE WEIRD. I THINK I'VE SEEN ENOUGH WOMEN DRESSED AS CAPTAIN AMERICA. OR DOCTOR DOOM. OR... YOU KNOW, ME.
ANYWAY, THE GOOD NEWS IS, WE FOUND HER. THE BAD NEWS IS...
...IT'S MADAME MASQUE. SHE'S A HIGH-RANKING MEMBER OF THE MAGGIA.
THE MAGGIA?
CRIMINALS. BUT... BETTER FINANCED. AND MUCH BETTER ARMED.
DADDY, I WANT A PIZZA!
AND VERY CAREFUL ABOUT NOT LEAVING ANY EVIDENCE OF THEIR CRIMES.
MOMMY, I WANT THIS ROOM! THIS ROOM SHOULD BE MY BEDROOM! THIS ROOM!
THE MAGGIA. THAT... DOESN'T SOUND GOOD.
IT'S NOT.
BUT SINCE THERE STILL DOESN'T SEEM TO BE ANY ALIEN ARMADAS ON THE HORIZON...MAYBE I'LL JUST SPEND MY DAY LOOKING AT A FEW APARTMENTS.

THIS IS THEIR OLD BUILDING.

SINCE NOBODY'S REALLY *LIVING* HERE ANYMORE, I THINK IT'S PROBABLY OKAY TO PEEK IN A FEW WINDOWS.

LASER RIFLES... NOT EXACTLY SURE I LIKE THE NEW FURNISHINGS IN THIS PLACE.

AND I'M NOT SURE I LIKE THE NEW *TENANTS.* WONDER WHAT KIND OF *DAMAGE DEPOSIT THOSE GUYS* HAD TO...

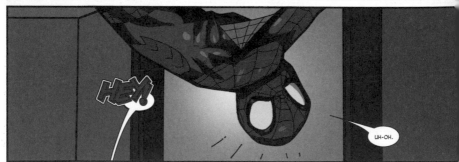

HEY!

UH-OH.

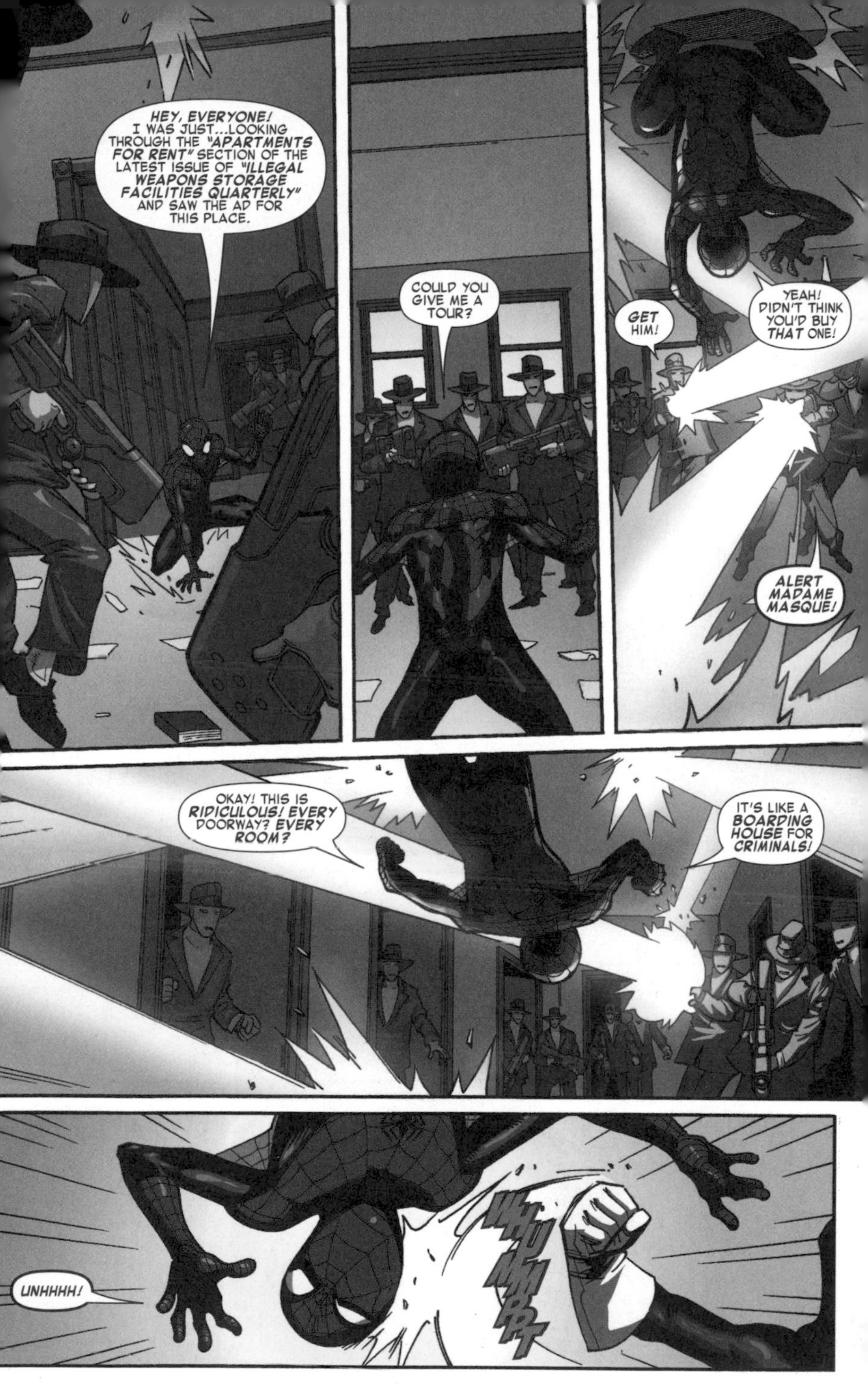
HEY, EVERYONE! I WAS JUST...LOOKING THROUGH THE "APARTMENTS FOR RENT" SECTION OF THE LATEST ISSUE OF "ILLEGAL WEAPONS STORAGE FACILITIES QUARTERLY" AND SAW THE AD FOR THIS PLACE.
COULD YOU GIVE ME A TOUR?
GET HIM!
YEAH! DIDN'T THINK YOU'D BUY THAT ONE!
ALERT MADAME MASQUE!
OKAY! THIS IS RIDICULOUS! EVERY DOORWAY? EVERY ROOM?
IT'S LIKE A BOARDING HOUSE FOR CRIMINALS!
WHUMMPT
UNHHHH!

AND...YOU'RE *MADAME MASQUE*. NICE TO *MEET* YOU, BUT FRANKLY A *HANDSHAKE* WOULD HAVE BEEN FINE.

I'M NOT SURE WHY YOU'RE *HERE*, SPIDER-MAN, OR WHO *SENT* YOU, BUT IT *DOESN'T* MATTER.

NO. IT DOESN'T MATTER BECAUSE *YOU'RE GOING TO STAY HERE*, FOREVER!

FOREVER? *HERE*? ONLY IF IT'S *RENT CONTROLLED*!

AND I'D HAVE TO DO SOMETHING ABOUT THE *WALLS*! AND ALL THE *WEAPONS* SCATTERED AROUND! MAYBE PUT IN A *POOL TABLE*?

ENOUGH! NOTHING YOU SAY MATTERS!

AFTER *FORGING* ALL THE LEGAL DOCUMENTS, AFTER *EVICTING* THE TENANTS, AFTER PAYING OFF *LAWYERS* AND *JUDGES* IN ORDER TO ESTABLISH THIS FACILITY, DID YOU *HONESTLY* THINK A *MAN* IN A *SPIDER COSTUME* WAS GOING TO STOP US?

GREAT! IF IT DOESN'T MATTER, THEN I'LL JUST BE ON MY WAY!

YOU'D BE *SURPRISED*! PEOPLE ARE *REALLY* AFRAID OF SPIDERS! I'LL *SHOW* YOU!

BOO!

WELL...*THAT* DIDN'T WORK! HMMM...LET'S TRY IT AGAIN!

BOO!

THERE? SEE? SCARY!

WUUUUU-WU

OH! HEAR *THAT*? SIRENS!

YOU PEOPLE *SURE* YOU WA[N]T TO LIVE HERE? I MEAN...WHAT W[ITH] ALL THE *NOIS[Y]* NEIGHBORS.

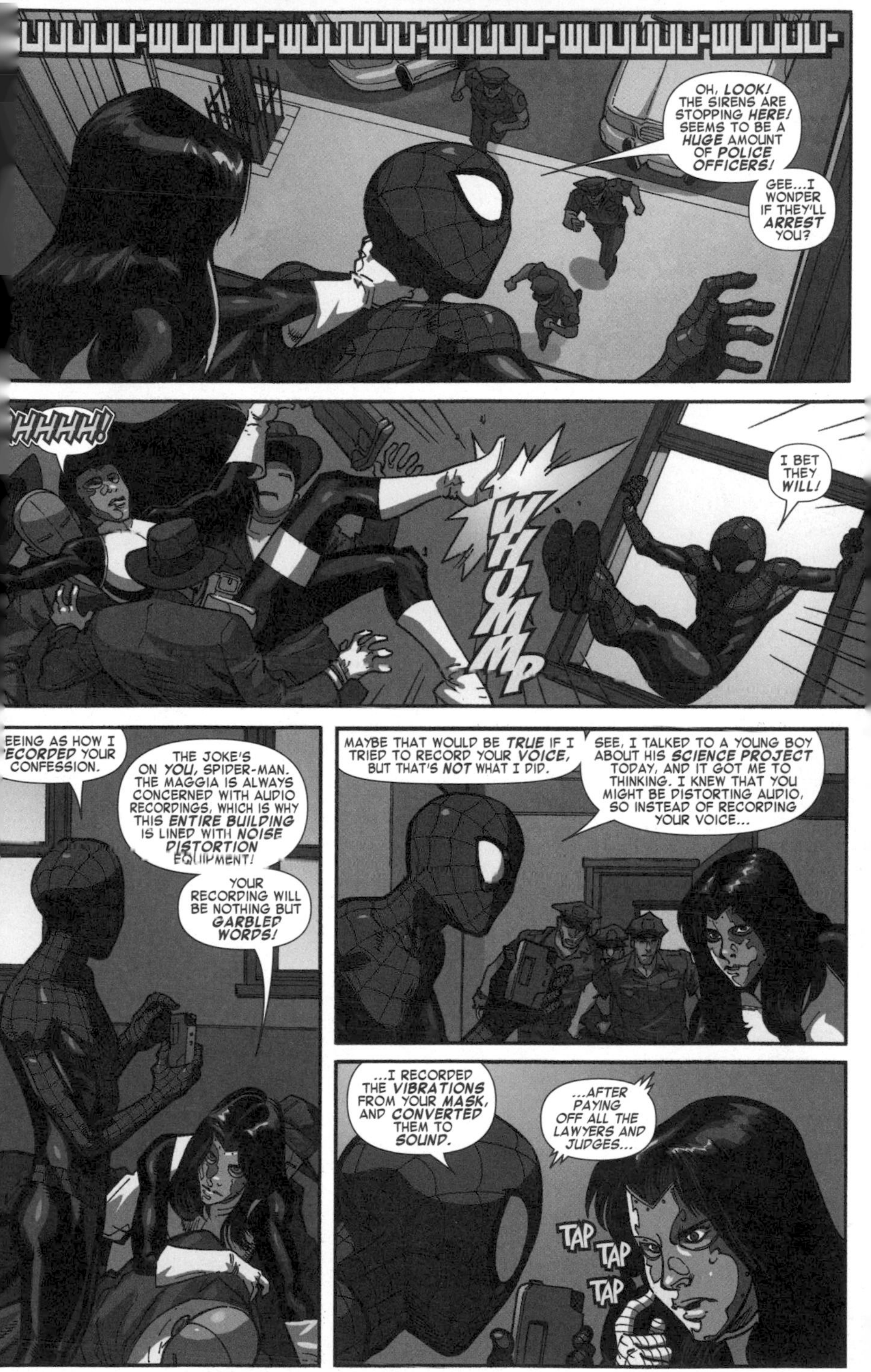

WUUUU-WUUUU-WUUUUU-WUUUU-WUUUUU-WUUUU-
OH, LOOK! THE SIRENS ARE STOPPING HERE! SEEMS TO BE A HUGE AMOUNT OF POLICE OFFICERS!
GEE...I WONDER IF THEY'LL ARREST YOU?
HHHH!
WHUMMP
I BET THEY WILL!
EEING AS HOW I ECORDED YOUR CONFESSION.
THE JOKE'S ON YOU, SPIDER-MAN. THE MAGGIA IS ALWAYS CONCERNED WITH AUDIO RECORDINGS, WHICH IS WHY THIS ENTIRE BUILDING IS LINED WITH NOISE DISTORTION EQUIPMENT!
YOUR RECORDING WILL BE NOTHING BUT GARBLED WORDS!
MAYBE THAT WOULD BE TRUE IF I TRIED TO RECORD YOUR VOICE, BUT THAT'S NOT WHAT I DID.
SEE, I TALKED TO A YOUNG BOY ABOUT HIS SCIENCE PROJECT TODAY, AND IT GOT ME TO THINKING. I KNEW THAT YOU MIGHT BE DISTORTING AUDIO, SO INSTEAD OF RECORDING YOUR VOICE...
...I RECORDED THE VIBRATIONS FROM YOUR MASK, AND CONVERTED THEM TO SOUND.
...AFTER PAYING OFF ALL THE LAWYERS AND JUDGES...
TAP
TAP
TAP

The next morning.

SO...MADAME MASQUE AND THE MAGGIA NEVER *LEGALLY* OWNED THE APARTMENT BUILDING AT ALL?

THAT'S RIGHT.

AND WE CAN *MOVE BACK IN* ANY TIME WE *WANT?*

THAT'S *ALSO* RIGHT.

ALL BECAUSE, *FOR ONCE*, SOMEBODY WAS ABLE TO *PROVE* SOMETHING AGAINST THE MAGGIA. THANKS TO *YOUR* SCIENCE PROJECT.

WOW! I TEAMED U_ WITH *SPIDE_ MAN!*

LET'S START MOVING THIS *FURNITURE* BACK, THEN. TIME FOR YOU FOLKS TO *GO HOME.*

MOMMY, I WANT A *RIDE!*

HMMM. IS IT OKAY?

WELL...

WHEEEEEEEEEEEEEEEEEEEEEEEE

WHEEEEEEEEEEEEEEE!!!

THE END.

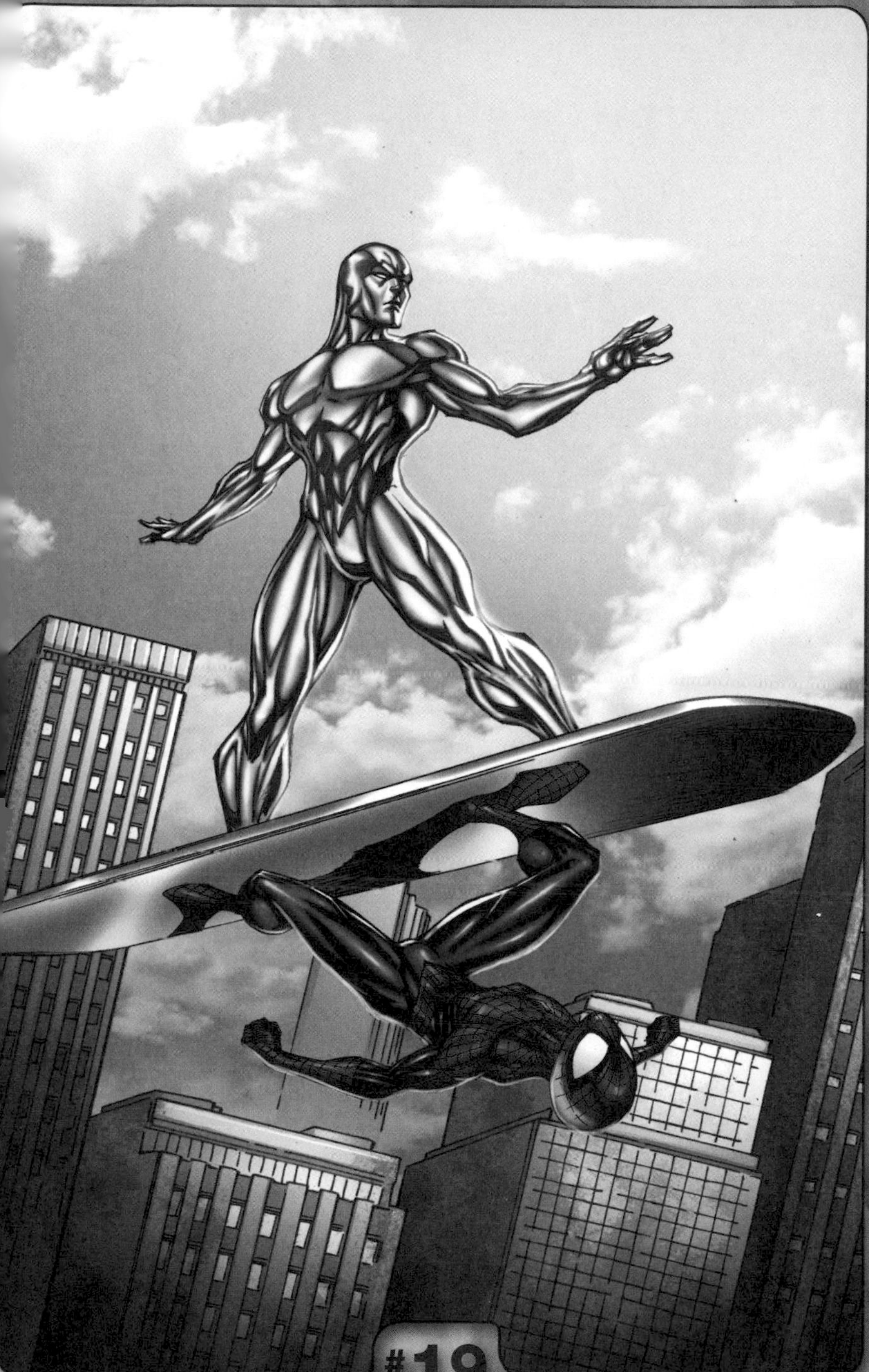

#19

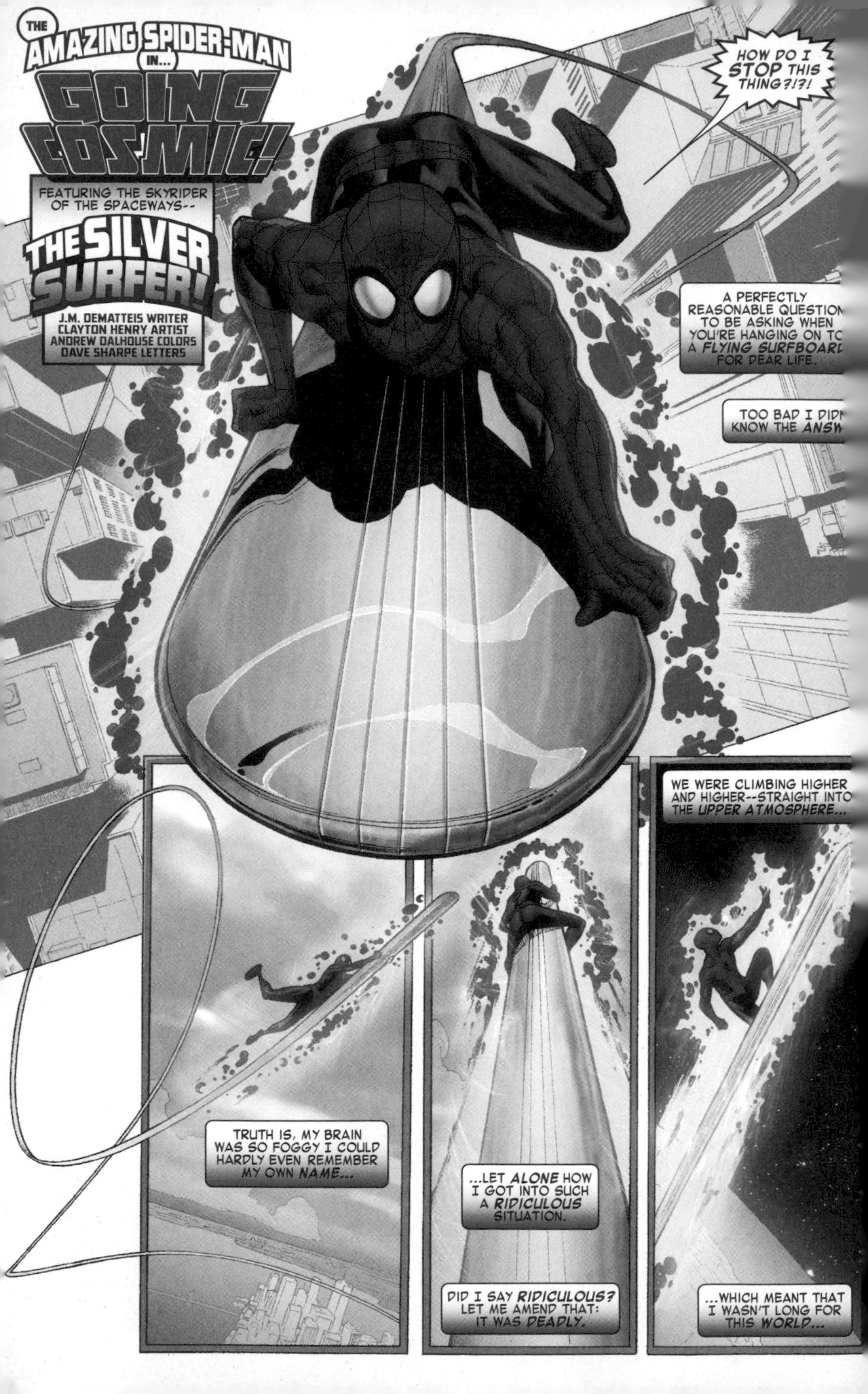
THE AMAZING SPIDER-MAN IN...
GOING COSMIC!
FEATURING THE SKYRIDER OF THE SPACEWAYS--
THE SILVER SURFER!
J.M. DEMATTEIS WRITER
CLAYTON HENRY ARTIST
ANDREW DALHOUSE COLORS
DAVE SHARPE LETTERS
HOW DO I STOP THIS THING?!?!
A PERFECTLY REASONABLE QUESTION TO BE ASKING WHEN YOU'RE HANGING ON TO A FLYING SURFBOAR FOR DEAR LIFE.
TOO BAD I DIDN KNOW THE ANSW
TRUTH IS, MY BRAIN WAS SO FOGGY I COULD HARDLY EVEN REMEMBER MY OWN NAME...
...LET ALONE HOW I GOT INTO SUCH A RIDICULOUS SITUATION.
DID I SAY RIDICULOUS? LET ME AMEND THAT: IT WAS DEADLY.
WE WERE CLIMBING HIGHER AND HIGHER--STRAIGHT INTO THE UPPER ATMOSPHERE...
...WHICH MEANT THAT I WASN'T LONG FOR THIS WORLD...

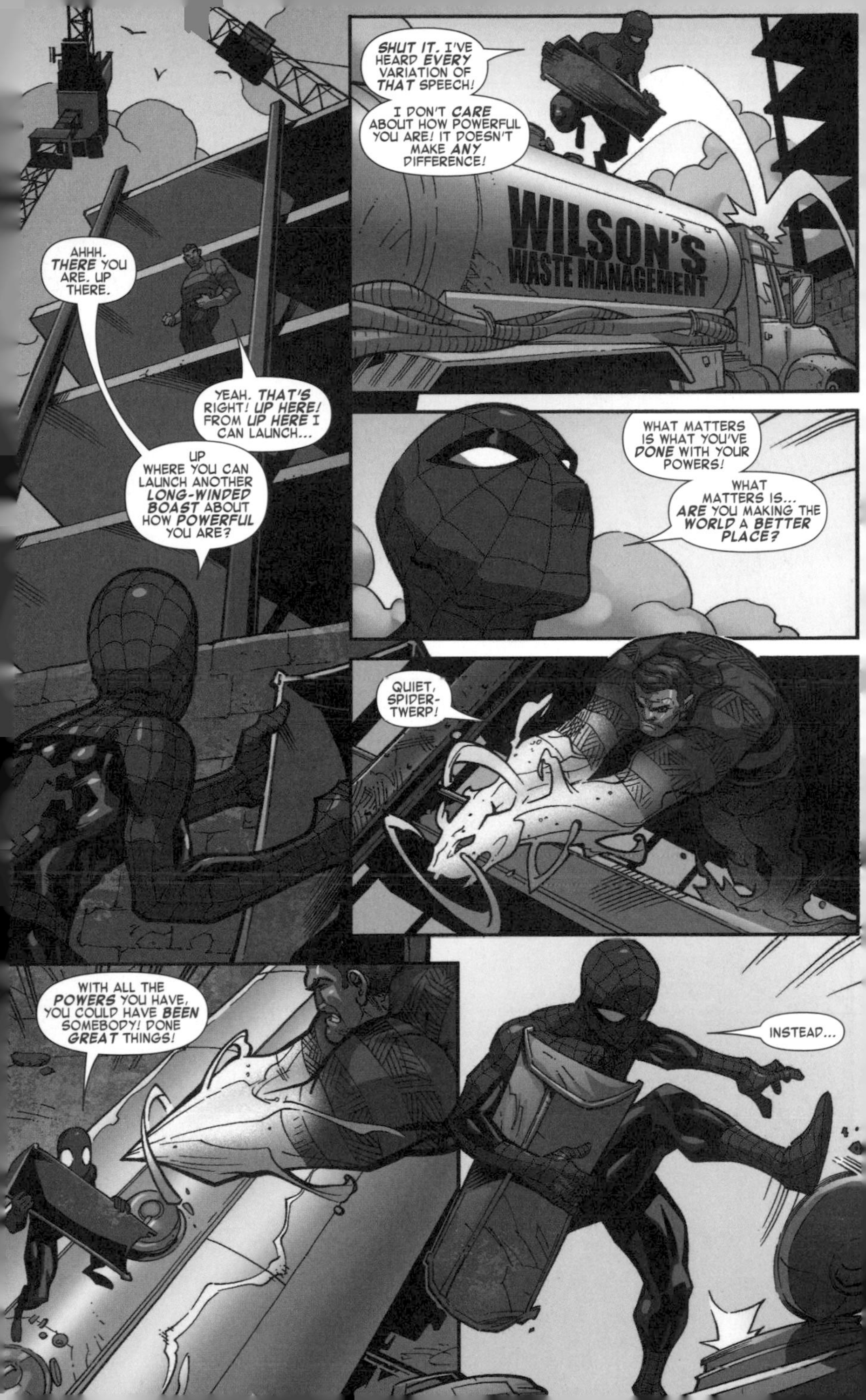
AHHH. THERE YOU ARE. UP THERE.
YEAH. THAT'S RIGHT! UP HERE! FROM UP HERE I CAN LAUNCH...
UP WHERE YOU CAN LAUNCH ANOTHER LONG-WINDED BOAST ABOUT HOW POWERFUL YOU ARE?
SHUT IT. I'VE HEARD EVERY VARIATION OF THAT SPEECH!
I DON'T CARE ABOUT HOW POWERFUL YOU ARE! IT DOESN'T MAKE ANY DIFFERENCE!
WILSON'S WASTE MANAGEMENT
WHAT MATTERS IS WHAT YOU'VE DONE WITH YOUR POWERS!
WHAT MATTERS IS... ARE YOU MAKING THE WORLD A BETTER PLACE?
QUIET, SPIDER-TWERP!
WITH ALL THE POWERS YOU HAVE, YOU COULD HAVE BEEN SOMEBODY! DONE GREAT THINGS!
INSTEAD...

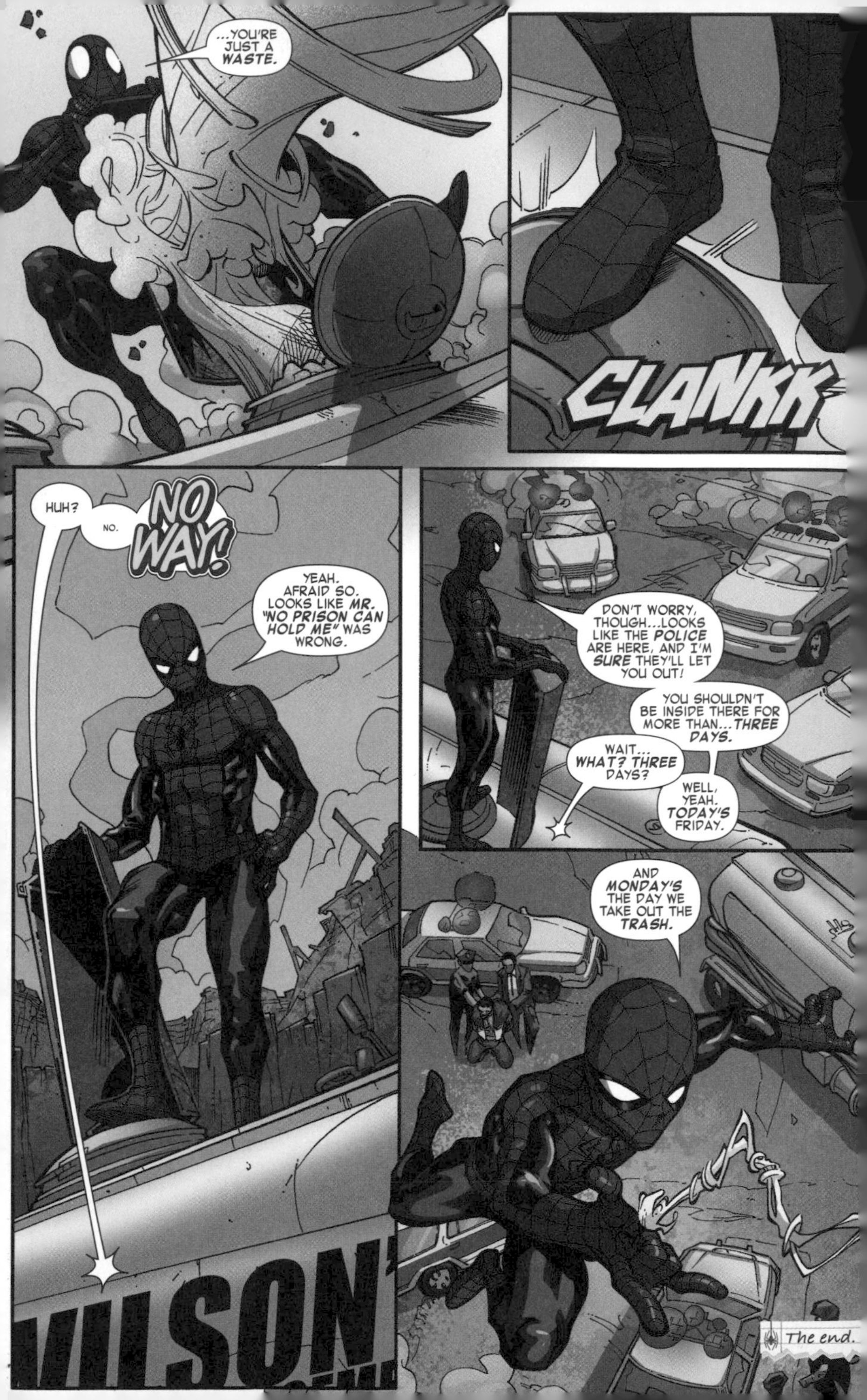
...YOU'RE JUST A WASTE.
CLANKK
HUH?
NO.
NO WAY!
YEAH. AFRAID SO. LOOKS LIKE MR. "NO PRISON CAN HOLD ME" WAS WRONG.
DON'T WORRY, THOUGH...LOOKS LIKE THE POLICE ARE HERE, AND I'M SURE THEY'LL LET YOU OUT!
YOU SHOULDN'T BE INSIDE THERE FOR MORE THAN...THREE DAYS.
WAIT... WHAT? THREE DAYS?
WELL, YEAH. TODAY'S FRIDAY.
AND MONDAY'S THE DAY WE TAKE OUT THE TRASH.
The end.

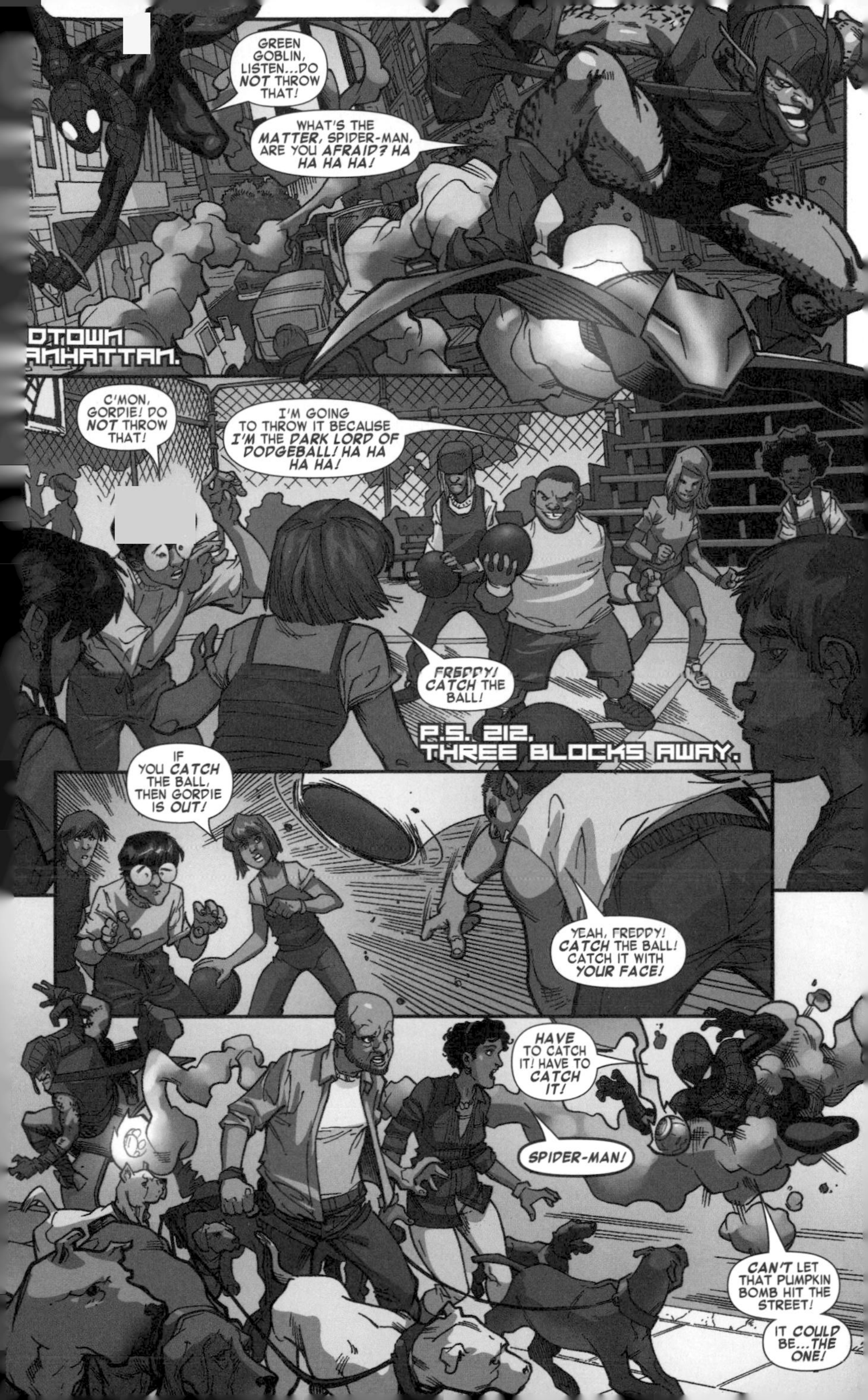
GREEN GOBLIN, LISTEN...DO NOT THROW THAT!
WHAT'S THE MATTER, SPIDER-MAN, ARE YOU AFRAID? HA HA HA HA!
DTOWN ANHATTAN.
C'MON, GORDIE! DO NOT THROW THAT!
I'M GOING TO THROW IT BECAUSE I'M THE DARK LORD OF DODGEBALL! HA HA HA HA!
FREDDY! CATCH THE BALL!
P.S. 212. THREE BLOCKS AWAY.
IF YOU CATCH THE BALL, THEN GORDIE IS OUT!
YEAH, FREDDY! CATCH THE BALL! CATCH IT WITH YOUR FACE!
HAVE TO CATCH IT! HAVE TO CATCH IT!
SPIDER-MAN!
CAN'T LET THAT PUMPKIN BOMB HIT THE STREET!
IT COULD BE...THE ONE!

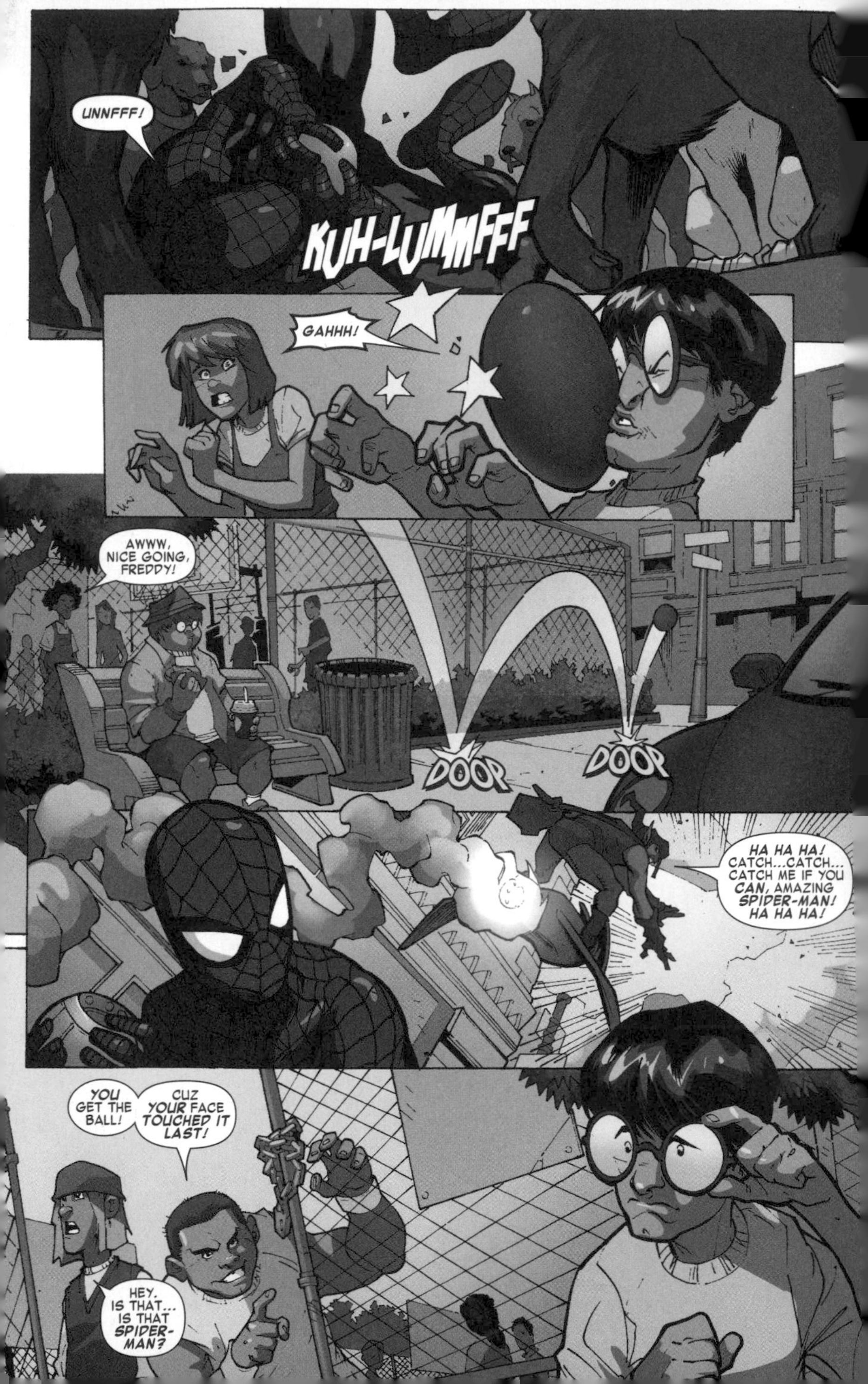
UNNFFF!
KUH-LUMMFFF
GAHHH!
AWWW, NICE GOING, FREDDY!
DOOP
DOOP
HA HA HA! CATCH...CATCH... CATCH ME IF YOU CAN, AMAZING SPIDER-MAN! HA HA HA!
YOU GET THE BALL!
CUZ YOUR FACE TOUCHED IT LAST!
HEY. IS THAT... IS THAT SPIDER-MAN?

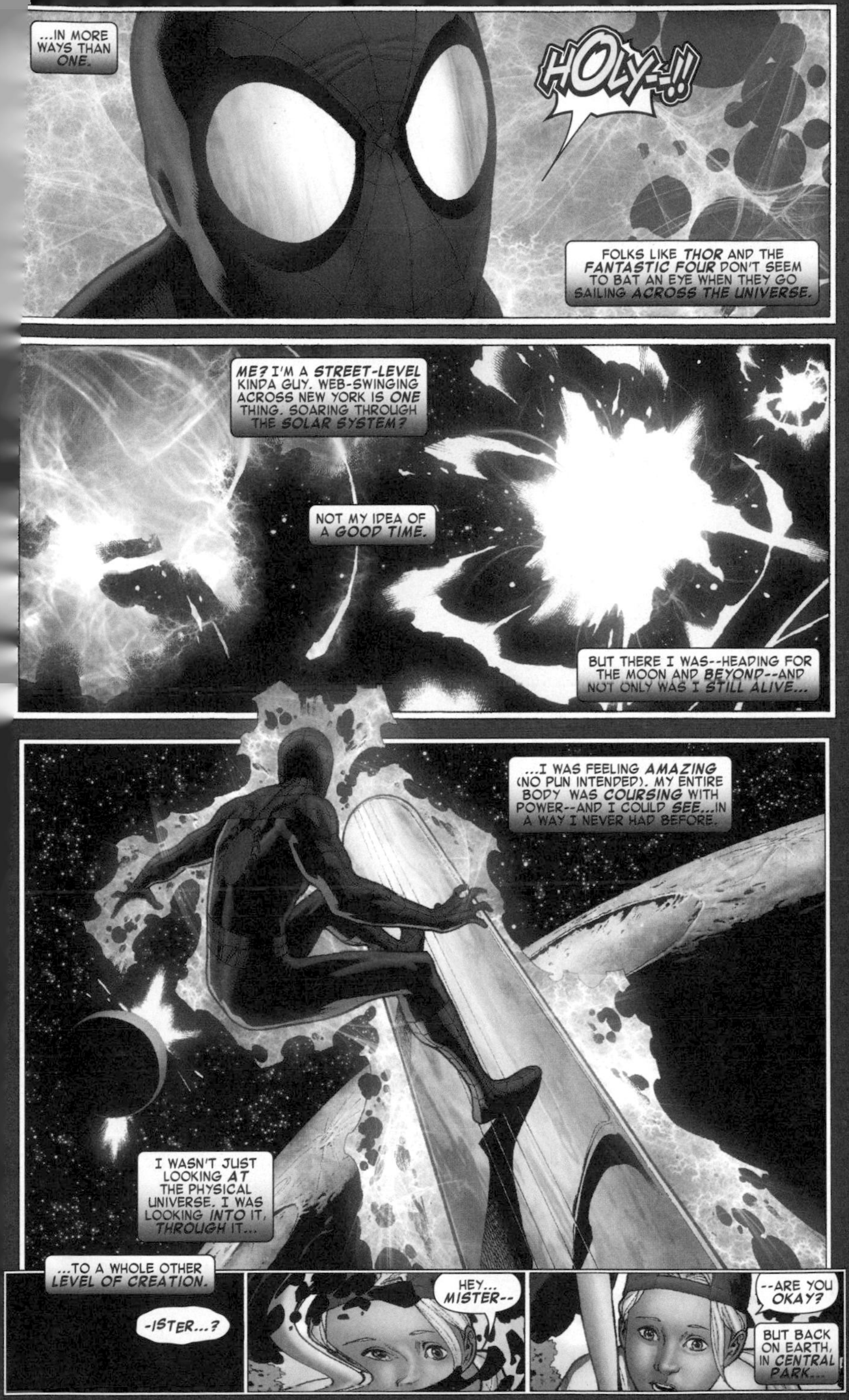
...IN MORE WAYS THAN ONE.
HOLY--!!
FOLKS LIKE THOR AND THE FANTASTIC FOUR DON'T SEEM TO BAT AN EYE WHEN THEY GO SAILING ACROSS THE UNIVERSE.
ME? I'M A STREET-LEVEL KINDA GUY. WEB-SWINGING ACROSS NEW YORK IS ONE THING. SOARING THROUGH THE SOLAR SYSTEM?
NOT MY IDEA OF A GOOD TIME.
BUT THERE I WAS--HEADING FOR THE MOON AND BEYOND--AND NOT ONLY WAS I STILL ALIVE...
...I WAS FEELING AMAZING (NO PUN INTENDED). MY ENTIRE BODY WAS COURSING WITH POWER--AND I COULD SEE...IN A WAY I NEVER HAD BEFORE.
I WASN'T JUST LOOKING AT THE PHYSICAL UNIVERSE. I WAS LOOKING INTO IT, THROUGH IT...
...TO A WHOLE OTHER LEVEL OF CREATION.
-ISTER...?
HEY... MISTER--
--ARE YOU OKAY?
BUT BACK ON EARTH, IN CENTRAL PARK...

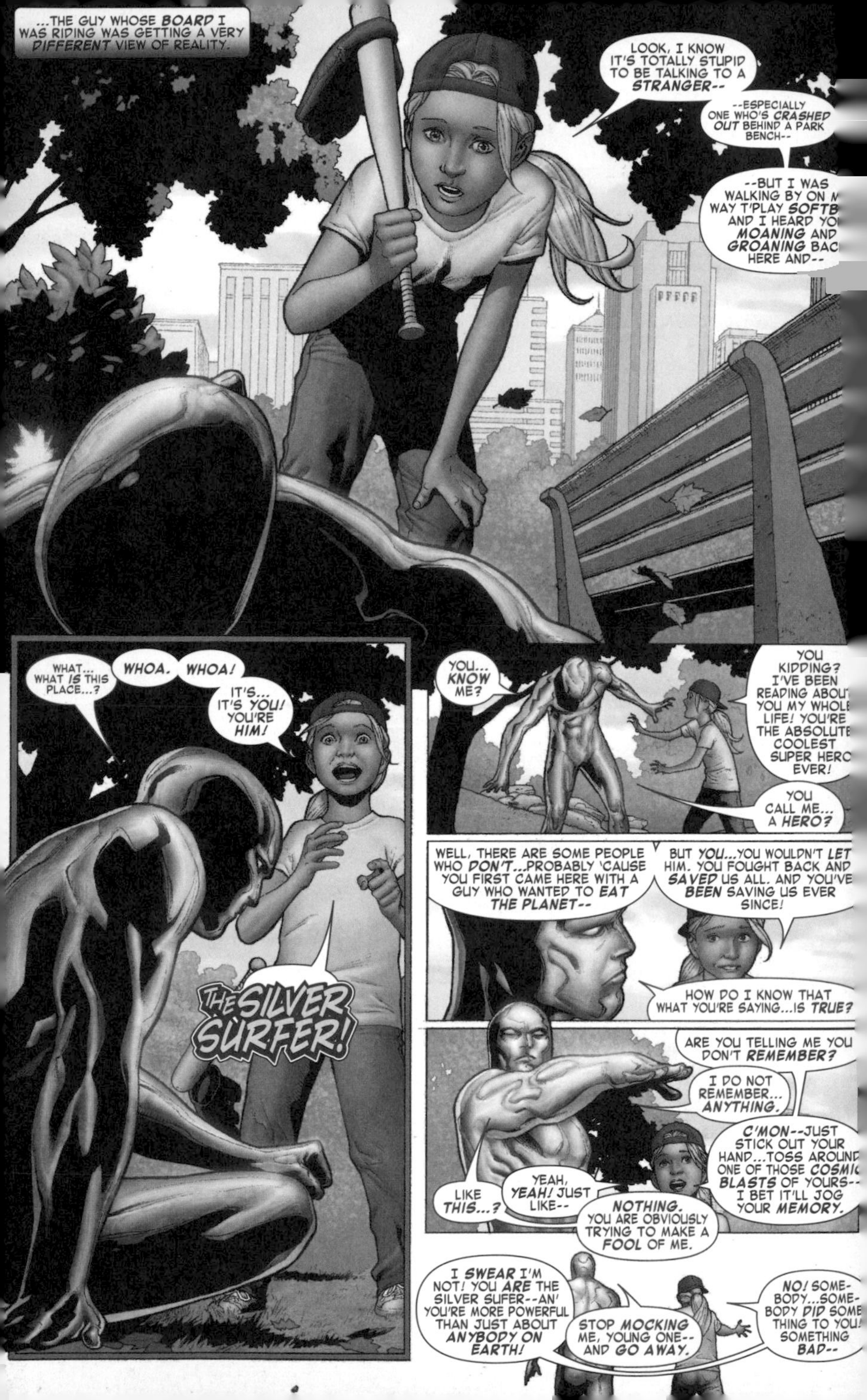
...THE GUY WHOSE BOARD I WAS RIDING WAS GETTING A VERY DIFFERENT VIEW OF REALITY.
LOOK, I KNOW IT'S TOTALLY STUPID TO BE TALKING TO A STRANGER--
--ESPECIALLY ONE WHO'S CRASHED OUT BEHIND A PARK BENCH--
--BUT I WAS WALKING BY ON M WAY T'PLAY SOFTB AND I HEARD YO MOANING AND GROANING BAC HERE AND--
WHAT... WHAT IS THIS PLACE...?
WHOA.
WHOA!
IT'S... IT'S YOU! YOU'RE HIM!
THE SILVER SURFER!
YOU... KNOW ME?
YOU KIDDING? I'VE BEEN READING ABOUT YOU MY WHOLE LIFE! YOU'RE THE ABSOLUTE COOLEST SUPER HERO EVER!
YOU CALL ME... A HERO?
WELL, THERE ARE SOME PEOPLE WHO DON'T...PROBABLY 'CAUSE YOU FIRST CAME HERE WITH A GUY WHO WANTED TO EAT THE PLANET--
BUT YOU...YOU WOULDN'T LET HIM. YOU FOUGHT BACK AND SAVED US ALL. AND YOU'VE BEEN SAVING US EVER SINCE!
HOW DO I KNOW THAT WHAT YOU'RE SAYING...IS TRUE?
ARE YOU TELLING ME YOU DON'T REMEMBER?
I DO NOT REMEMBER... ANYTHING.
C'MON--JUST STICK OUT YOUR HAND...TOSS AROUND ONE OF THOSE COSMIC BLASTS OF YOURS-- I BET IT'LL JOG YOUR MEMORY.
LIKE THIS...?
YEAH, YEAH! JUST LIKE--
NOTHING. YOU ARE OBVIOUSLY TRYING TO MAKE A FOOL OF ME.
I SWEAR I'M NOT! YOU ARE THE SILVER SUFER--AN' YOU'RE MORE POWERFUL THAN JUST ABOUT ANYBODY ON EARTH!
STOP MOCKING ME, YOUNG ONE-- AND GO AWAY.
NO! SOME-BODY...SOME-BODY DID SOME THING TO YOU! SOMETHING BAD--

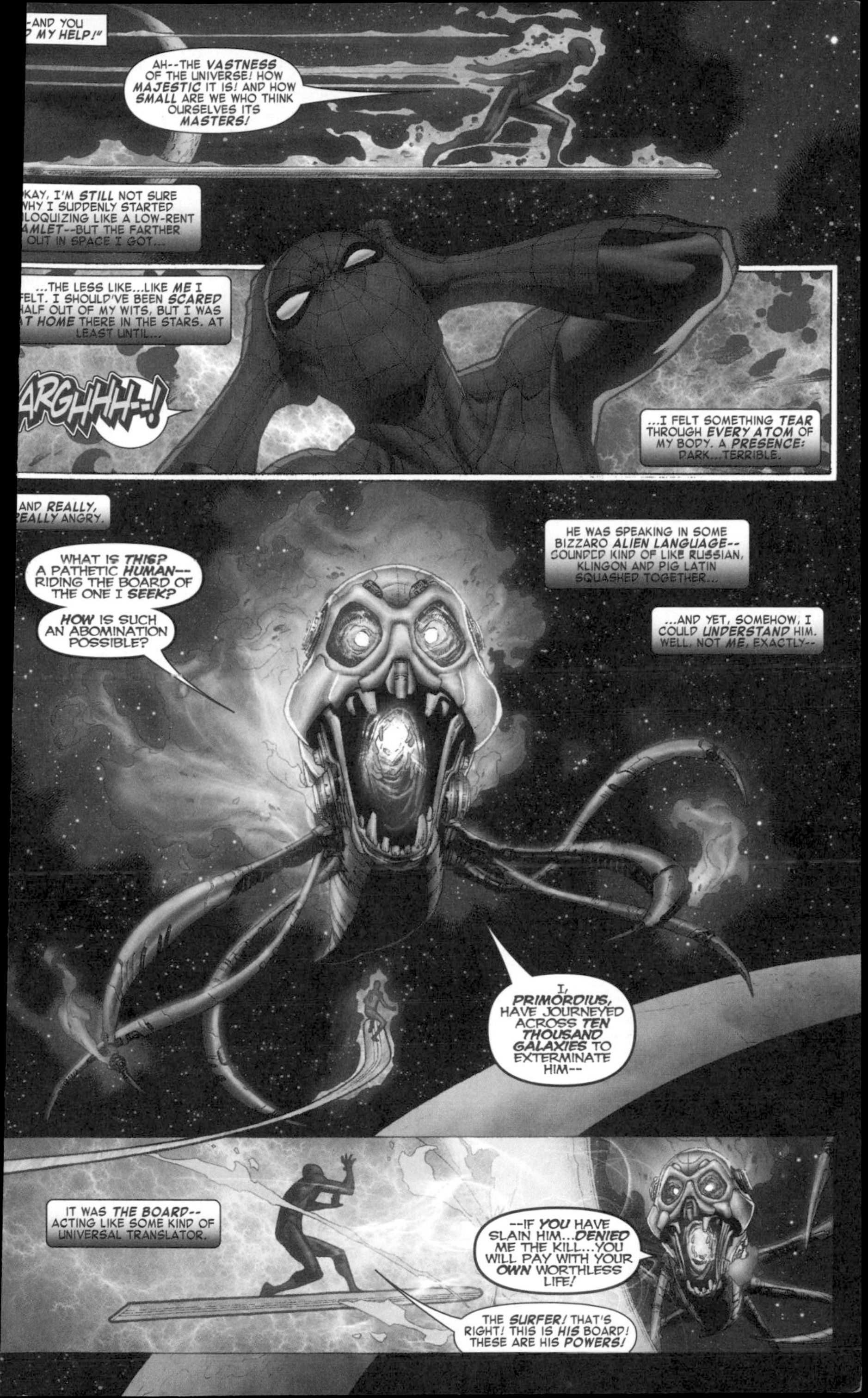
-AND YOU
D MY HELP!"
AH--THE VASTNESS OF THE UNIVERSE! HOW MAJESTIC IT IS! AND HOW SMALL ARE WE WHO THINK OURSELVES ITS MASTERS!
KAY, I'M STILL NOT SURE WHY I SUDDENLY STARTED LOQUIZING LIKE A LOW-RENT AMLET--BUT THE FARTHER OUT IN SPACE I GOT...
...THE LESS LIKE...LIKE ME I FELT. I SHOULD'VE BEEN SCARED HALF OUT OF MY WITS, BUT I WAS AT HOME THERE IN THE STARS. AT LEAST UNTIL...
ARGHHH--!
...I FELT SOMETHING TEAR THROUGH EVERY ATOM OF MY BODY. A PRESENCE: DARK...TERRIBLE.
AND REALLY, REALLY ANGRY.
WHAT IS THIS? A PATHETIC HUMAN--RIDING THE BOARD OF THE ONE I SEEK?
HOW IS SUCH AN ABOMINATION POSSIBLE?
HE WAS SPEAKING IN SOME BIZZARO ALIEN LANGUAGE--SOUNDED KIND OF LIKE RUSSIAN, KLINGON AND PIG LATIN SQUASHED TOGETHER...
...AND YET, SOMEHOW, I COULD UNDERSTAND HIM. WELL, NOT ME, EXACTLY--
I, PRIMORDIUS, HAVE JOURNEYED ACROSS TEN THOUSAND GALAXIES TO EXTERMINATE HIM--
IT WAS THE BOARD--ACTING LIKE SOME KIND OF UNIVERSAL TRANSLATOR.
--IF YOU HAVE SLAIN HIM...DENIED ME THE KILL...YOU WILL PAY WITH YOUR OWN WORTHLESS LIFE!
THE SURFER! THAT'S RIGHT! THIS IS HIS BOARD! THESE ARE HIS POWERS!

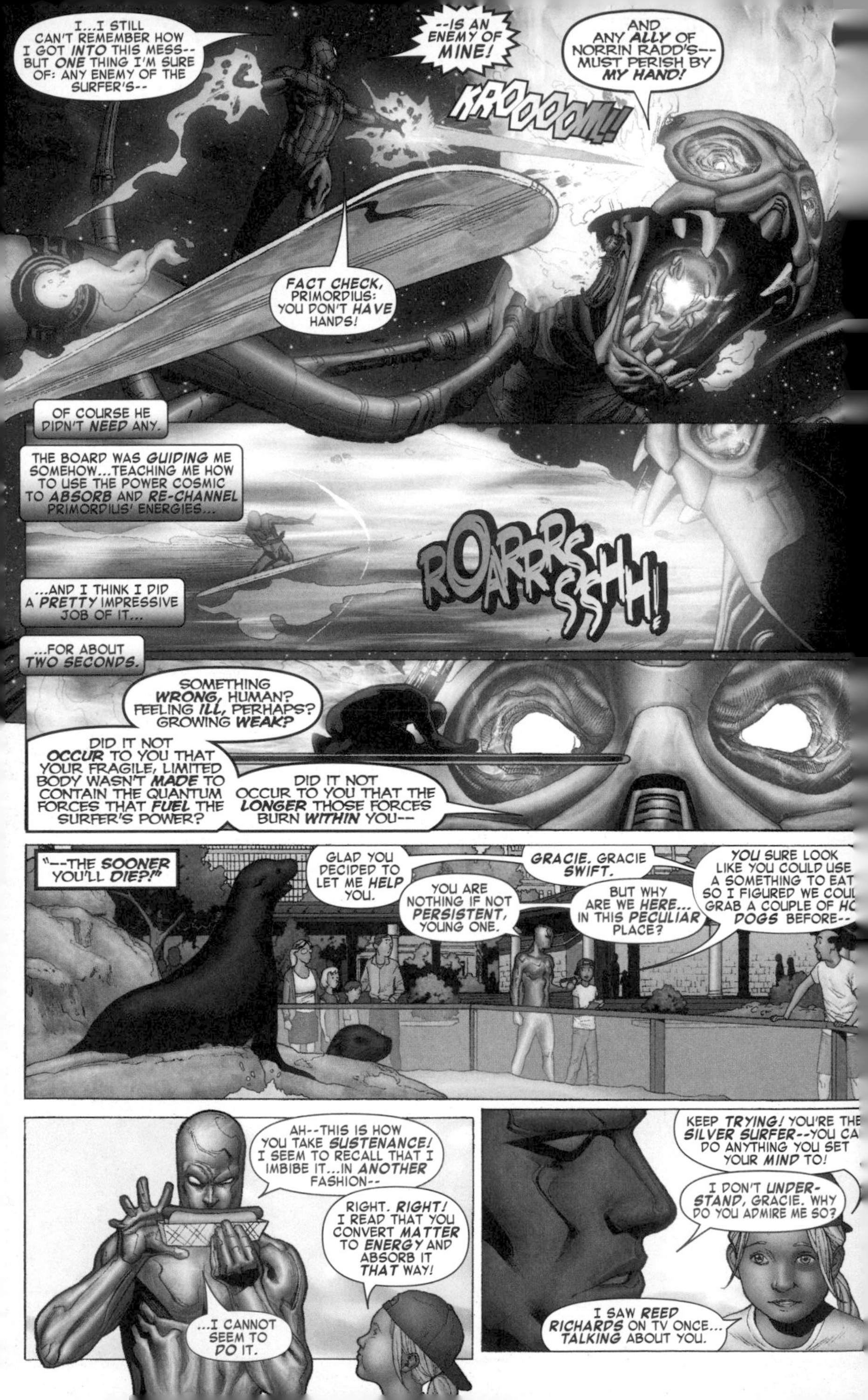
I...I STILL CAN'T REMEMBER HOW I GOT INTO THIS MESS--BUT ONE THING I'M SURE OF: ANY ENEMY OF THE SURFER'S--
--IS AN ENEMY OF MINE!
AND ANY ALLY OF NORRIN RADD'S--MUST PERISH BY MY HAND!
KROOOOOM!!
FACT CHECK, PRIMORDIUS: YOU DON'T HAVE HANDS!
OF COURSE HE DIDN'T NEED ANY.
THE BOARD WAS GUIDING ME SOMEHOW...TEACHING ME HOW TO USE THE POWER COSMIC TO ABSORB AND RE-CHANNEL PRIMORDIUS' ENERGIES...
...AND I THINK I DID A PRETTY IMPRESSIVE JOB OF IT...
ROARRRSSHH!
...FOR ABOUT TWO SECONDS.
SOMETHING WRONG, HUMAN? FEELING ILL, PERHAPS? GROWING WEAK?
DID IT NOT OCCUR TO YOU THAT YOUR FRAGILE, LIMITED BODY WASN'T MADE TO CONTAIN THE QUANTUM FORCES THAT FUEL THE SURFER'S POWER?
DID IT NOT OCCUR TO YOU THAT THE LONGER THOSE FORCES BURN WITHIN YOU--
"--THE SOONER YOU'LL DIE?!"
GLAD YOU DECIDED TO LET ME HELP YOU.
YOU ARE NOTHING IF NOT PERSISTENT, YOUNG ONE.
GRACIE. GRACIE SWIFT.
BUT WHY ARE WE HERE... IN THIS PECULIAR PLACE?
YOU SURE LOOK LIKE YOU COULD USE A SOMETHING TO EAT SO I FIGURED WE COUL GRAB A COUPLE OF HO DOGS BEFORE--
AH--THIS IS HOW YOU TAKE SUSTENANCE! I SEEM TO RECALL THAT I IMBIBE IT...IN ANOTHER FASHION--
RIGHT. RIGHT! I READ THAT YOU CONVERT MATTER TO ENERGY AND ABSORB IT THAT WAY!
...I CANNOT SEEM TO DO IT.
KEEP TRYING! YOU'RE THE SILVER SURFER--YOU CA DO ANYTHING YOU SET YOUR MIND TO!
I DON'T UNDERSTAND, GRACIE. WHY DO YOU ADMIRE ME SO?
I SAW REED RICHARDS ON TV ONCE... TALKING ABOUT YOU.

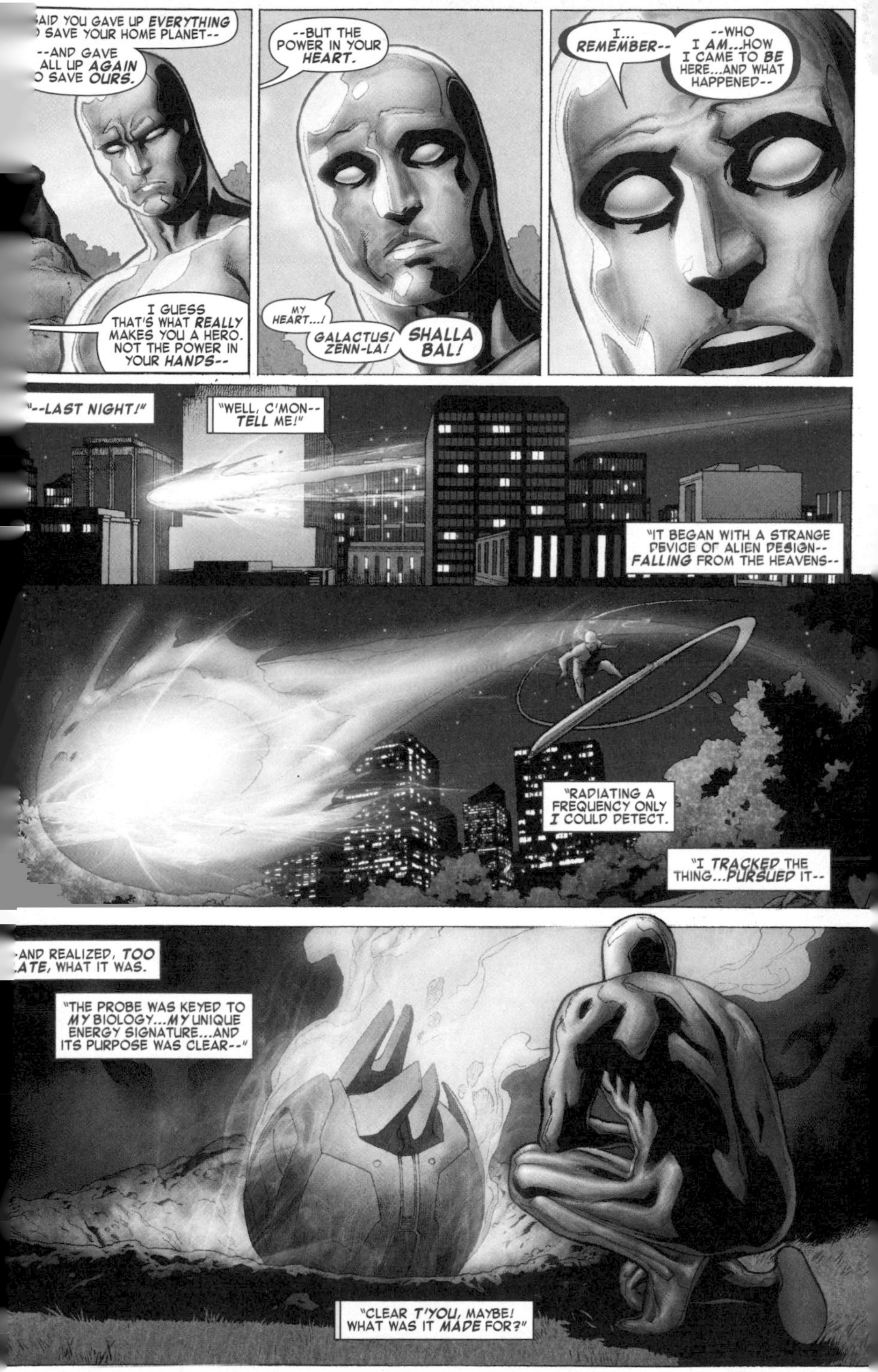
SAID YOU GAVE UP EVERYTHING
O SAVE YOUR HOME PLANET--
--AND GAVE
ALL UP AGAIN
O SAVE OURS.
I GUESS THAT'S WHAT REALLY MAKES YOU A HERO. NOT THE POWER IN YOUR HANDS--
--BUT THE POWER IN YOUR HEART.
MY HEART...!
GALACTUS! ZENN-LA!
SHALLA BAL!
I... REMEMBER--
--WHO I AM...HOW I CAME TO BE HERE...AND WHAT HAPPENED--
"--LAST NIGHT!"
"WELL, C'MON-- TELL ME!"
"IT BEGAN WITH A STRANGE DEVICE OF ALIEN DESIGN-- FALLING FROM THE HEAVENS--
"RADIATING A FREQUENCY ONLY I COULD DETECT.
"I TRACKED THE THING...PURSUED IT--
-AND REALIZED, TOO
ATE, WHAT IT WAS.
"THE PROBE WAS KEYED TO MY BIOLOGY...MY UNIQUE ENERGY SIGNATURE...AND ITS PURPOSE WAS CLEAR--"
"CLEAR T'YOU, MAYBE! WHAT WAS IT MADE FOR?"

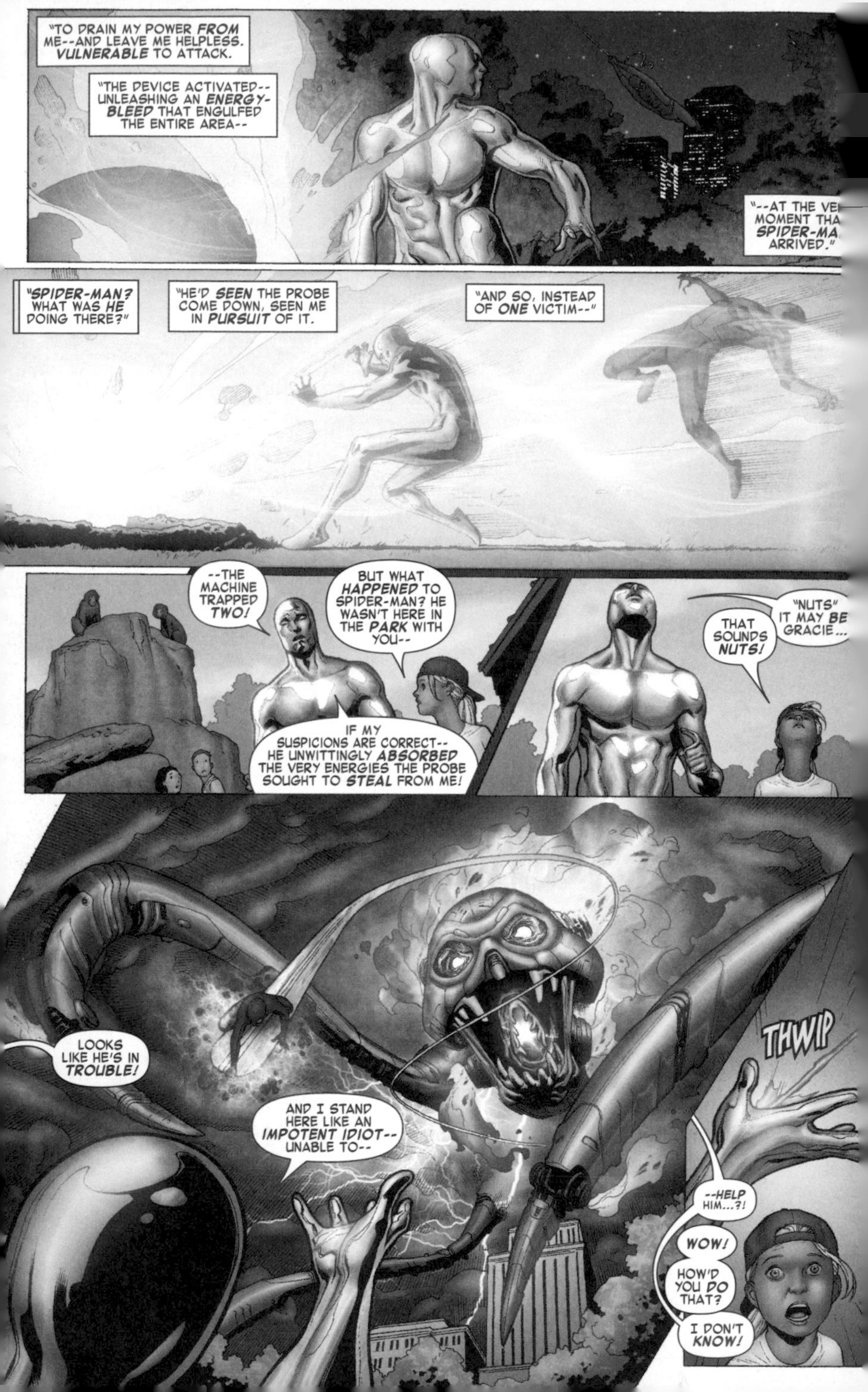
"TO DRAIN MY POWER *FROM* ME--AND LEAVE ME HELPLESS. *VULNERABLE* TO ATTACK.
"THE DEVICE ACTIVATED--UNLEASHING AN *ENERGY-BLEED* THAT ENGULFED THE ENTIRE AREA--
"--AT THE VE MOMENT THA *SPIDER-MA* ARRIVED."
"*SPIDER-MAN?* WHAT WAS *HE* DOING THERE?"
"HE'D *SEEN* THE PROBE COME DOWN, SEEN ME IN *PURSUIT* OF IT.
"AND SO, INSTEAD OF *ONE* VICTIM--"
--THE MACHINE TRAPPED *TWO!*
BUT WHAT *HAPPENED* TO SPIDER-MAN? HE WASN'T HERE IN THE *PARK* WITH YOU--
IF MY SUSPICIONS ARE CORRECT--HE UNWITTINGLY *ABSORBED* THE VERY ENERGIES THE PROBE SOUGHT TO *STEAL* FROM ME!
THAT SOUNDS *NUTS!*
"NUTS" IT MAY *BE* GRACIE...
LOOKS LIKE HE'S IN *TROUBLE!*
AND I STAND HERE LIKE AN *IMPOTENT IDIOT*--UNABLE TO--
THWIP
--HELP HIM...?!
WOW!
HOW'D YOU *DO* THAT?
I DON'T *KNOW!*

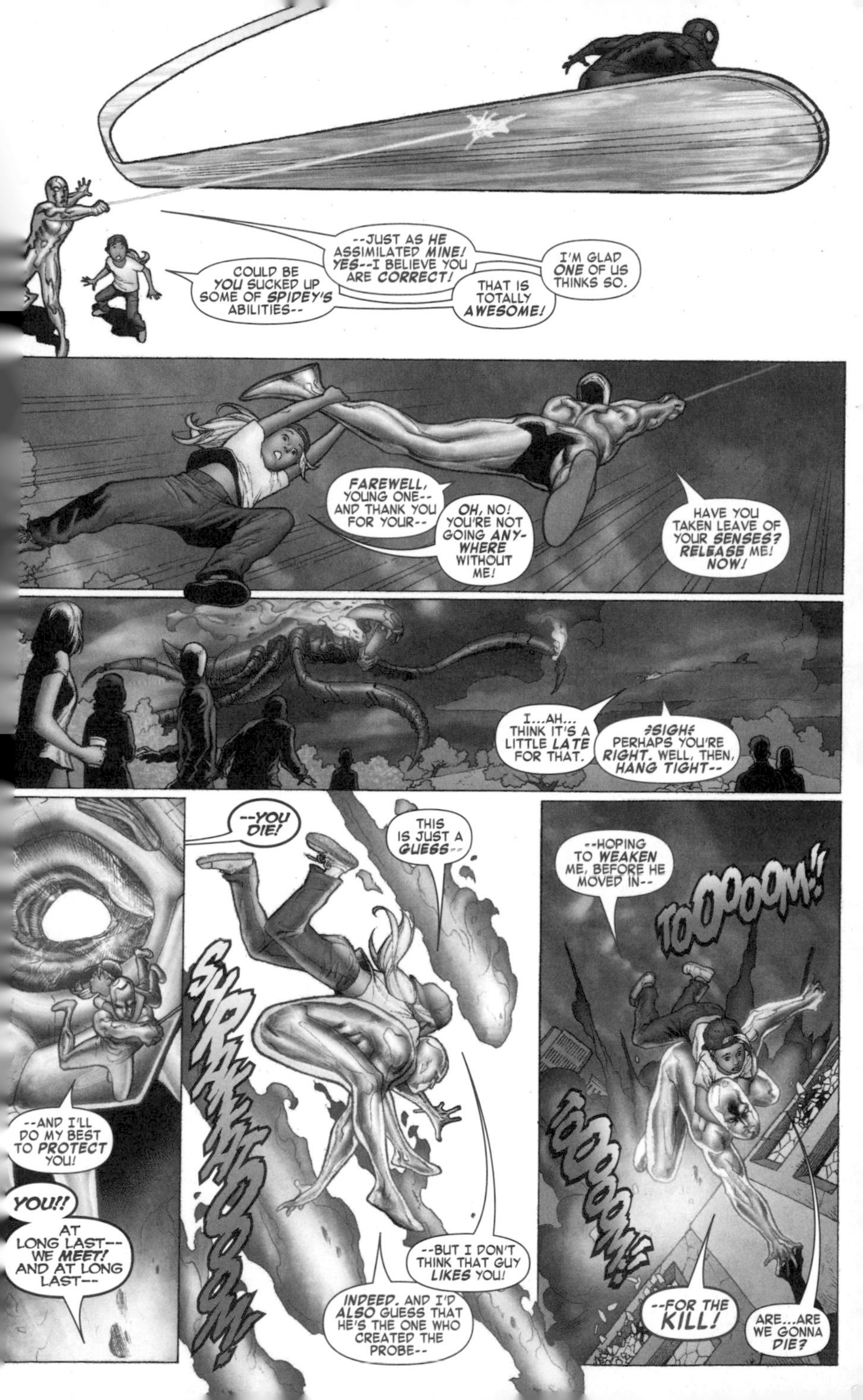
COULD BE YOU SUCKED UP SOME OF SPIDEY'S ABILITIES--
--JUST AS HE ASSIMILATED MINE! YES--I BELIEVE YOU ARE CORRECT!
THAT IS TOTALLY AWESOME!
I'M GLAD ONE OF US THINKS SO.
FAREWELL, YOUNG ONE--AND THANK YOU FOR YOUR--
OH, NO! YOU'RE NOT GOING ANY-WHERE WITHOUT ME!
HAVE YOU TAKEN LEAVE OF YOUR SENSES? RELEASE ME! NOW!
I...AH... THINK IT'S A LITTLE LATE FOR THAT.
SIGH PERHAPS YOU'RE RIGHT. WELL, THEN, HANG TIGHT--
--AND I'LL DO MY BEST TO PROTECT YOU!
YOU!!
AT LONG LAST--WE MEET! AND AT LONG LAST--
--YOU DIE!
THIS IS JUST A GUESS--
--BUT I DON'T THINK THAT GUY LIKES YOU!
INDEED. AND I'D ALSO GUESS THAT HE'S THE ONE WHO CREATED THE PROBE--
--HOPING TO WEAKEN ME, BEFORE HE MOVED IN--
TOOOOOM!!
TOOOOOOM!
--FOR THE KILL!
ARE...ARE WE GONNA DIE?

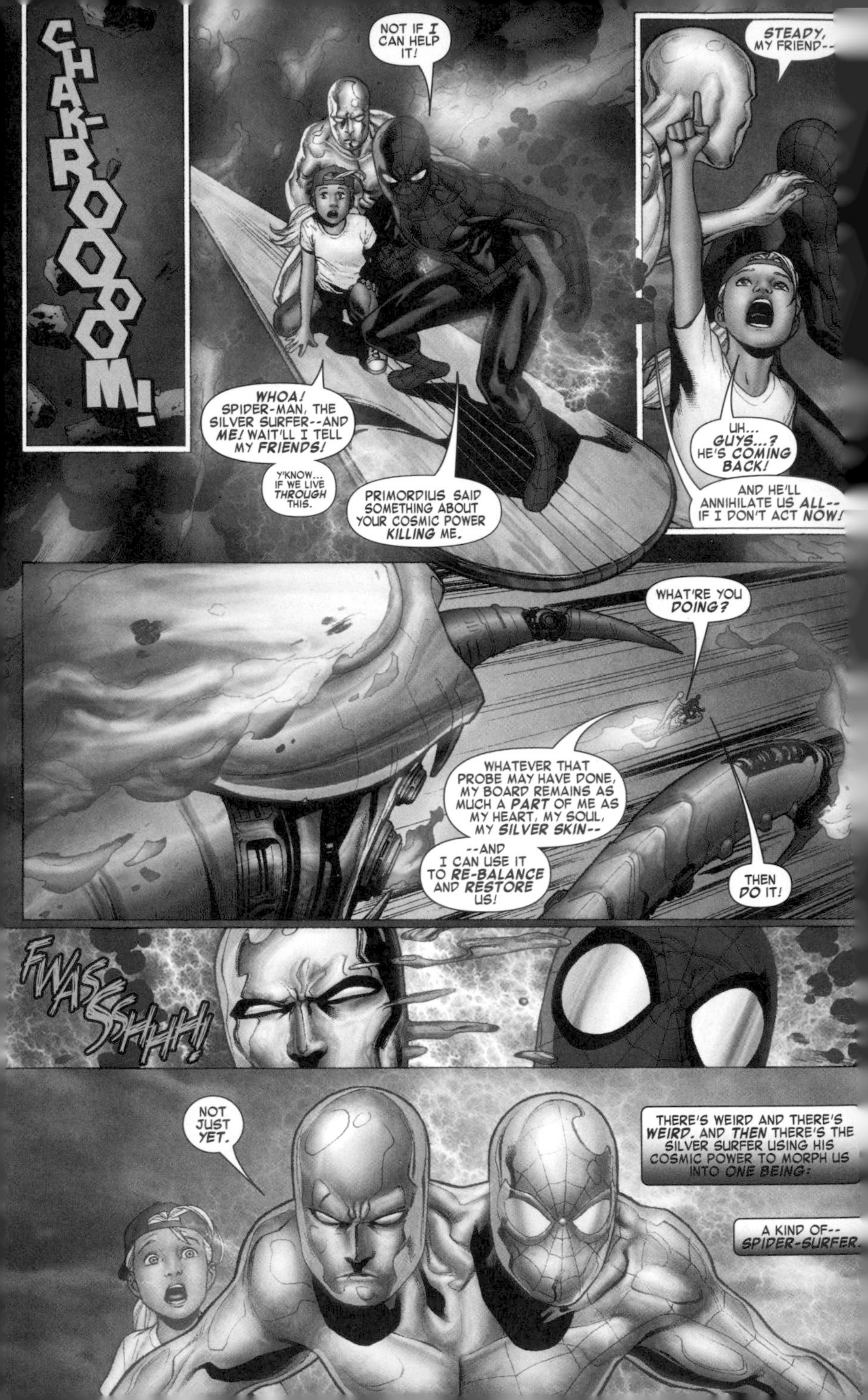
CHAK-ROOOOM!
NOT IF I CAN HELP IT!
STEADY, MY FRIEND--
WHOA! SPIDER-MAN, THE SILVER SURFER--AND ME! WAIT'LL I TELL MY FRIENDS!
Y'KNOW... IF WE LIVE THROUGH THIS.
PRIMORDIUS SAID SOMETHING ABOUT YOUR COSMIC POWER KILLING ME.
UH... GUYS...? HE'S COMING BACK!
AND HE'LL ANNIHILATE US ALL-- IF I DON'T ACT NOW!
WHAT'RE YOU DOING?
WHATEVER THAT PROBE MAY HAVE DONE, MY BOARD REMAINS AS MUCH A PART OF ME AS MY HEART, MY SOUL, MY SILVER SKIN--
--AND I CAN USE IT TO RE-BALANCE AND RESTORE US!
THEN DO IT!
FWASSHHH!
NOT JUST YET.
THERE'S WEIRD AND THERE'S WEIRD. AND THEN THERE'S THE SILVER SURFER USING HIS COSMIC POWER TO MORPH US INTO ONE BEING:
A KIND OF-- SPIDER-SURFER.

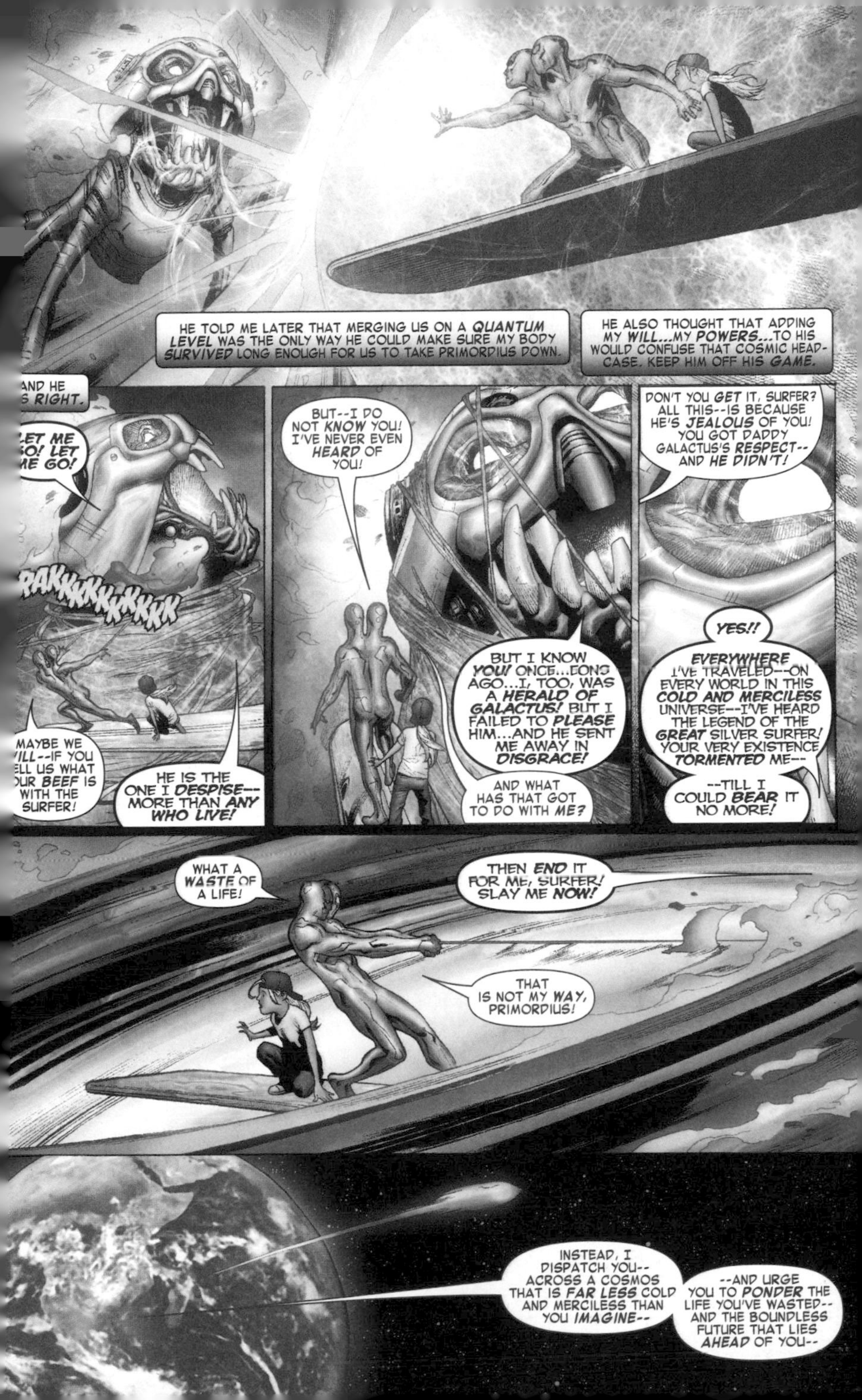
HE TOLD ME LATER THAT MERGING US ON A QUANTUM LEVEL WAS THE ONLY WAY HE COULD MAKE SURE MY BODY SURVIVED LONG ENOUGH FOR US TO TAKE PRIMORDIUS DOWN.
HE ALSO THOUGHT THAT ADDING MY WILL...MY POWERS...TO HIS WOULD CONFUSE THAT COSMIC HEAD-CASE. KEEP HIM OFF HIS GAME.
AND HE S RIGHT.
LET ME GO! LET ME GO!
RAKKKKKKKKK
MAYBE WE WILL--IF YOU ELL US WHAT OUR BEEF IS WITH THE SURFER!
HE IS THE ONE I DESPISE--MORE THAN ANY WHO LIVE!
BUT--I DO NOT KNOW YOU! I'VE NEVER EVEN HEARD OF YOU!
BUT I KNOW YOU! ONCE...LONG AGO...I, TOO, WAS A HERALD OF GALACTUS! BUT I FAILED TO PLEASE HIM...AND HE SENT ME AWAY IN DISGRACE!
AND WHAT HAS THAT GOT TO DO WITH ME?
DON'T YOU GET IT, SURFER? ALL THIS--IS BECAUSE HE'S JEALOUS OF YOU! YOU GOT DADDY GALACTUS'S RESPECT--AND HE DIDN'T!
YES!!
EVERYWHERE I'VE TRAVELED--ON EVERY WORLD IN THIS COLD AND MERCILESS UNIVERSE--I'VE HEARD THE LEGEND OF THE GREAT SILVER SURFER! YOUR VERY EXISTENCE TORMENTED ME--
--TILL I COULD BEAR IT NO MORE!
WHAT A WASTE OF A LIFE!
THEN END IT FOR ME, SURFER! SLAY ME NOW!
THAT IS NOT MY WAY, PRIMORDIUS!
INSTEAD, I DISPATCH YOU--ACROSS A COSMOS THAT IS FAR LESS COLD AND MERCILESS THAN YOU IMAGINE--
--AND URGE YOU TO PONDER THE LIFE YOU'VE WASTED--AND THE BOUNDLESS FUTURE THAT LIES AHEAD OF YOU--

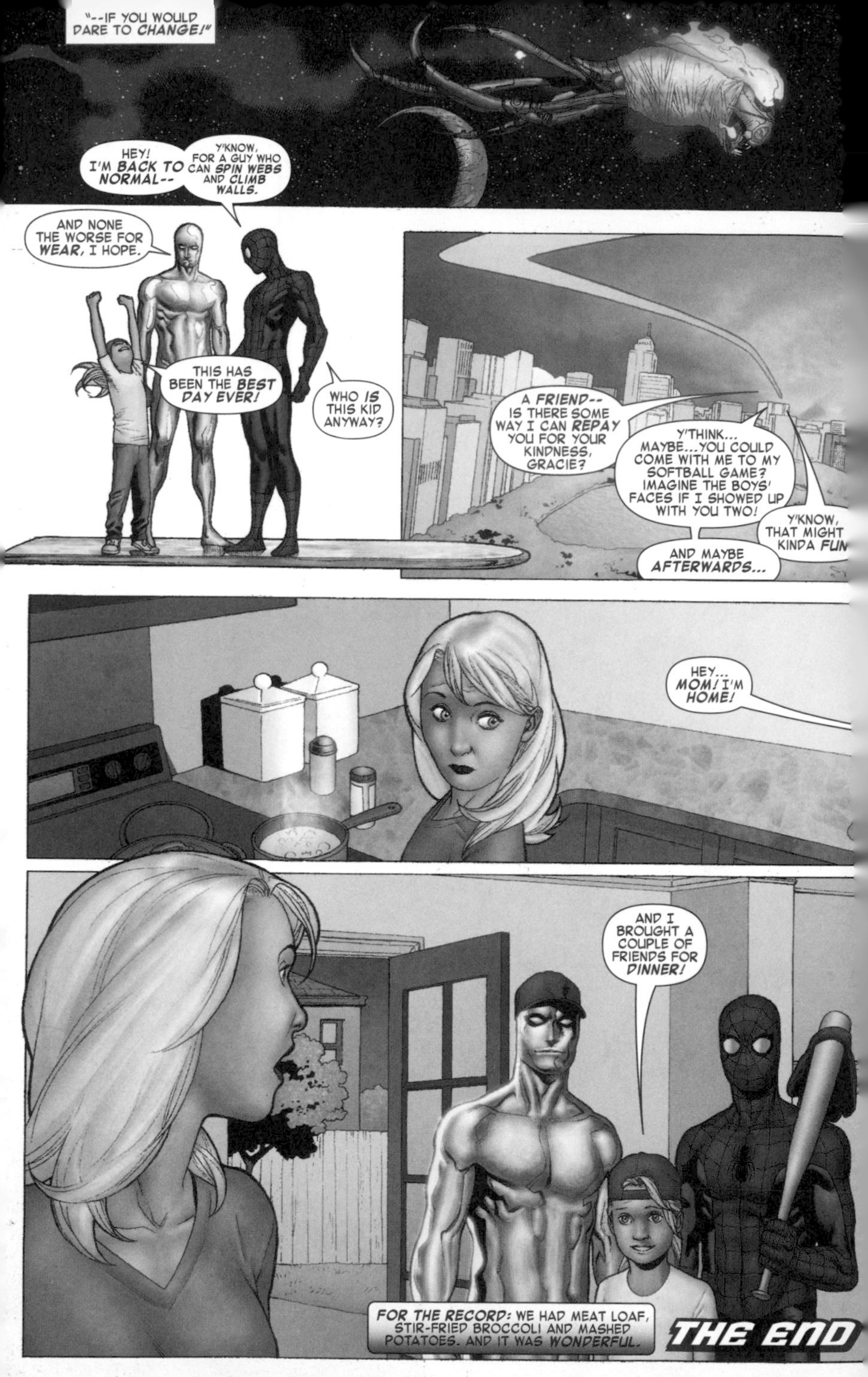
"--IF YOU WOULD DARE TO CHANGE!"
HEY! I'M BACK TO NORMAL--
Y'KNOW, FOR A GUY WHO CAN SPIN WEBS AND CLIMB WALLS.
AND NONE THE WORSE FOR WEAR, I HOPE.
THIS HAS BEEN THE BEST DAY EVER!
WHO IS THIS KID ANYWAY?
A FRIEND-- IS THERE SOME WAY I CAN REPAY YOU FOR YOUR KINDNESS, GRACIE?
Y'THINK... MAYBE... YOU COULD COME WITH ME TO MY SOFTBALL GAME? IMAGINE THE BOYS' FACES IF I SHOWED UP WITH YOU TWO!
Y'KNOW, THAT MIGHT KINDA FUN
AND MAYBE AFTERWARDS...
HEY... MOM! I'M HOME!
AND I BROUGHT A COUPLE OF FRIENDS FOR DINNER!
FOR THE RECORD: WE HAD MEAT LOAF, STIR-FRIED BROCCOLI AND MASHED POTATOES. AND IT WAS WONDERFUL.
THE END

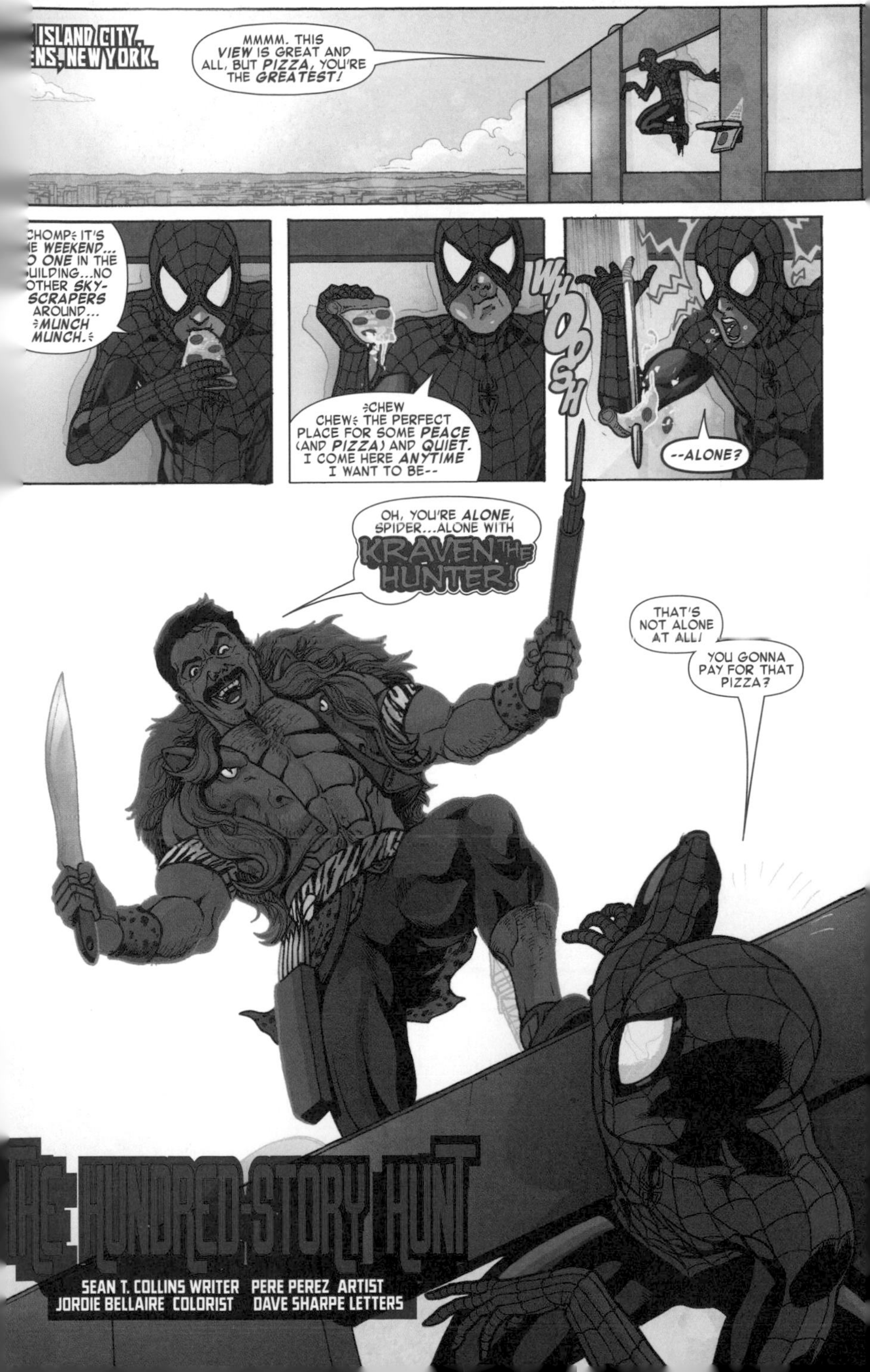
ISLAND CITY,
ENS, NEW YORK.
MMMM. THIS VIEW IS GREAT AND ALL, BUT PIZZA, YOU'RE THE GREATEST!
CHOMP IT'S E WEEKEND... O ONE IN THE UILDING...NO OTHER SKY-SCRAPERS AROUND... MUNCH MUNCH.
CHEW CHEW THE PERFECT PLACE FOR SOME PEACE (AND PIZZA) AND QUIET. I COME HERE ANYTIME I WANT TO BE--
WHOOSH
--ALONE?
OH, YOU'RE ALONE, SPIDER...ALONE WITH KRAVEN THE HUNTER!
THAT'S NOT ALONE AT ALL!
YOU GONNA PAY FOR THAT PIZZA?
THE HUNDRED-STORY HUNT
SEAN T. COLLINS WRITER PERE PEREZ ARTIST
JORDIE BELLAIRE COLORIST DAVE SHARPE LETTERS

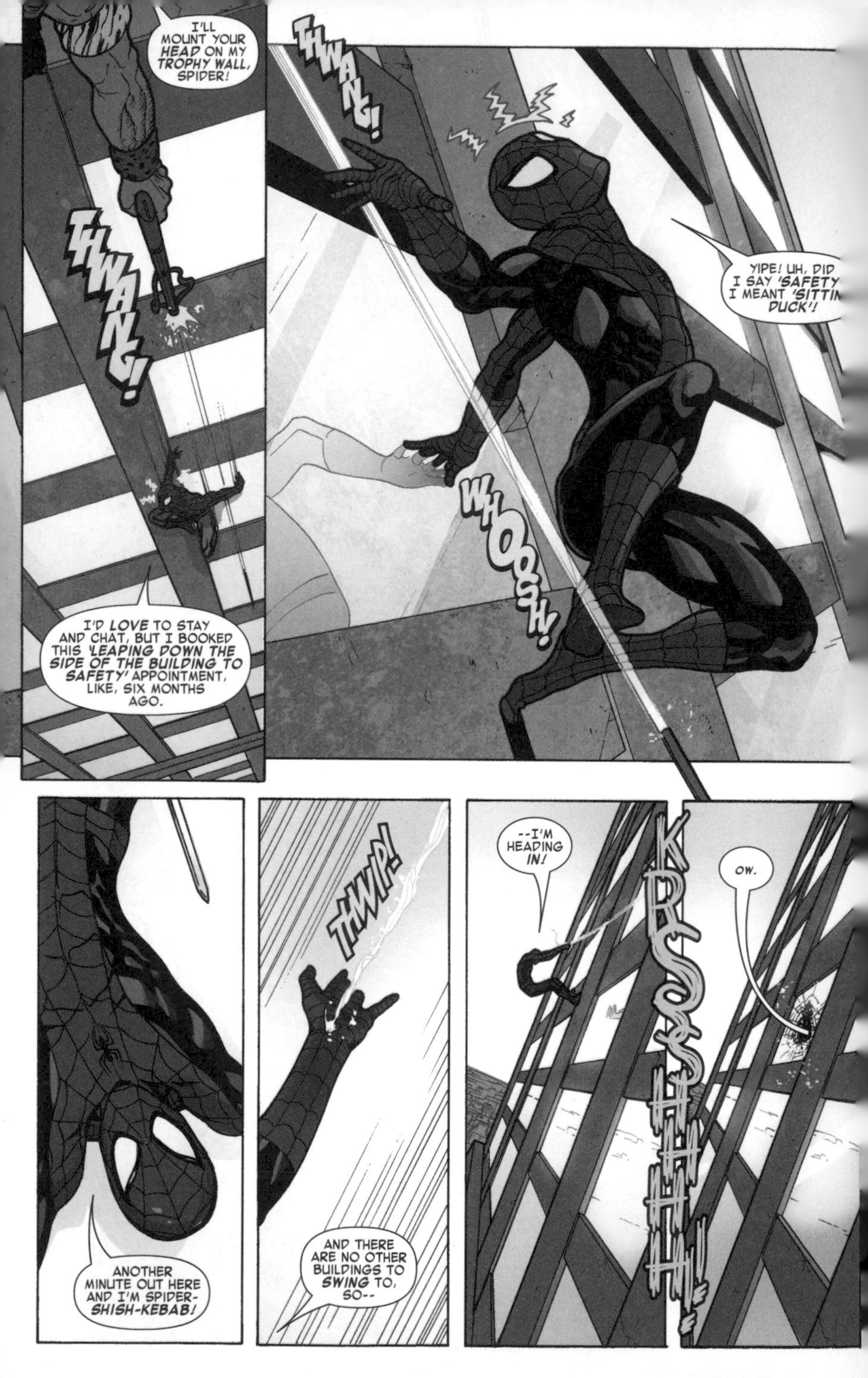

I'LL MOUNT YOUR HEAD ON MY TROPHY WALL, SPIDER!
THWANG!
I'D LOVE TO STAY AND CHAT, BUT I BOOKED THIS 'LEAPING DOWN THE SIDE OF THE BUILDING TO SAFETY' APPOINTMENT, LIKE, SIX MONTHS AGO.
THWANG!
YIPE! UH, DID I SAY 'SAFETY'? I MEANT 'SITTING DUCK'!
WHOOSH!
ANOTHER MINUTE OUT HERE AND I'M SPIDER-SHISH-KEBAB!
THWIP!
AND THERE ARE NO OTHER BUILDINGS TO SWING TO, SO--
--I'M HEADING IN!
KRSSHHHHHHHE
OW.

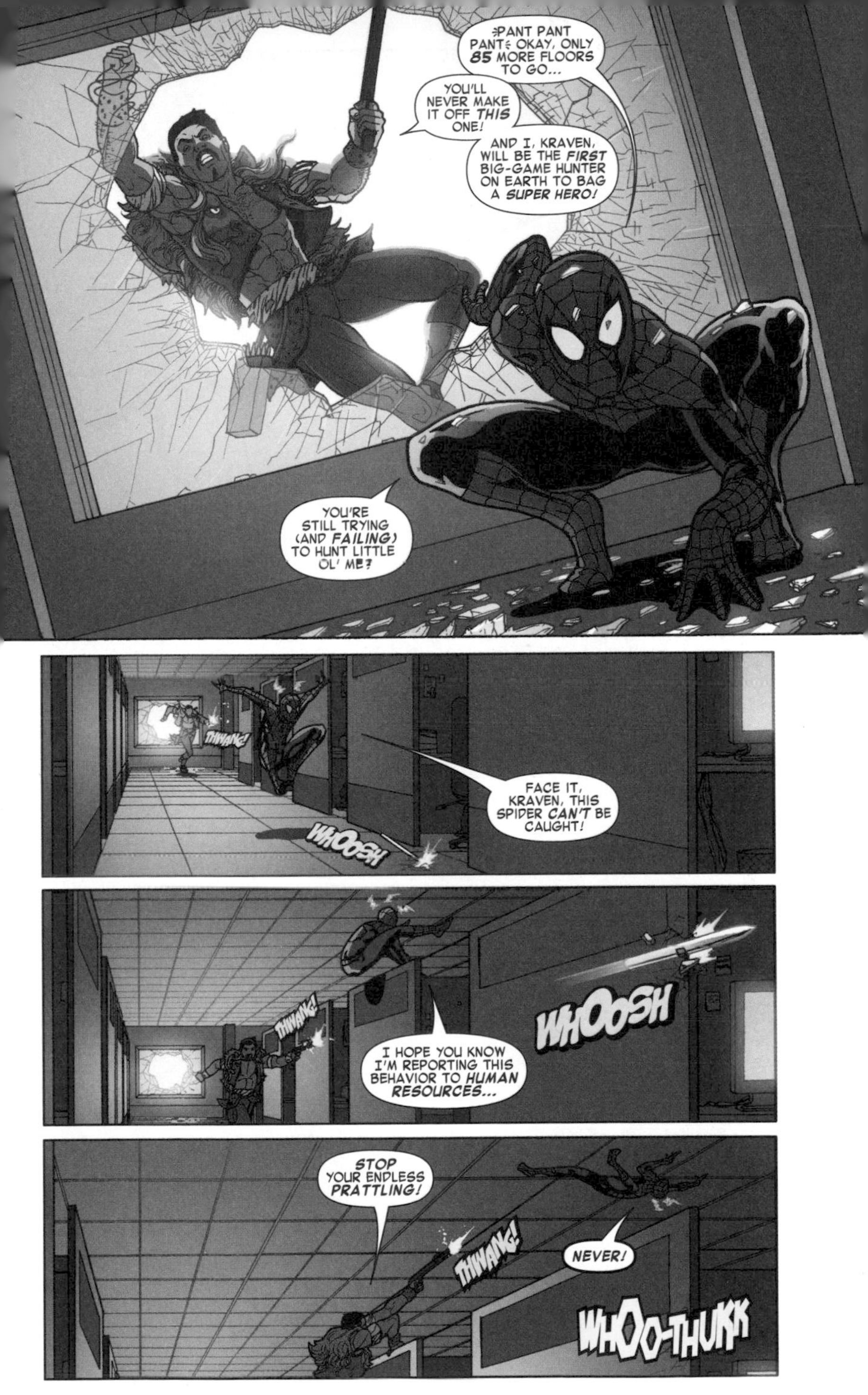

PANT PANT PANT OKAY, ONLY 85 MORE FLOORS TO GO...
YOU'LL NEVER MAKE IT OFF THIS ONE!
AND I, KRAVEN, WILL BE THE FIRST BIG-GAME HUNTER ON EARTH TO BAG A SUPER HERO!
YOU'RE STILL TRYING (AND FAILING) TO HUNT LITTLE OL' ME?
THWANG!
FACE IT, KRAVEN, THIS SPIDER CAN'T BE CAUGHT!
WHOOSH
THWANG!
WHOOSH
I HOPE YOU KNOW I'M REPORTING THIS BEHAVIOR TO HUMAN RESOURCES...
STOP YOUR ENDLESS PRATTLING!
THWANG!
NEVER!
WHOO-THUKK

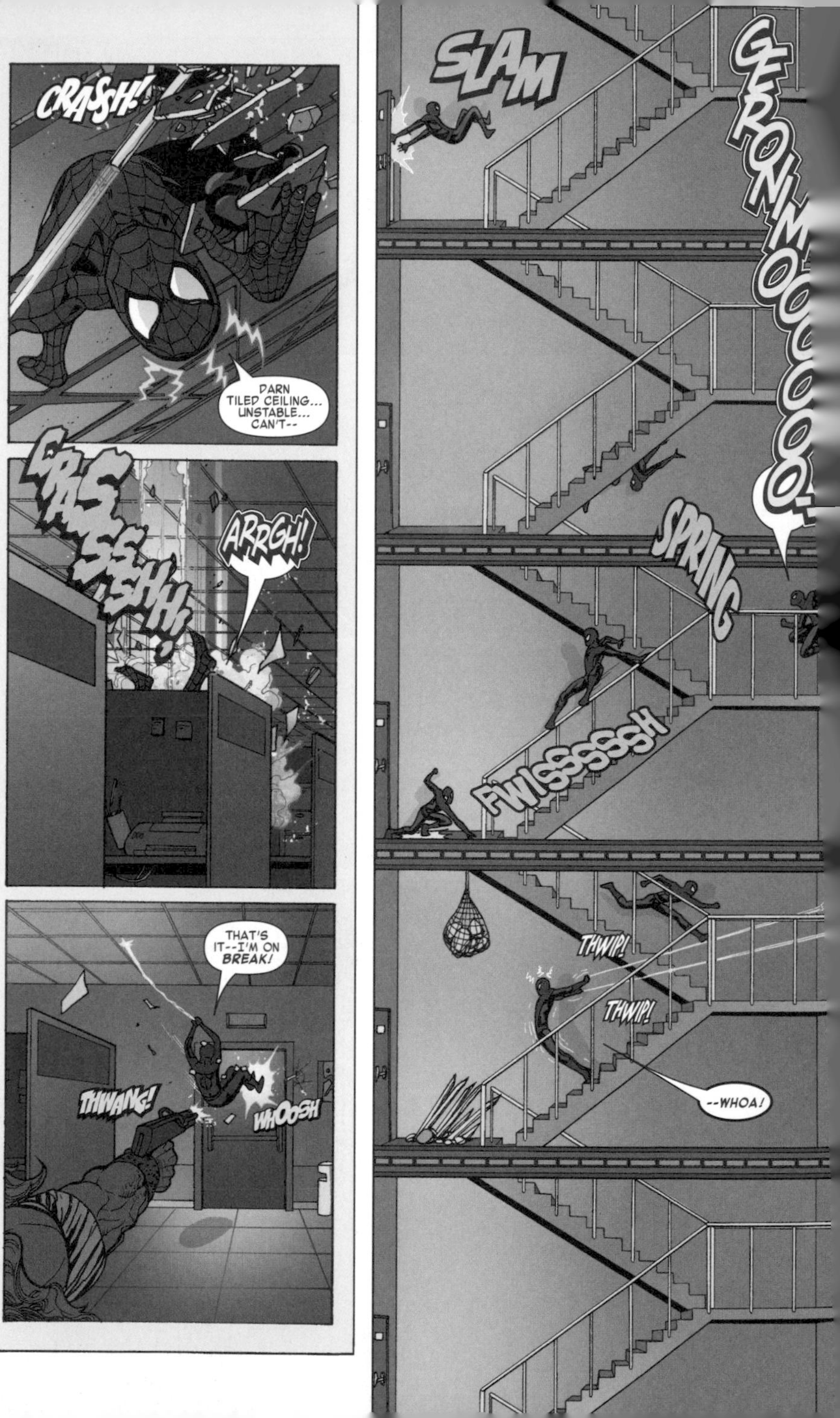
CRASSH!
DARN TILED CEILING... UNSTABLE... CAN'T--
CRASSSHH!
ARRGH!
THAT'S IT--I'M ON BREAK!
THWANG!
WHOOSH
SLAM
GERONIMOOOOOOOO-
SPRING
FWISSSSSH
THWIP!
THWIP!
--WHOA!

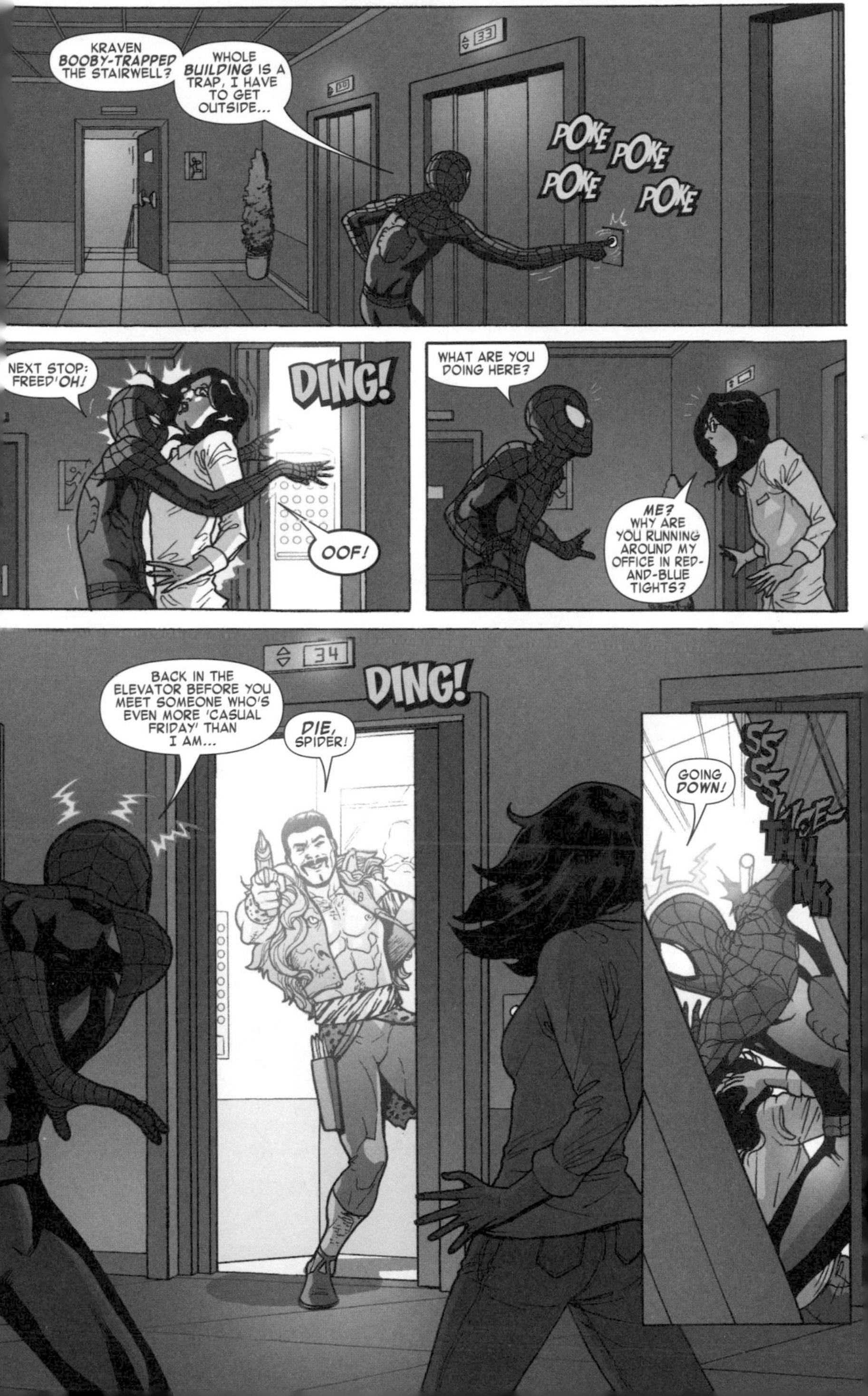
KRAVEN BOOBY-TRAPPED THE STAIRWELL?
WHOLE BUILDING IS A TRAP, I HAVE TO GET OUTSIDE...
POKE POKE POKE POKE
NEXT STOP: FREED'OH!
DING!
OOF!
WHAT ARE YOU DOING HERE?
ME? WHY ARE YOU RUNNING AROUND MY OFFICE IN RED-AND-BLUE TIGHTS?
34
BACK IN THE ELEVATOR BEFORE YOU MEET SOMEONE WHO'S EVEN MORE 'CASUAL FRIDAY' THAN I AM...
DING!
DIE, SPIDER!
GOING DOWN!

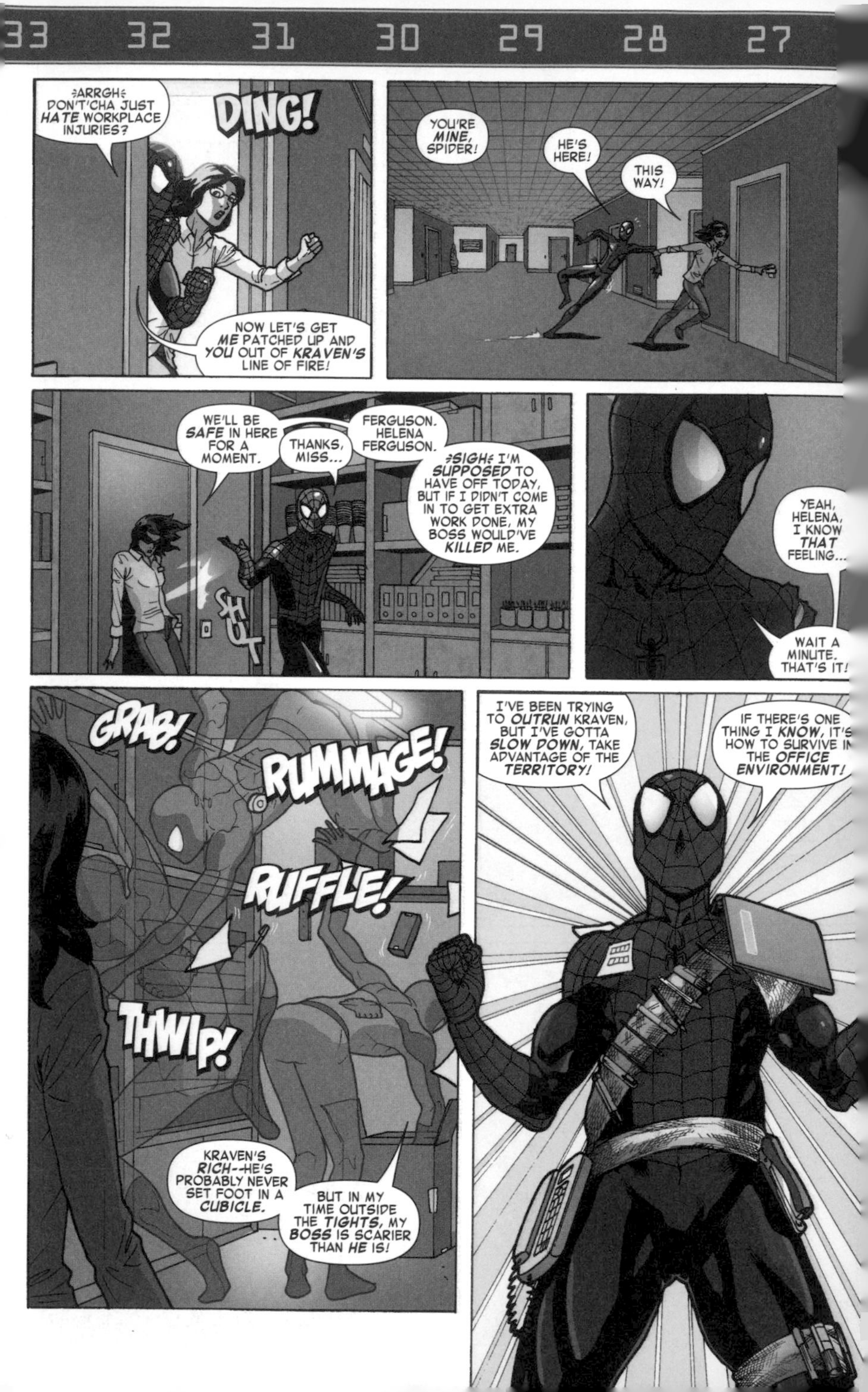
33 32 31 30 29 28 27
≠ARRGH≠ DON'T'CHA JUST HATE WORKPLACE INJURIES?
DING!
NOW LET'S GET ME PATCHED UP AND YOU OUT OF KRAVEN'S LINE OF FIRE!
YOU'RE MINE, SPIDER!
HE'S HERE!
THIS WAY!
WE'LL BE SAFE IN HERE FOR A MOMENT.
THANKS, MISS...
FERGUSON. HELENA FERGUSON.
≠SIGH≠ I'M SUPPOSED TO HAVE OFF TODAY, BUT IF I DIDN'T COME IN TO GET EXTRA WORK DONE, MY BOSS WOULD'VE KILLED ME.
SHUT
YEAH, HELENA, I KNOW THAT FEELING...
WAIT A MINUTE. THAT'S IT!
GRAB!
RUMMAGE!
RUFFLE!
THWIP!
KRAVEN'S RICH--HE'S PROBABLY NEVER SET FOOT IN A CUBICLE.
BUT IN MY TIME OUTSIDE THE TIGHTS, MY BOSS IS SCARIER THAN HE IS!
I'VE BEEN TRYING TO OUTRUN KRAVEN, BUT I'VE GOTTA SLOW DOWN, TAKE ADVANTAGE OF THE TERRITORY!
IF THERE'S ONE THING I KNOW, IT'S HOW TO SURVIVE IN THE OFFICE ENVIRONMENT!

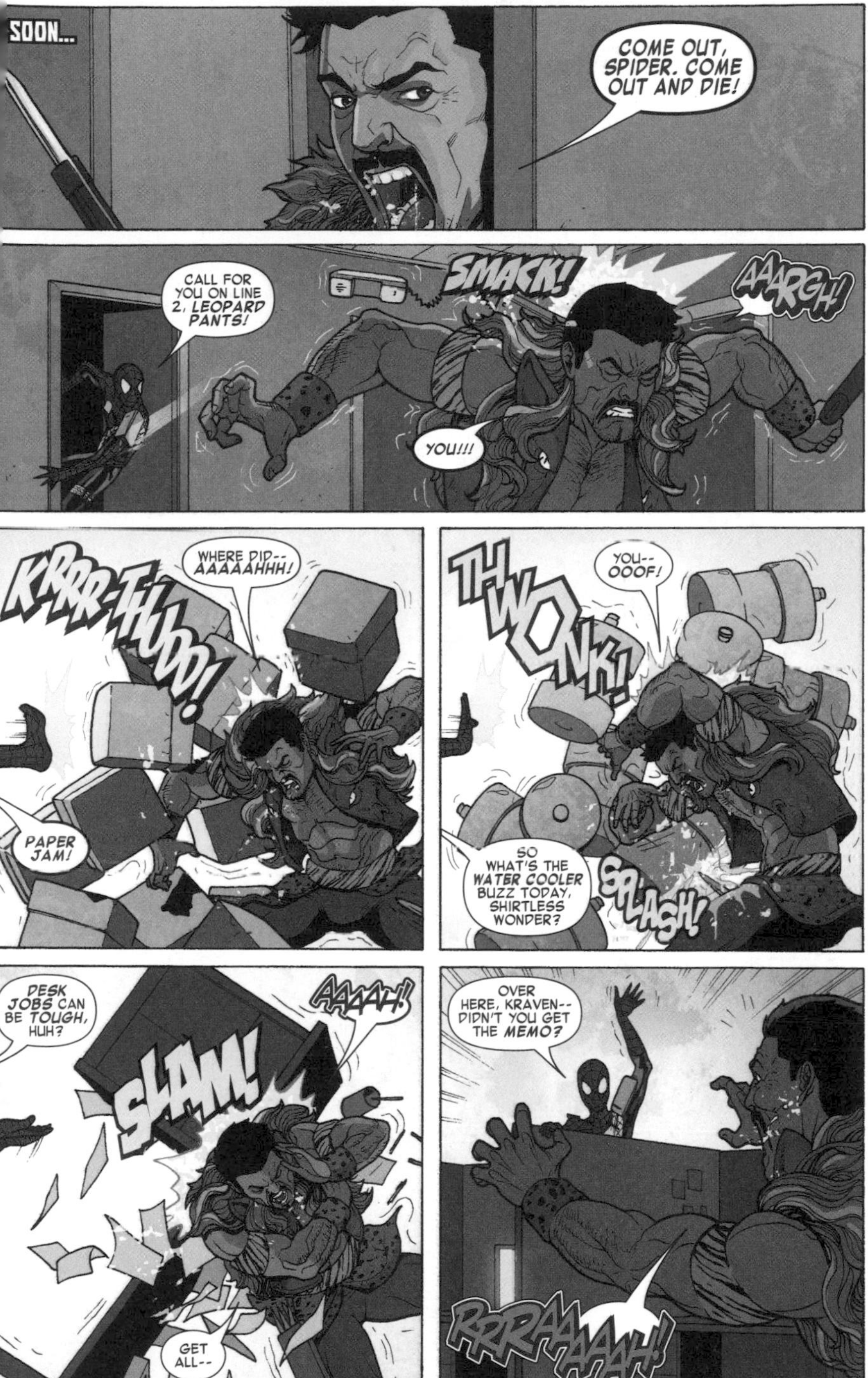
SOON...
COME OUT, SPIDER. COME OUT AND DIE!
CALL FOR YOU ON LINE 2, LEOPARD PANTS!
SMACK!
AAARGH!
YOU!!!
KRRR-THUDD!
WHERE DID-- AAAAAHHH!
PAPER JAM!
THWONK!
YOU-- OOOF!
SO WHAT'S THE WATER COOLER BUZZ TODAY, SHIRTLESS WONDER?
SPLASH!
DESK JOBS CAN BE TOUGH, HUH?
AAAAH!
SLAM!
GET ALL--
OVER HERE, KRAVEN-- DIDN'T YOU GET THE MEMO?
RRRAAAAAH!

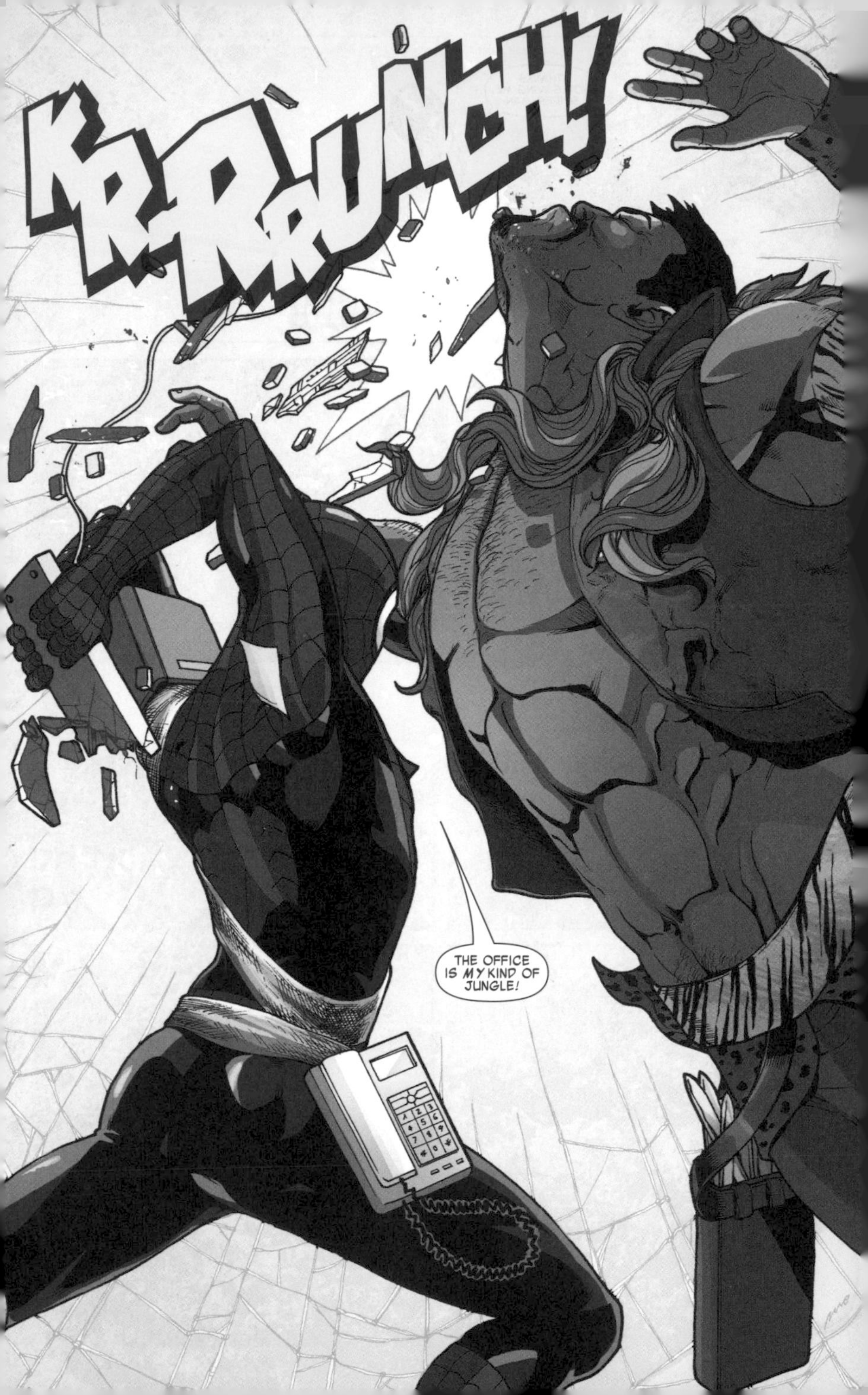
KRRRUNCH!
THE OFFICE IS MY KIND OF JUNGLE!

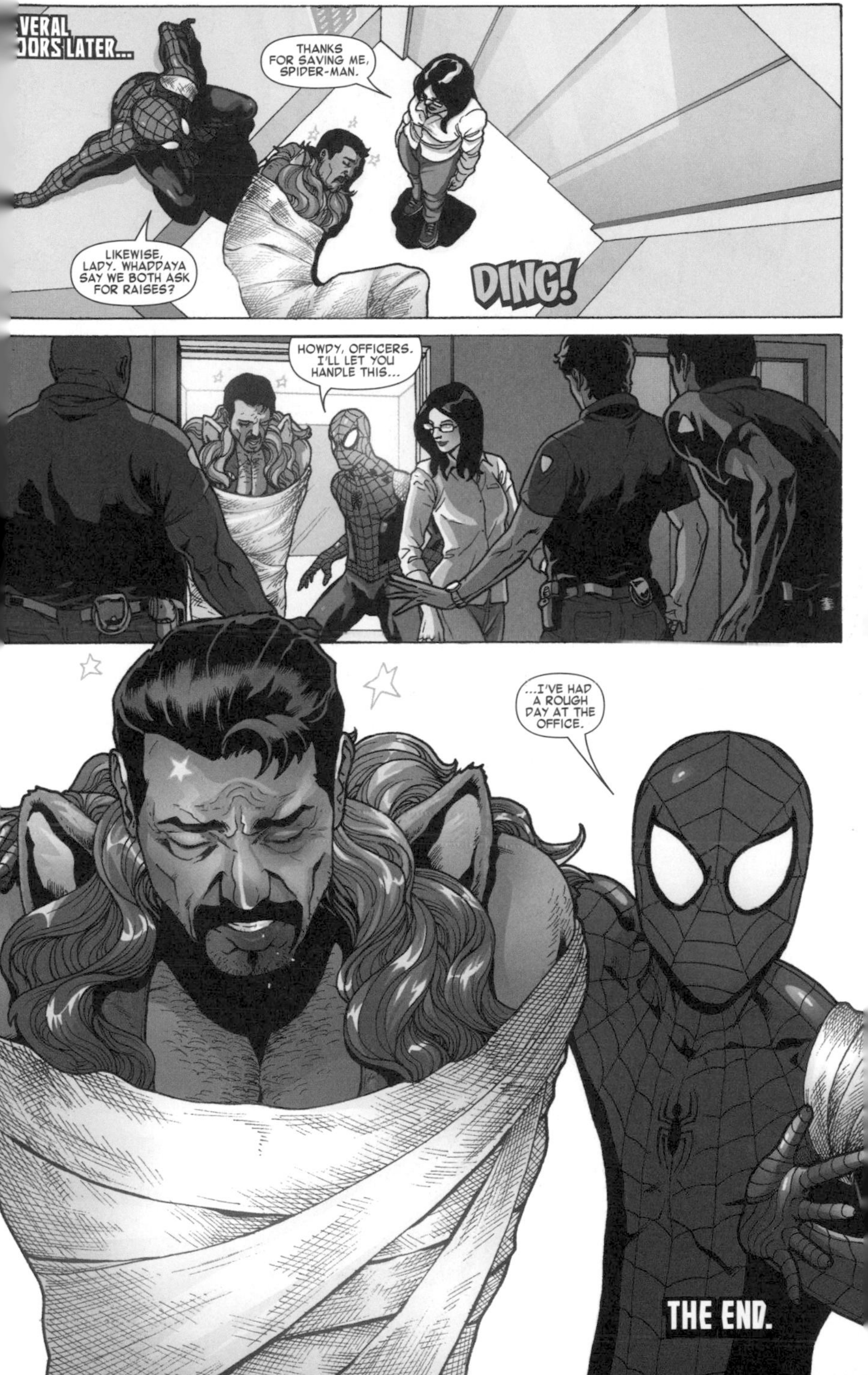
VERAL
OORS LATER...
THANKS FOR SAVING ME, SPIDER-MAN.
LIKEWISE, LADY. WHADDAYA SAY WE BOTH ASK FOR RAISES?
DING!
HOWDY, OFFICERS. I'LL LET YOU HANDLE THIS...
...I'VE HAD A ROUGH DAY AT THE OFFICE.
THE END.

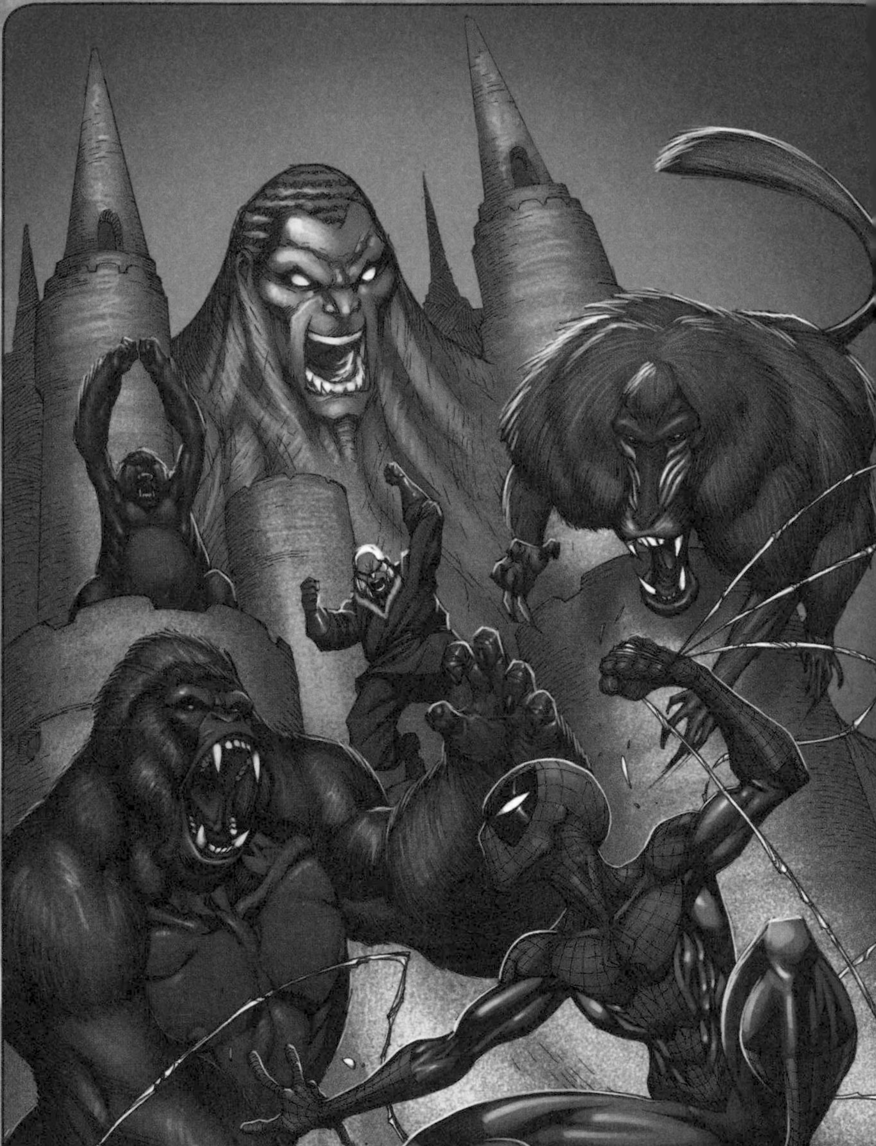

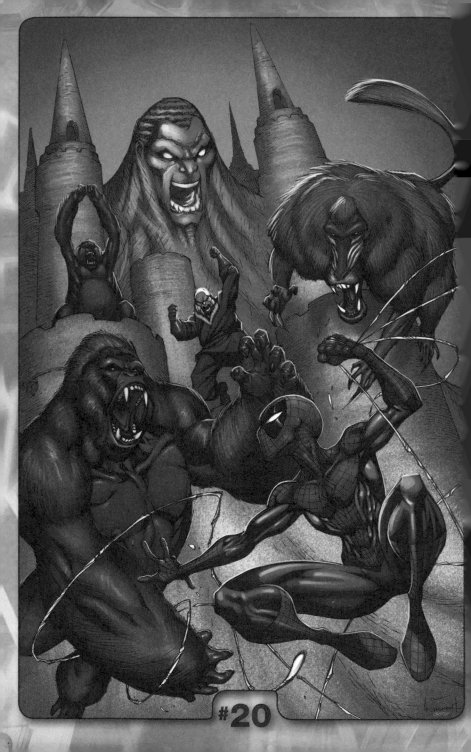

#20

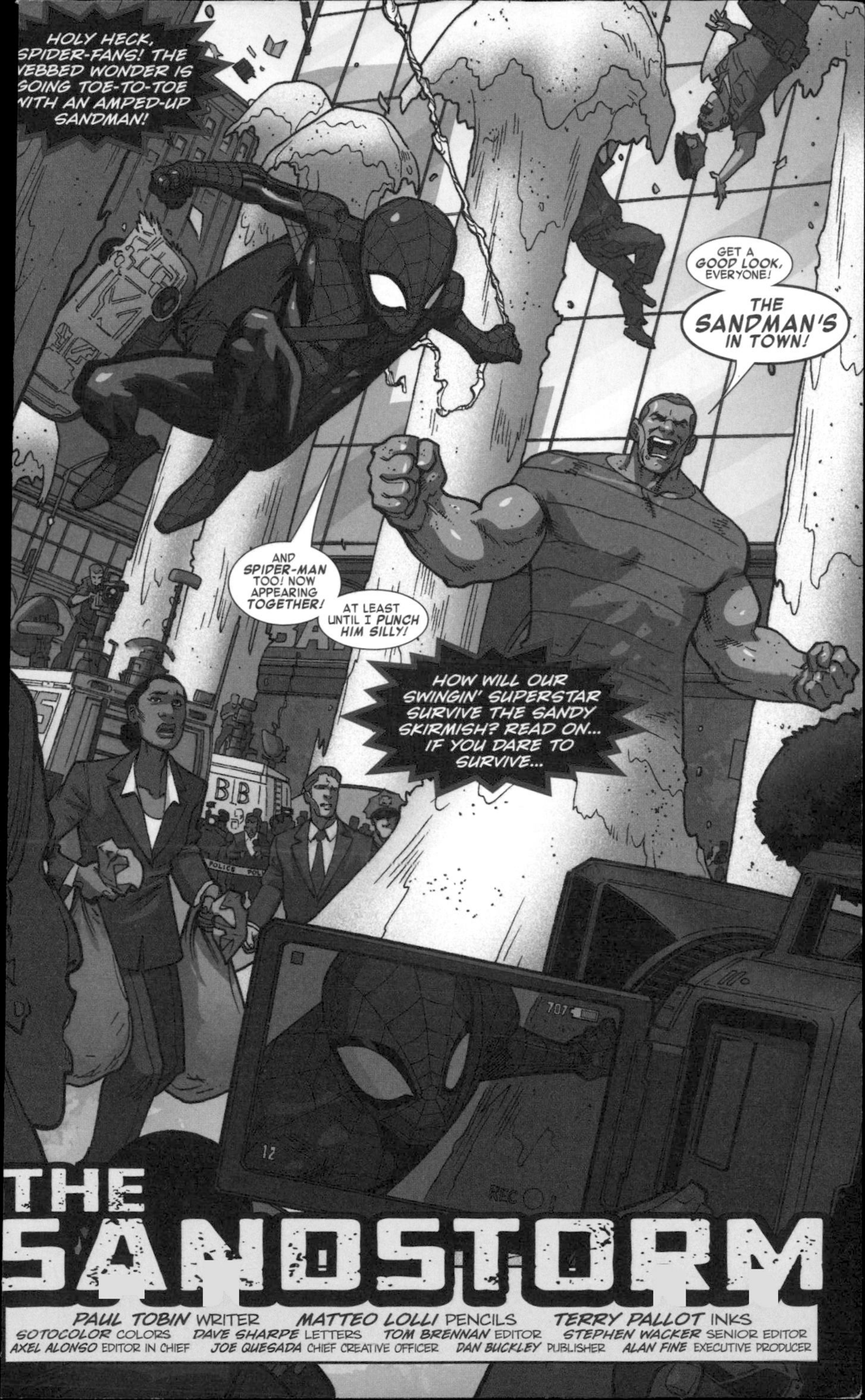
HOLY HECK, SPIDER-FANS! THE WEBBED WONDER IS GOING TOE-TO-TOE WITH AN AMPED-UP SANDMAN!
GET A GOOD LOOK, EVERYONE!
THE SANDMAN'S IN TOWN!
AND SPIDER-MAN TOO! NOW APPEARING TOGETHER!
AT LEAST UNTIL I PUNCH HIM SILLY!
HOW WILL OUR SWINGIN' SUPERSTAR SURVIVE THE SANDY SKIRMISH? READ ON... IF YOU DARE TO SURVIVE...
THE SANDSTORM
PAUL TOBIN WRITER MATTEO LOLLI PENCILS TERRY PALLOT INKS
SOTOCOLOR COLORS DAVE SHARPE LETTERS TOM BRENNAN EDITOR STEPHEN WACKER SENIOR EDITOR
AXEL ALONSO EDITOR IN CHIEF JOE QUESADA CHIEF CREATIVE OFFICER DAN BUCKLEY PUBLISHER ALAN FINE EXECUTIVE PRODUCER

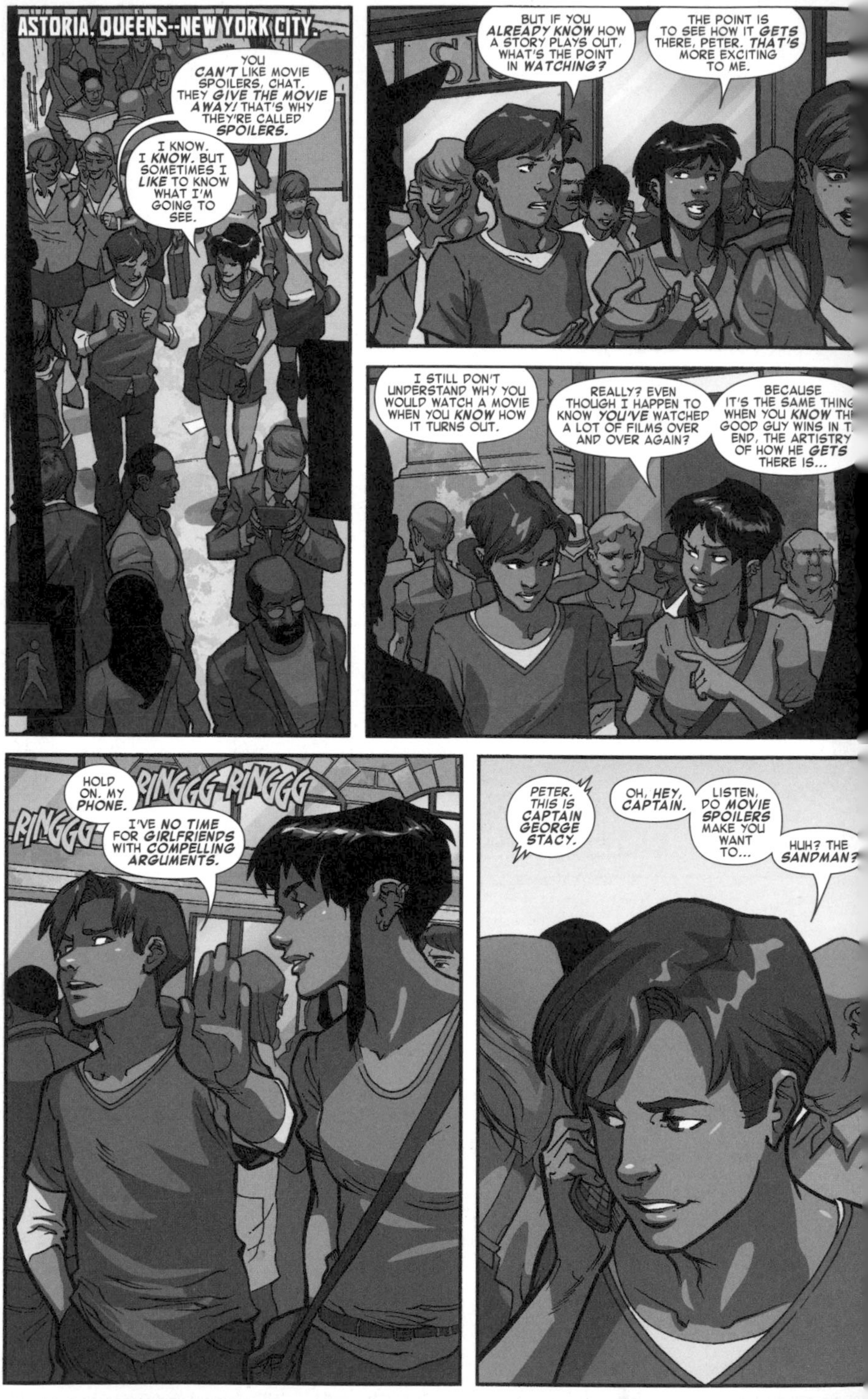
ASTORIA, QUEENS--NEW YORK CITY.
YOU CAN'T LIKE MOVIE SPOILERS, CHAT. THEY GIVE THE MOVIE AWAY! THAT'S WHY THEY'RE CALLED SPOILERS.
I KNOW. I KNOW. BUT SOMETIMES I LIKE TO KNOW WHAT I'M GOING TO SEE.
BUT IF YOU ALREADY KNOW HOW A STORY PLAYS OUT, WHAT'S THE POINT IN WATCHING?
THE POINT IS TO SEE HOW IT GETS THERE, PETER. THAT'S MORE EXCITING TO ME.
I STILL DON'T UNDERSTAND WHY YOU WOULD WATCH A MOVIE WHEN YOU KNOW HOW IT TURNS OUT.
REALLY? EVEN THOUGH I HAPPEN TO KNOW YOU'VE WATCHED A LOT OF FILMS OVER AND OVER AGAIN?
BECAUSE IT'S THE SAME THING WHEN YOU KNOW TH GOOD GUY WINS IN T END, THE ARTISTRY OF HOW HE GETS THERE IS...
RINGGG RINGGG
RINGGG
HOLD ON. MY PHONE.
I'VE NO TIME FOR GIRLFRIENDS WITH COMPELLING ARGUMENTS.
PETER. THIS IS CAPTAIN GEORGE STACY.
OH, HEY, CAPTAIN.
LISTEN, DO MOVIE SPOILERS MAKE YOU WANT TO...
HUH? THE SANDMAN?

the AMAZING SPIDER-MAN

in

GOBLIN BALL

Paul Tobin	Roberto Di Salvo	Olazaba w/Pallot
Writer	Pencils	Inks

Sotocolor	Dave Sharpe	Garza & Soto
Colors	Letterer	Cover Art

Taylor Esposito	Tom Brennan	Stephen Wacker
Production	Editor	Senior Editor

Axel Alonso	Joe Quesada	Dan Buckley	Alan Fine
Editor in Chief	Chief Creative Officer	Publisher	Exec. Producer

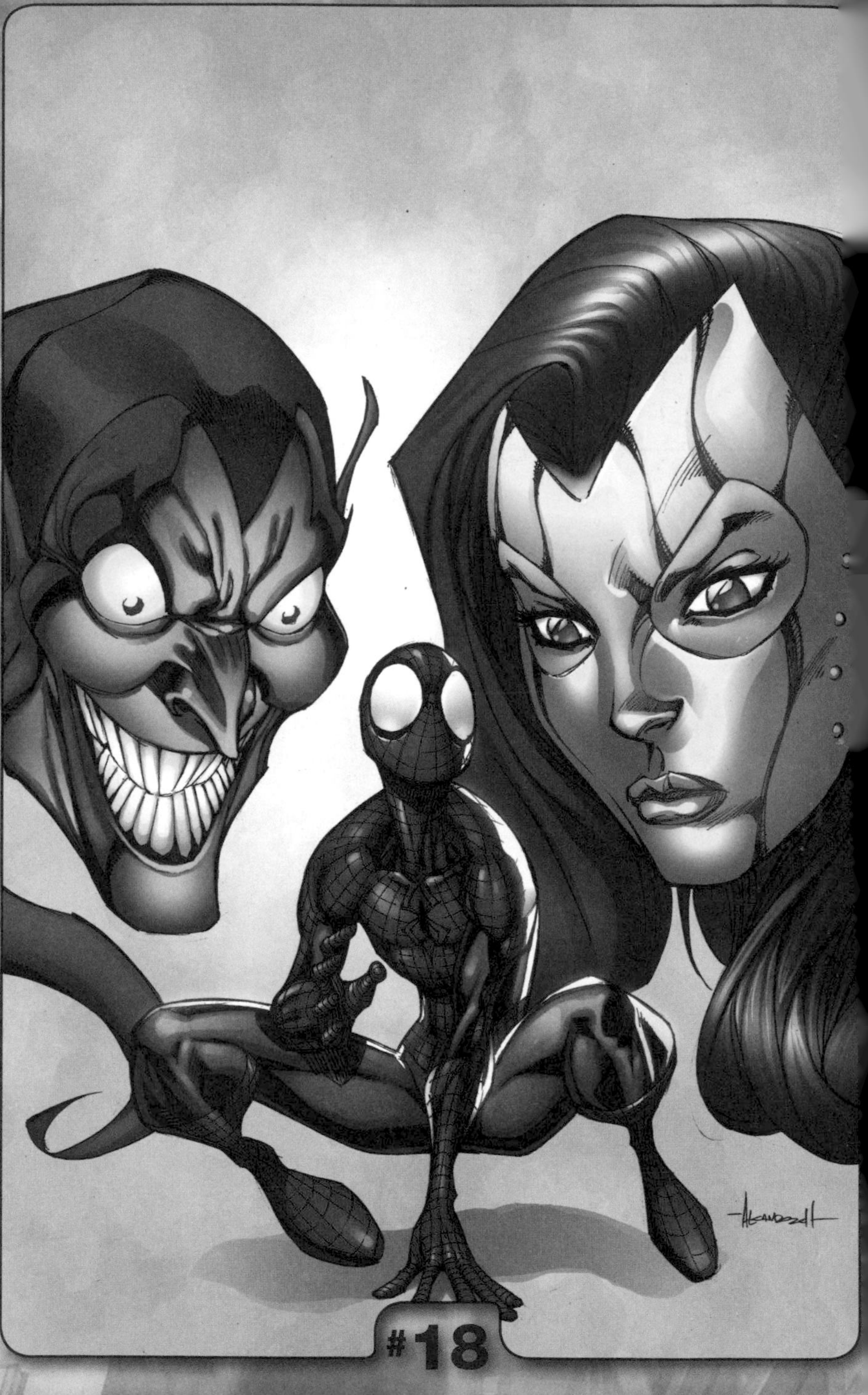
#18

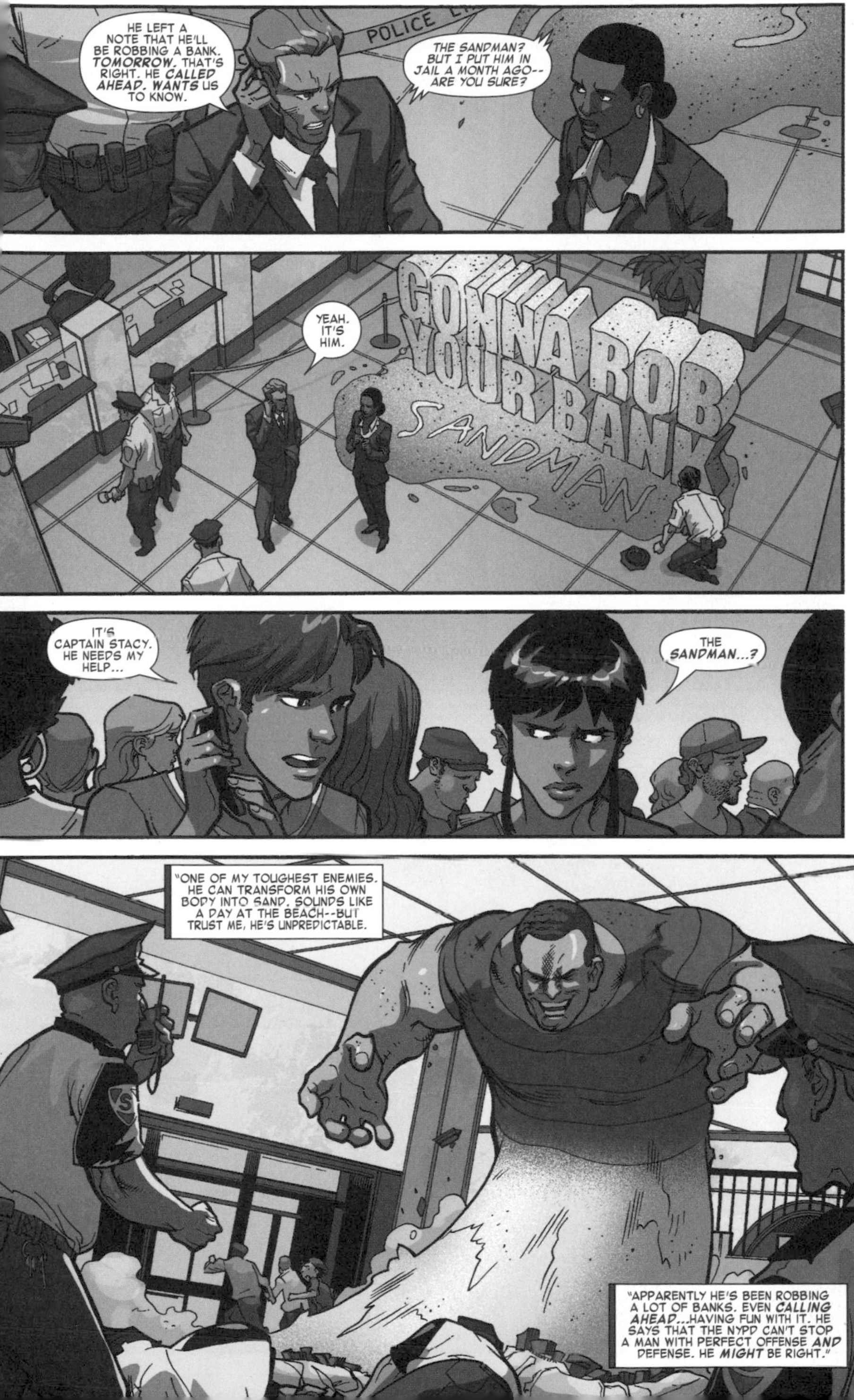
HE LEFT A NOTE THAT HE'LL BE ROBBING A BANK. TOMORROW. THAT'S RIGHT. HE CALLED AHEAD. WANTS US TO KNOW.
POLICE LI
THE SANDMAN? BUT I PUT HIM IN JAIL A MONTH AGO-- ARE YOU SURE?
YEAH. IT'S HIM.
GONNA ROB YOUR BANK
SANDMAN
IT'S CAPTAIN STACY. HE NEEDS MY HELP...
THE SANDMAN...?
"ONE OF MY TOUGHEST ENEMIES. HE CAN TRANSFORM HIS OWN BODY INTO SAND. SOUNDS LIKE A DAY AT THE BEACH--BUT TRUST ME, HE'S UNPREDICTABLE.
"APPARENTLY HE'S BEEN ROBBING A LOT OF BANKS. EVEN CALLING AHEAD...HAVING FUN WITH IT. HE SAYS THAT THE NYPD CAN'T STOP A MAN WITH PERFECT OFFENSE AND DEFENSE. HE MIGHT BE RIGHT."

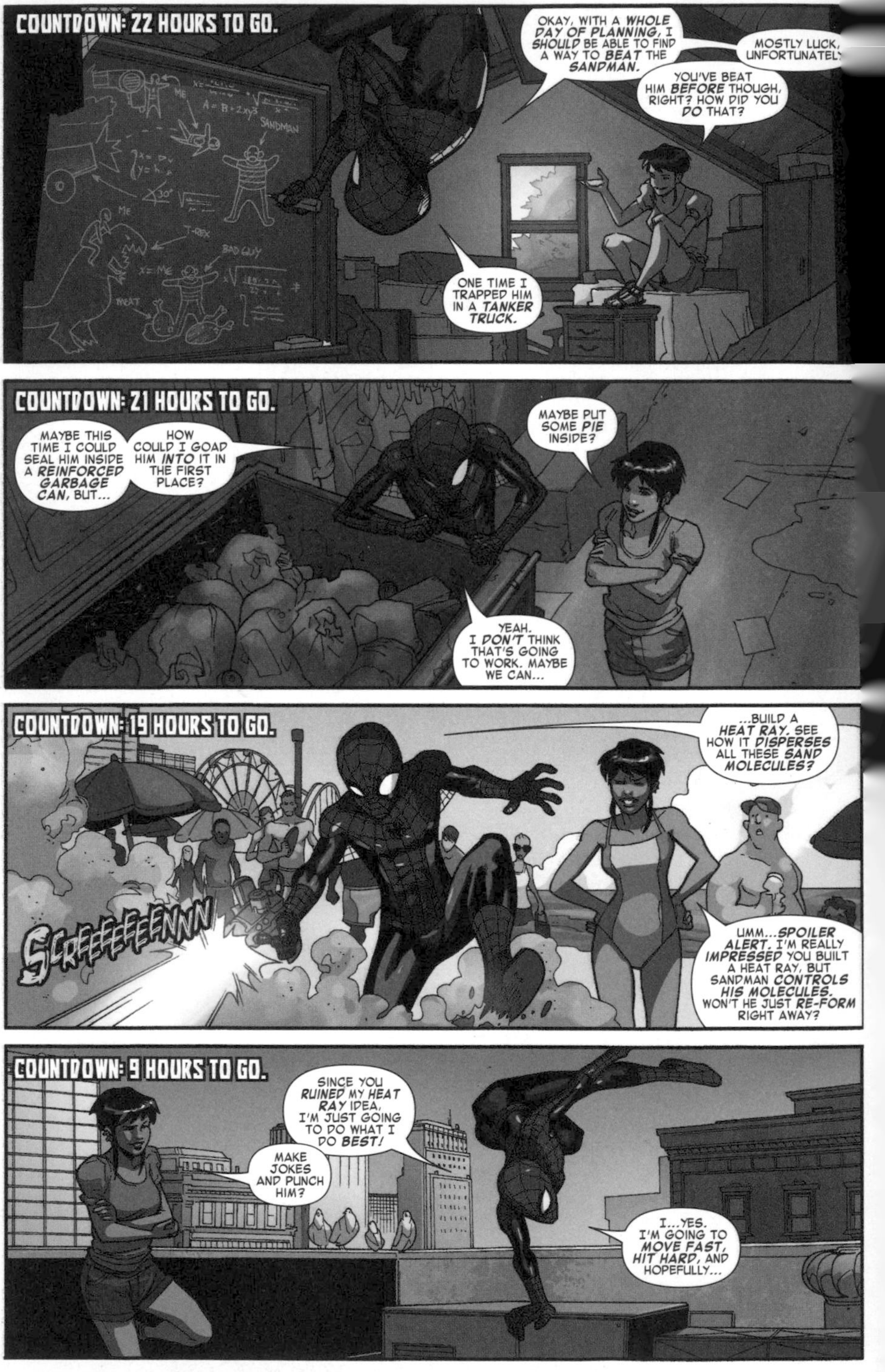
COUNTDOWN: 22 HOURS TO GO.
OKAY, WITH A WHOLE DAY OF PLANNING, I SHOULD BE ABLE TO FIND A WAY TO BEAT THE SANDMAN.
MOSTLY LUCK, UNFORTUNATELY.
YOU'VE BEAT HIM BEFORE THOUGH, RIGHT? HOW DID YOU DO THAT?
ONE TIME I TRAPPED HIM IN A TANKER TRUCK.
ME
SANDMAN
ME
T-REX
BAD GUY
X=ME
MEAT
COUNTDOWN: 21 HOURS TO GO.
MAYBE THIS TIME I COULD SEAL HIM INSIDE A REINFORCED GARBAGE CAN, BUT...
HOW COULD I GOAD HIM INTO IT IN THE FIRST PLACE?
MAYBE PUT SOME PIE INSIDE?
YEAH. I DON'T THINK THAT'S GOING TO WORK. MAYBE WE CAN...
COUNTDOWN: 19 HOURS TO GO.
...BUILD A HEAT RAY. SEE HOW IT DISPERSES ALL THESE SAND MOLECULES?
SCREEEEEEENNN
UMM...SPOILER ALERT. I'M REALLY IMPRESSED YOU BUILT A HEAT RAY, BUT SANDMAN CONTROLS HIS MOLECULES. WON'T HE JUST RE-FORM RIGHT AWAY?
COUNTDOWN: 9 HOURS TO GO.
SINCE YOU RUINED MY HEAT RAY IDEA, I'M JUST GOING TO DO WHAT I DO BEST!
MAKE JOKES AND PUNCH HIM?
I...YES. I'M GOING TO MOVE FAST, HIT HARD, AND HOPEFULLY...

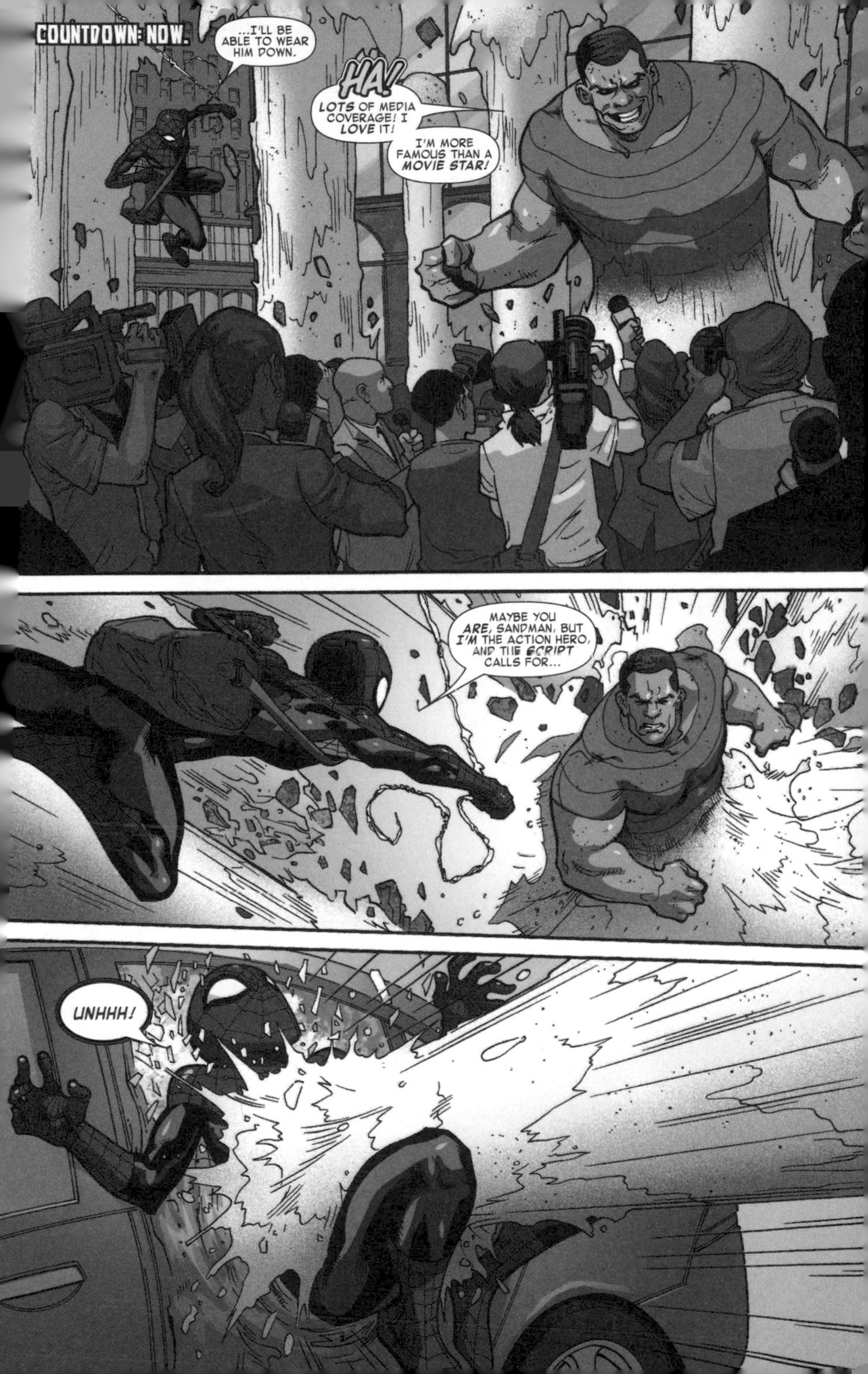
COUNTDOWN: NOW.
...I'LL BE ABLE TO WEAR HIM DOWN.
HA! LOTS OF MEDIA COVERAGE! I LOVE IT!
I'M MORE FAMOUS THAN A MOVIE STAR!
MAYBE YOU ARE, SANDMAN, BUT I'M THE ACTION HERO, AND THE SCRIPT CALLS FOR...
UNHHH!

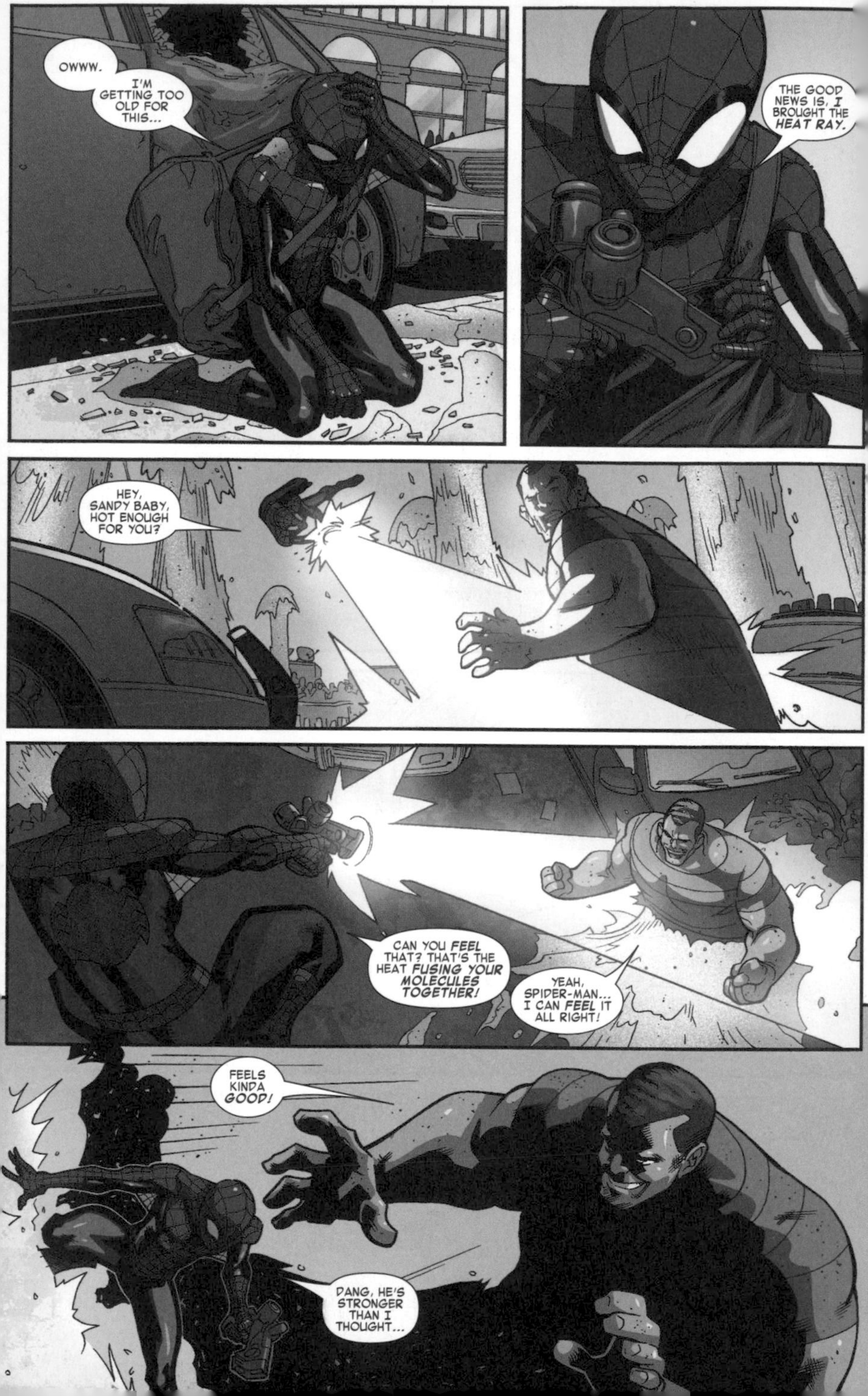
OWWW.
I'M GETTING TOO OLD FOR THIS...
THE GOOD NEWS IS, I BROUGHT THE HEAT RAY.
HEY, SANDY BABY, HOT ENOUGH FOR YOU?
CAN YOU FEEL THAT? THAT'S THE HEAT FUSING YOUR MOLECULES TOGETHER!
YEAH, SPIDER-MAN... I CAN FEEL IT ALL RIGHT!
FEELS KINDA GOOD!
DANG, HE'S STRONGER THAN I THOUGHT...

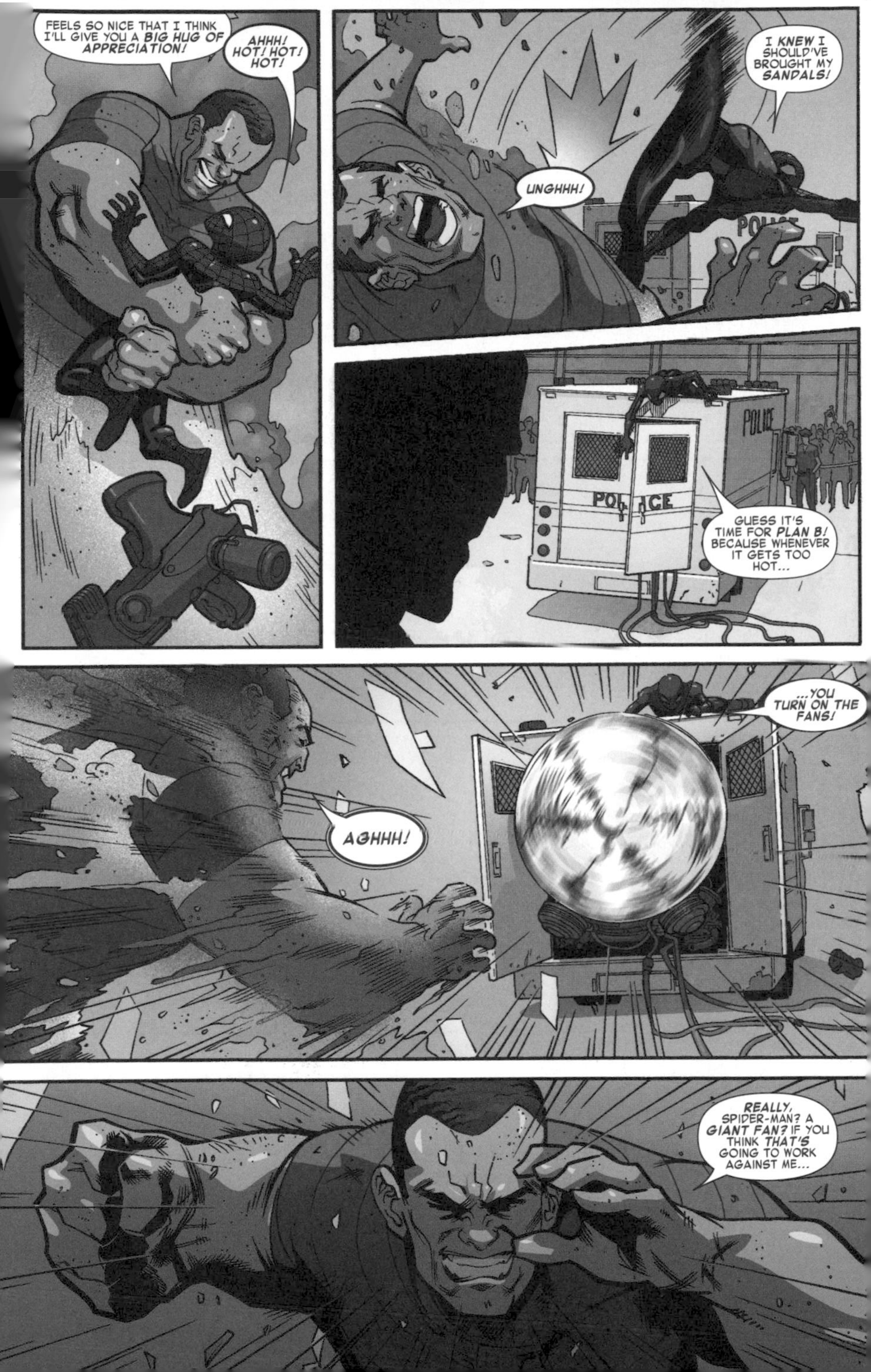
FEELS SO NICE THAT I THINK I'LL GIVE YOU A BIG HUG OF APPRECIATION!
AHHH! HOT! HOT! HOT!
I KNEW I SHOULD'VE BROUGHT MY SANDALS!
UNGHHH!
POLICE
POLICE
POLICE
GUESS IT'S TIME FOR PLAN B! BECAUSE WHENEVER IT GETS TOO HOT...
...YOU TURN ON THE FANS!
AGHHH!
REALLY, SPIDER-MAN? A GIANT FAN? IF YOU THINK THAT'S GOING TO WORK AGAINST ME...

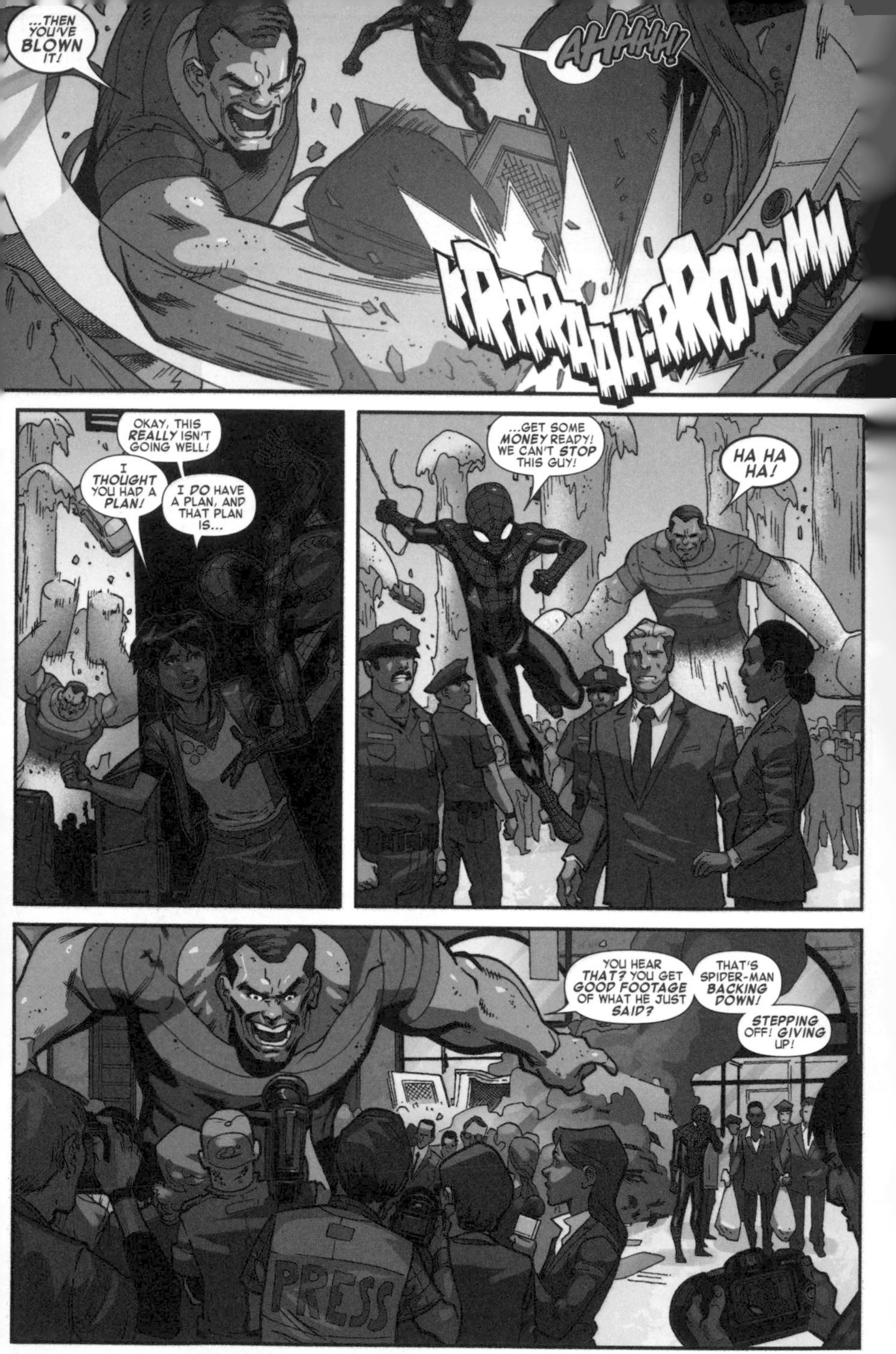
...THEN YOU'VE BLOWN IT!
AHHHH!
KRRRRAAA-RROOOMM
OKAY, THIS REALLY ISN'T GOING WELL!
I THOUGHT YOU HAD A PLAN!
I DO HAVE A PLAN, AND THAT PLAN IS...
...GET SOME MONEY READY! WE CAN'T STOP THIS GUY!
HA HA HA!
YOU HEAR THAT? YOU GET GOOD FOOTAGE OF WHAT HE JUST SAID?
THAT'S SPIDER-MAN BACKING DOWN!
STEPPING OFF! GIVING UP!
PRESS

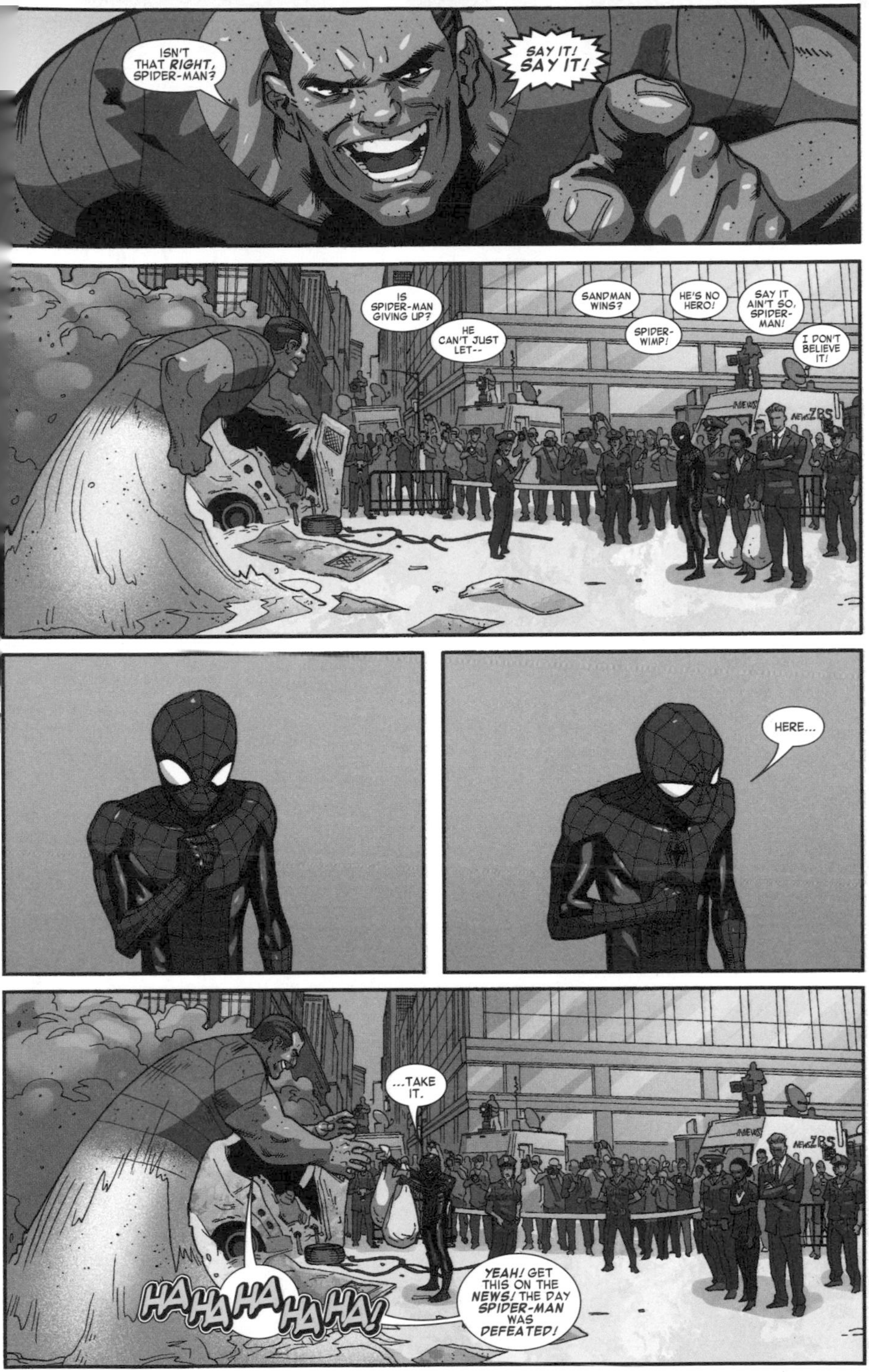

ISN'T THAT RIGHT, SPIDER-MAN?
SAY IT! SAY IT!
IS SPIDER-MAN GIVING UP?
HE CAN'T JUST LET--
SANDMAN WINS?
SPIDER-WIMP!
HE'S NO HERO!
SAY IT AIN'T SO, SPIDER-MAN!
I DON'T BELIEVE IT!
HERE...
...TAKE IT.
HA HA HA HA HA!
YEAH! GET THIS ON THE NEWS! THE DAY SPIDER-MAN WAS DEFEATED!

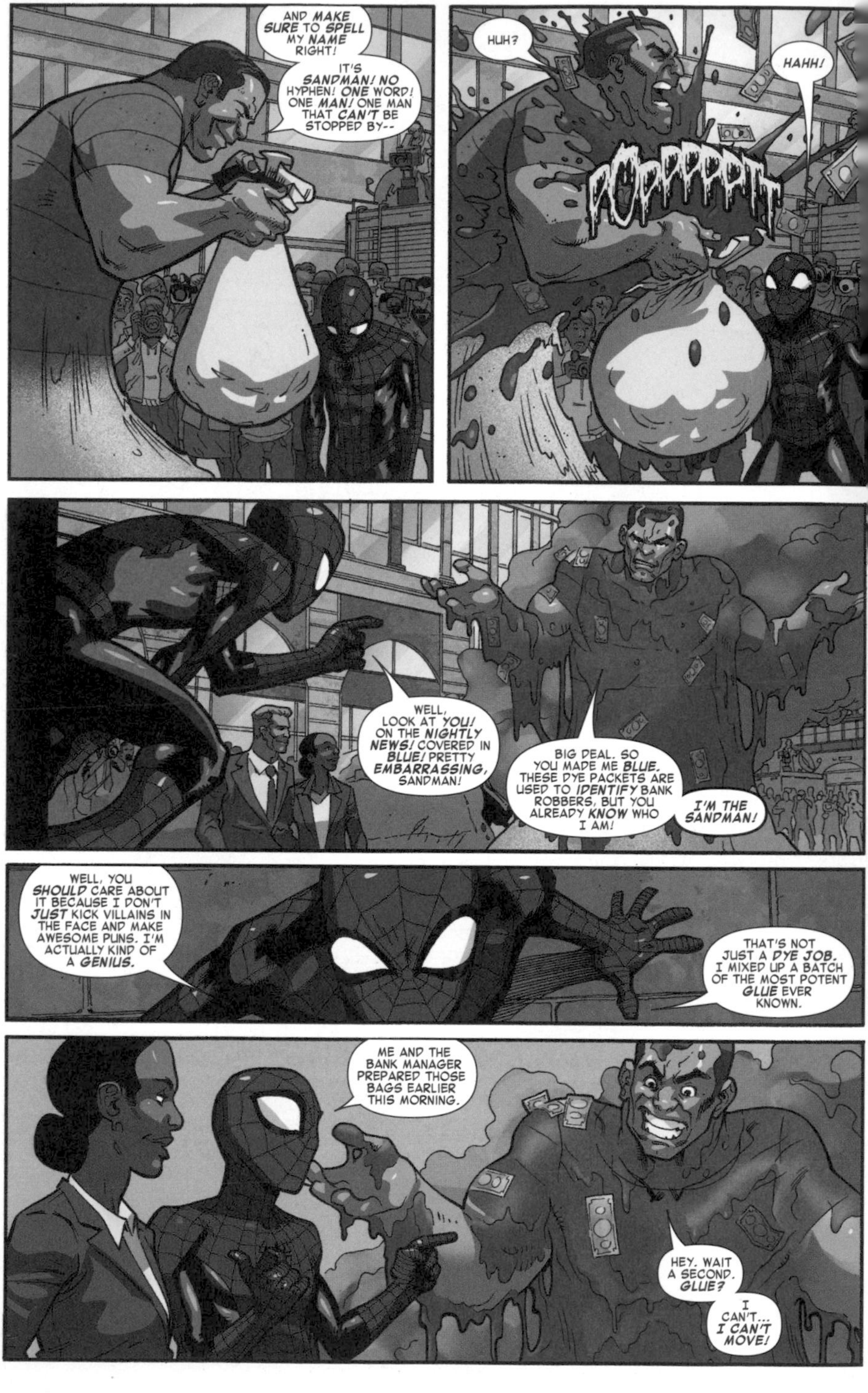
AND MAKE SURE TO SPELL MY NAME RIGHT!
IT'S SANDMAN! NO HYPHEN! ONE WORD! ONE MAN! ONE MAN THAT CAN'T BE STOPPED BY--
HUH?
HAHH!
POPPPPPT!
WELL, LOOK AT YOU! ON THE NIGHTLY NEWS! COVERED IN BLUE! PRETTY EMBARRASSING, SANDMAN!
BIG DEAL. SO YOU MADE ME BLUE. THESE DYE PACKETS ARE USED TO IDENTIFY BANK ROBBERS, BUT YOU ALREADY KNOW WHO I AM!
I'M THE SANDMAN!
WELL, YOU SHOULD CARE ABOUT IT BECAUSE I DON'T JUST KICK VILLAINS IN THE FACE AND MAKE AWESOME PUNS. I'M ACTUALLY KIND OF A GENIUS.
THAT'S NOT JUST A DYE JOB. I MIXED UP A BATCH OF THE MOST POTENT GLUE EVER KNOWN.
ME AND THE BANK MANAGER PREPARED THOSE BAGS EARLIER THIS MORNING.
HEY. WAIT A SECOND. GLUE?
I CAN'T... I CAN'T MOVE!

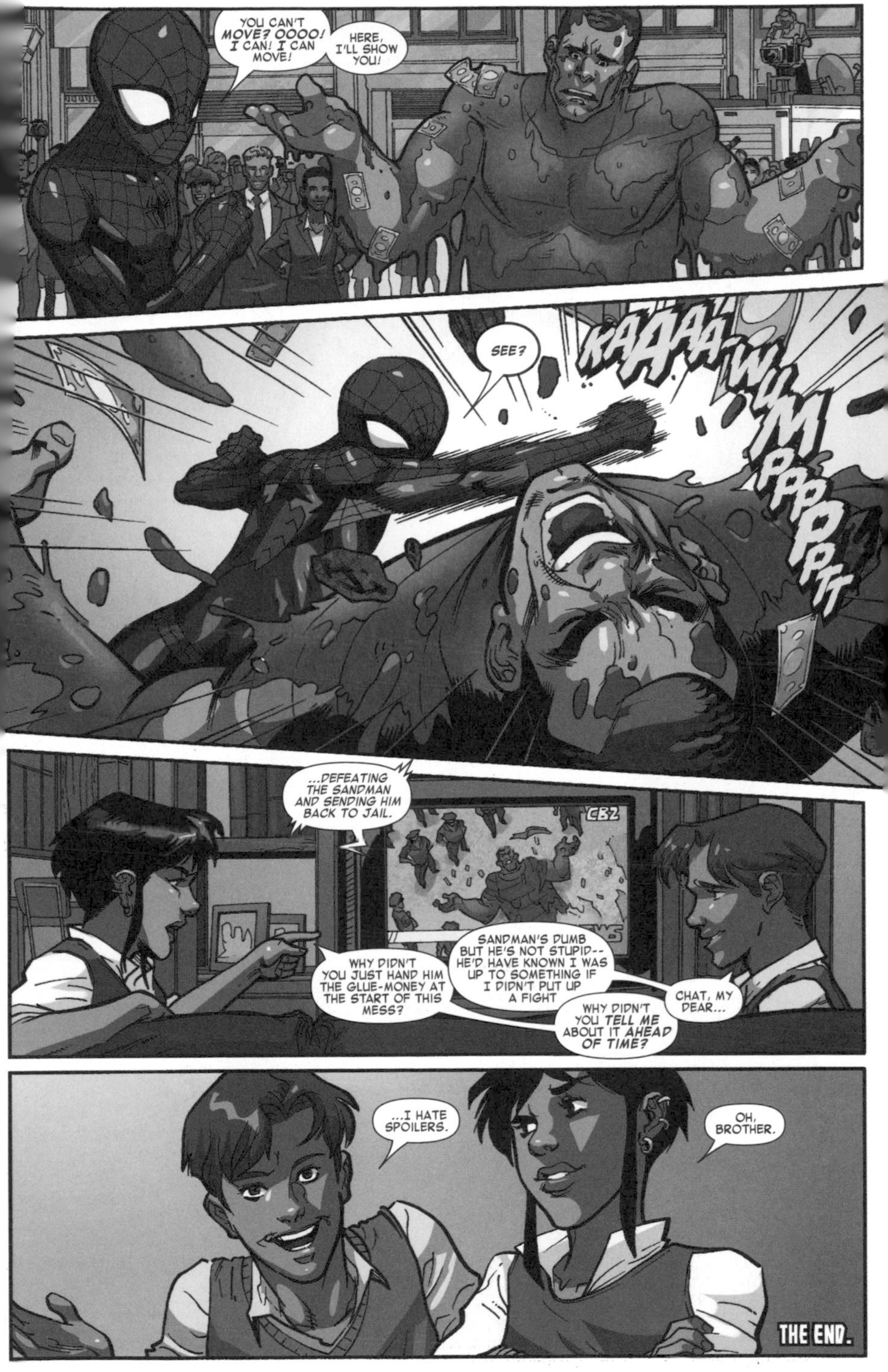
YOU CAN'T MOVE? OOOO! I CAN! I CAN MOVE!
HERE, I'LL SHOW YOU!
SEE?
KAAAA-WUMPPPPTT
...DEFEATING THE SANDMAN AND SENDING HIM BACK TO JAIL.
CB2
WHY DIDN'T YOU JUST HAND HIM THE GLUE-MONEY AT THE START OF THIS MESS?
SANDMAN'S DUMB BUT HE'S NOT STUPID--HE'D HAVE KNOWN I WAS UP TO SOMETHING IF I DIDN'T PUT UP A FIGHT
CHAT, MY DEAR...
WHY DIDN'T YOU TELL ME ABOUT IT AHEAD OF TIME?
...I HATE SPOILERS.
OH, BROTHER.
THE END.

WALLOPING WEB-SWINGERS! SPIDEY'S IN COMBAT WITH THE RED GHOST AND HIS SUPER-APES! MIKHLO, THE SUPER-STRONG GORILLA, HAS RIPPED UP THE STREET!
IGOR THE BABOON CAN CHANGE SHAPES!
PEOTR THE ORANGUTAN CAN CONTROL GRAVITY!
AND ALL THE WHILE THE RED GHOST WILL JOKE FROM THE SIDELINES ABOUT SQUISHING A SPIDER!
HA! TIME TO SQUASH YOU LIKE THE SPIDER YOU ARE!
SADDLE UP, SPIDER-FANS, AS THE AMAZING SPIDER-MAN FACES...
JUNGLE EVIL!
PAUL TOBIN WRITER ROB DI SALVO PENCILS
VICTOR OLAZABA INKS SOTOCOLOR COLORS
DAVE SHARPE LETTERER TOM BRENNAN EDITOR

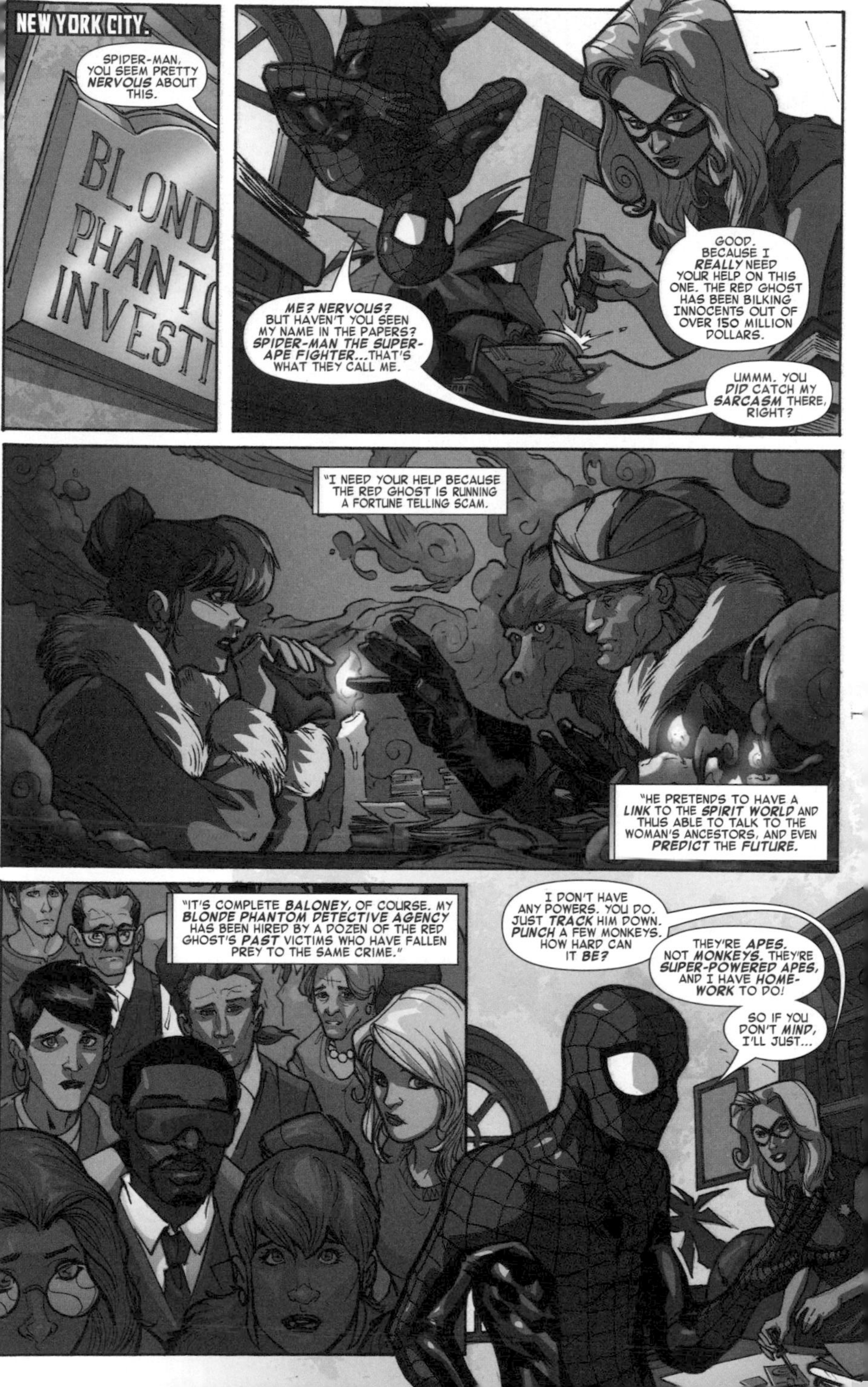
NEW YORK CITY.
SPIDER-MAN, YOU SEEM PRETTY NERVOUS ABOUT THIS.
BLOND PHANTO INVESTI
ME? NERVOUS? BUT HAVEN'T YOU SEEN MY NAME IN THE PAPERS? SPIDER-MAN THE SUPER-APE FIGHTER...THAT'S WHAT THEY CALL ME.
GOOD. BECAUSE I REALLY NEED YOUR HELP ON THIS ONE. THE RED GHOST HAS BEEN BILKING INNOCENTS OUT OF OVER 150 MILLION DOLLARS.
UMMM. YOU DID CATCH MY SARCASM THERE, RIGHT?
"I NEED YOUR HELP BECAUSE THE RED GHOST IS RUNNING A FORTUNE TELLING SCAM.
"HE PRETENDS TO HAVE A LINK TO THE SPIRIT WORLD AND THUS ABLE TO TALK TO THE WOMAN'S ANCESTORS, AND EVEN PREDICT THE FUTURE.
"IT'S COMPLETE BALONEY, OF COURSE. MY BLONDE PHANTOM DETECTIVE AGENCY HAS BEEN HIRED BY A DOZEN OF THE RED GHOST'S PAST VICTIMS WHO HAVE FALLEN PREY TO THE SAME CRIME."
I DON'T HAVE ANY POWERS. YOU DO. JUST TRACK HIM DOWN. PUNCH A FEW MONKEYS. HOW HARD CAN IT BE?
THEY'RE APES. NOT MONKEYS. THEY'RE SUPER-POWERED APES, AND I HAVE HOME-WORK TO DO!
SO IF YOU DON'T MIND, I'LL JUST...

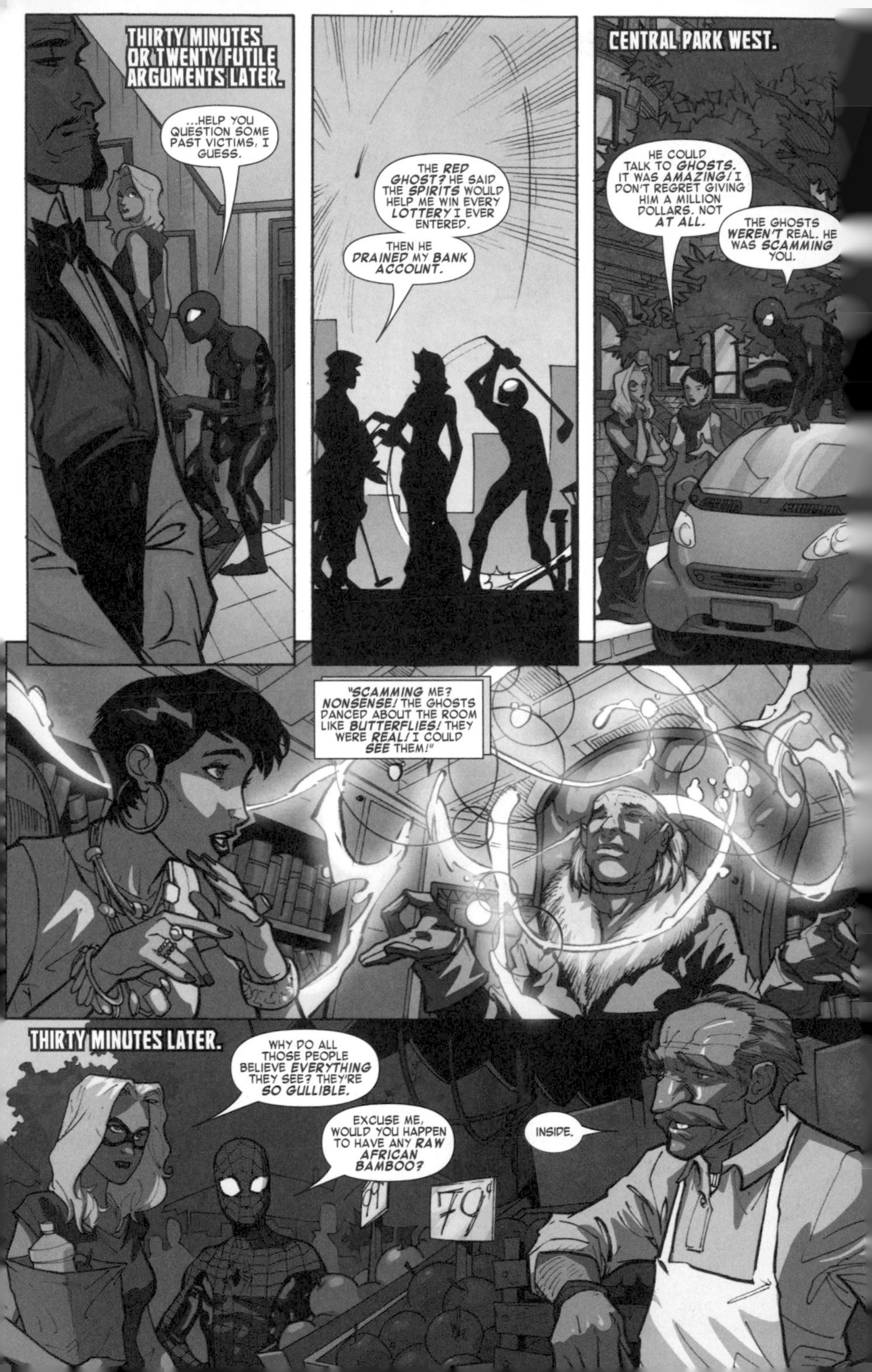
THIRTY MINUTES OR TWENTY FUTILE ARGUMENTS LATER.
...HELP YOU QUESTION SOME PAST VICTIMS, I GUESS.
THE RED GHOST? HE SAID THE SPIRITS WOULD HELP ME WIN EVERY LOTTERY I EVER ENTERED.
THEN HE DRAINED MY BANK ACCOUNT.
CENTRAL PARK WEST.
HE COULD TALK TO GHOSTS. IT WAS AMAZING! I DON'T REGRET GIVING HIM A MILLION DOLLARS. NOT AT ALL.
THE GHOSTS WEREN'T REAL. HE WAS SCAMMING YOU.
"SCAMMING ME? NONSENSE! THE GHOSTS DANCED ABOUT THE ROOM LIKE BUTTERFLIES! THEY WERE REAL! I COULD SEE THEM!"
THIRTY MINUTES LATER.
WHY DO ALL THOSE PEOPLE BELIEVE EVERYTHING THEY SEE? THEY'RE SO GULLIBLE.
EXCUSE ME, WOULD YOU HAPPEN TO HAVE ANY RAW AFRICAN BAMBOO?
INSIDE.
79¢

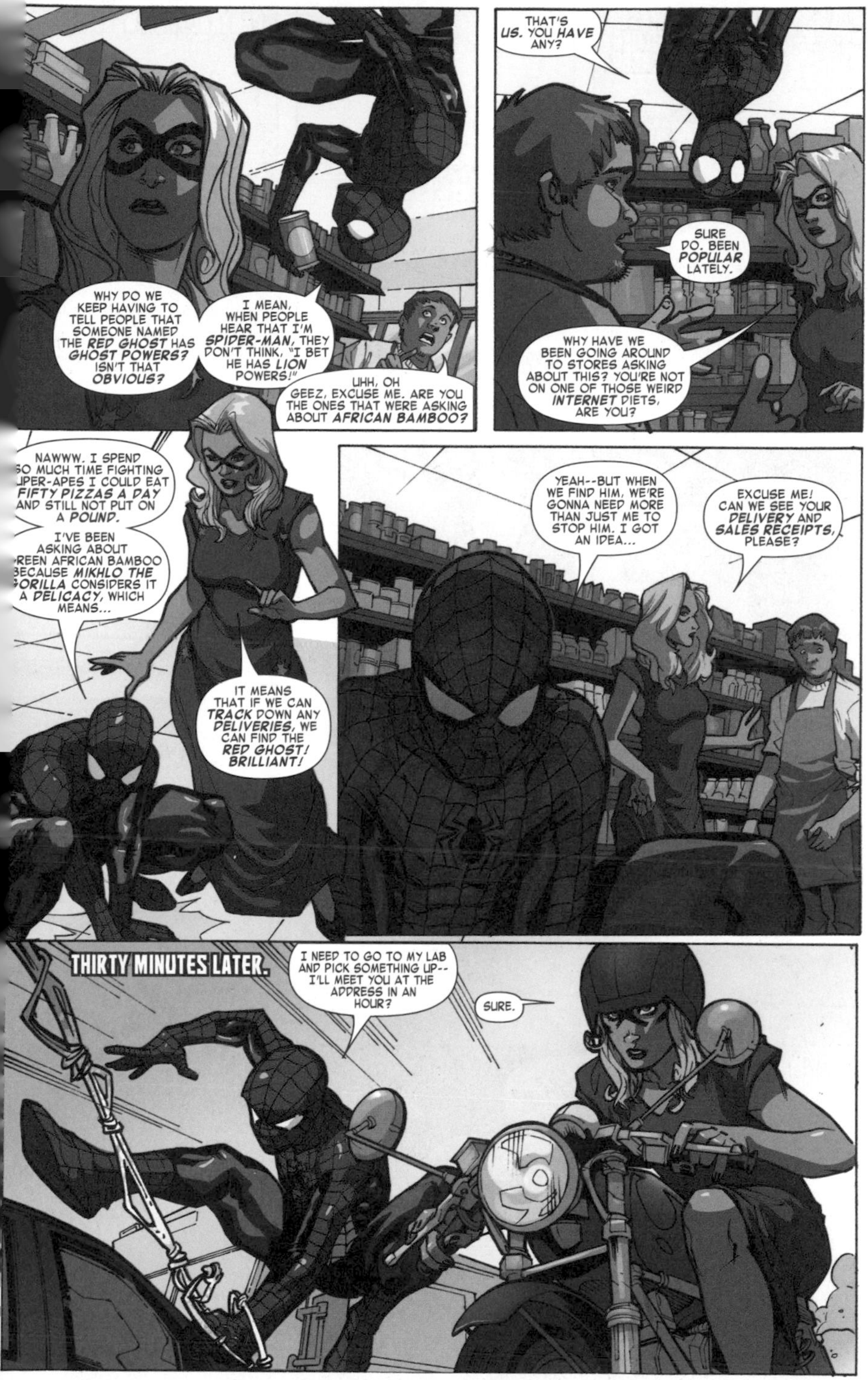
WHY DO WE KEEP HAVING TO TELL PEOPLE THAT SOMEONE NAMED THE RED GHOST HAS GHOST POWERS? ISN'T THAT OBVIOUS?
I MEAN, WHEN PEOPLE HEAR THAT I'M SPIDER-MAN, THEY DON'T THINK, "I BET HE HAS LION POWERS!"
UHH, OH GEEZ, EXCUSE ME. ARE YOU THE ONES THAT WERE ASKING ABOUT AFRICAN BAMBOO?
THAT'S US. YOU HAVE ANY?
SURE DO. BEEN POPULAR LATELY.
WHY HAVE WE BEEN GOING AROUND TO STORES ASKING ABOUT THIS? YOU'RE NOT ON ONE OF THOSE WEIRD INTERNET DIETS, ARE YOU?
NAWWW. I SPEND SO MUCH TIME FIGHTING SUPER-APES I COULD EAT FIFTY PIZZAS A DAY AND STILL NOT PUT ON A POUND.
I'VE BEEN ASKING ABOUT GREEN AFRICAN BAMBOO BECAUSE MIKHLO THE GORILLA CONSIDERS IT A DELICACY, WHICH MEANS...
IT MEANS THAT IF WE CAN TRACK DOWN ANY DELIVERIES, WE CAN FIND THE RED GHOST! BRILLIANT!
YEAH--BUT WHEN WE FIND HIM, WE'RE GONNA NEED MORE THAN JUST ME TO STOP HIM. I GOT AN IDEA...
EXCUSE ME! CAN WE SEE YOUR DELIVERY AND SALES RECEIPTS, PLEASE?
THIRTY MINUTES LATER.
I NEED TO GO TO MY LAB AND PICK SOMETHING UP-- I'LL MEET YOU AT THE ADDRESS IN AN HOUR?
SURE.

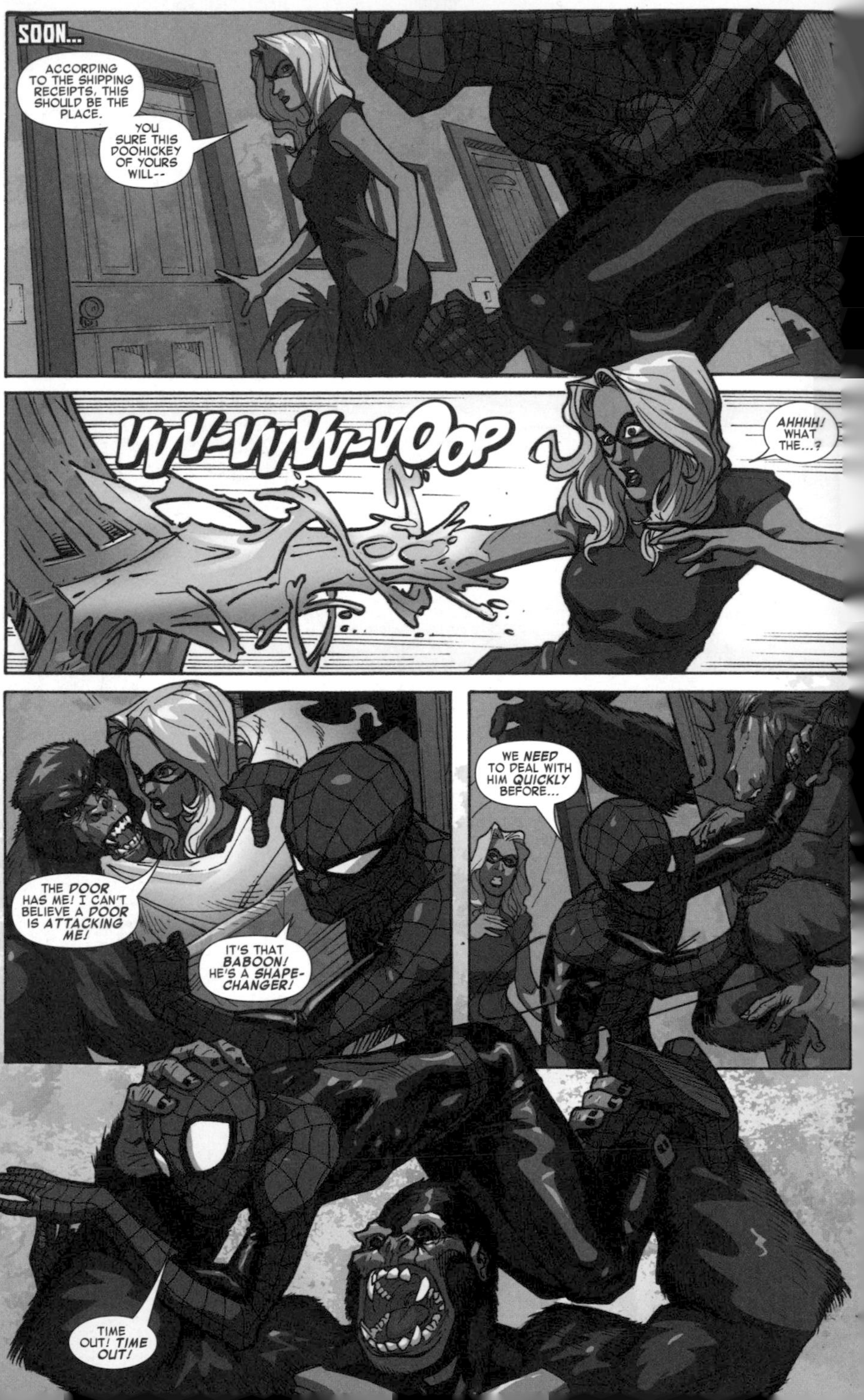
SOON...
ACCORDING TO THE SHIPPING RECEIPTS, THIS SHOULD BE THE PLACE.
YOU SURE THIS DOOHICKEY OF YOURS WILL--
VVV-VVVV-VOOP
AHHHH! WHAT THE...?
THE DOOR HAS ME! I CAN'T BELIEVE A DOOR IS ATTACKING ME!
IT'S THAT BABOON! HE'S A SHAPE-CHANGER!
WE NEED TO DEAL WITH HIM QUICKLY BEFORE...
TIME OUT! TIME OUT!

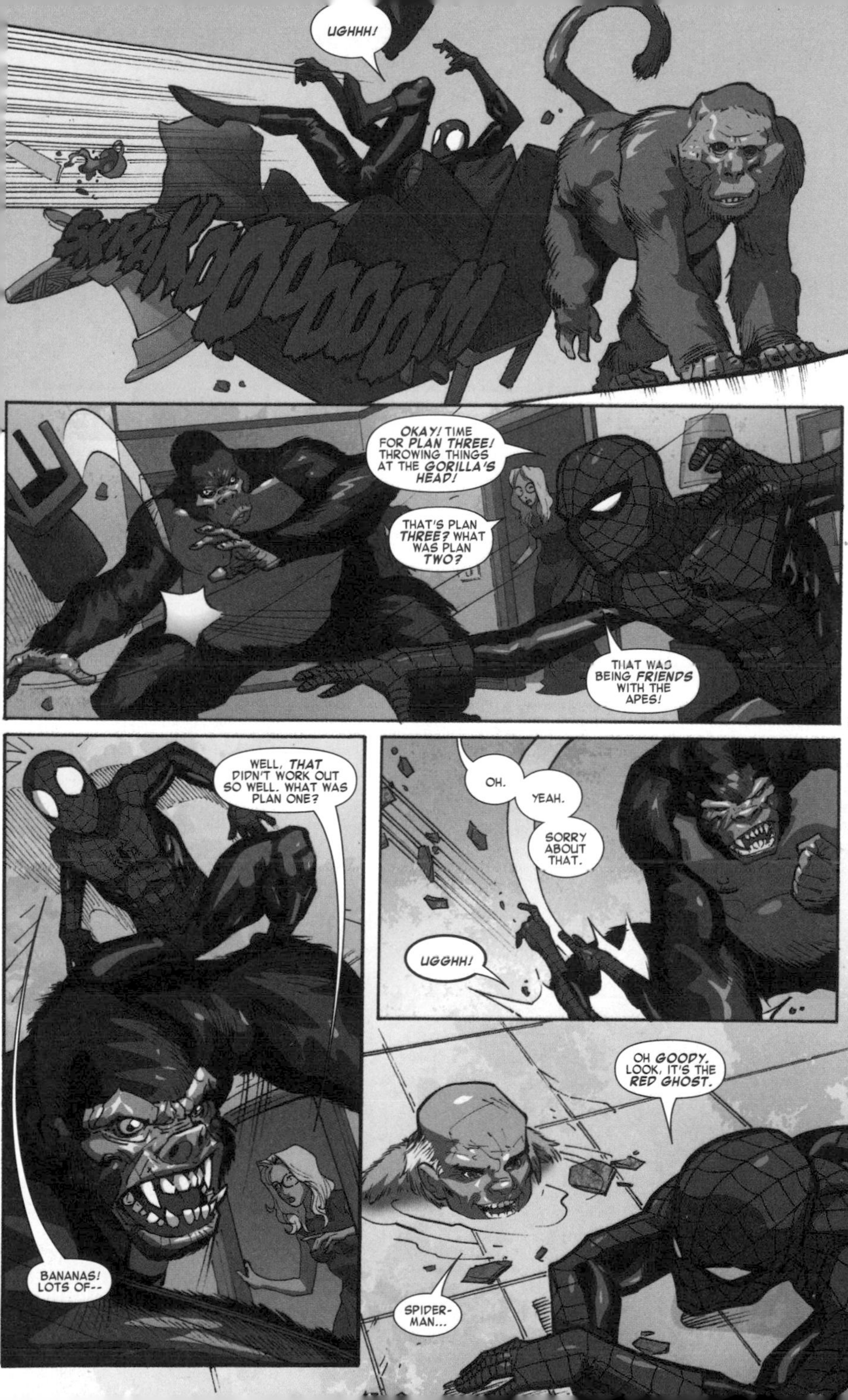
UGHHH!
SKRAKOOOOOOOM
OKAY! TIME FOR PLAN THREE! THROWING THINGS AT THE GORILLA'S HEAD!
THAT'S PLAN THREE? WHAT WAS PLAN TWO?
THAT WAS BEING FRIENDS WITH THE APES!
WELL, THAT DIDN'T WORK OUT SO WELL. WHAT WAS PLAN ONE?
BANANAS! LOTS OF--
OH.
YEAH.
SORRY ABOUT THAT.
UGGHH!
OH GOODY. LOOK, IT'S THE RED GHOST.
SPIDER-MAN...

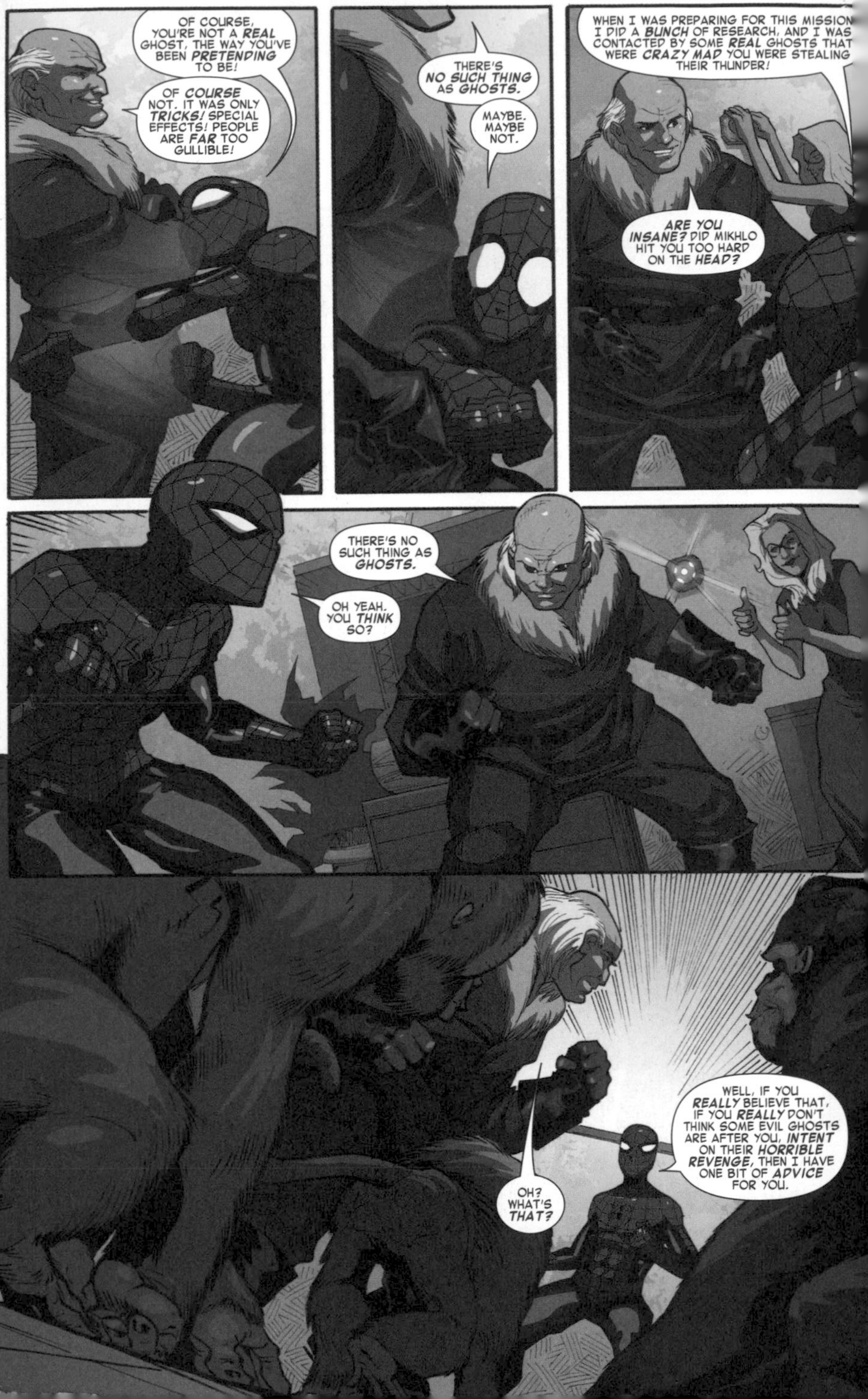
OF COURSE, YOU'RE NOT A REAL GHOST, THE WAY YOU'VE BEEN PRETENDING TO BE!
OF COURSE NOT. IT WAS ONLY TRICKS! SPECIAL EFFECTS! PEOPLE ARE FAR TOO GULLIBLE!
THERE'S NO SUCH THING AS GHOSTS.
MAYBE. MAYBE NOT.
WHEN I WAS PREPARING FOR THIS MISSION I DID A BUNCH OF RESEARCH, AND I WAS CONTACTED BY SOME REAL GHOSTS THAT WERE CRAZY MAD YOU WERE STEALING THEIR THUNDER!
ARE YOU INSANE? DID MIKHLO HIT YOU TOO HARD ON THE HEAD?
THERE'S NO SUCH THING AS GHOSTS.
OH YEAH. YOU THINK SO?
WELL, IF YOU REALLY BELIEVE THAT, IF YOU REALLY DON'T THINK SOME EVIL GHOSTS ARE AFTER YOU, INTENT ON THEIR HORRIBLE REVENGE, THEN I HAVE ONE BIT OF ADVICE FOR YOU.
OH? WHAT'S THAT?

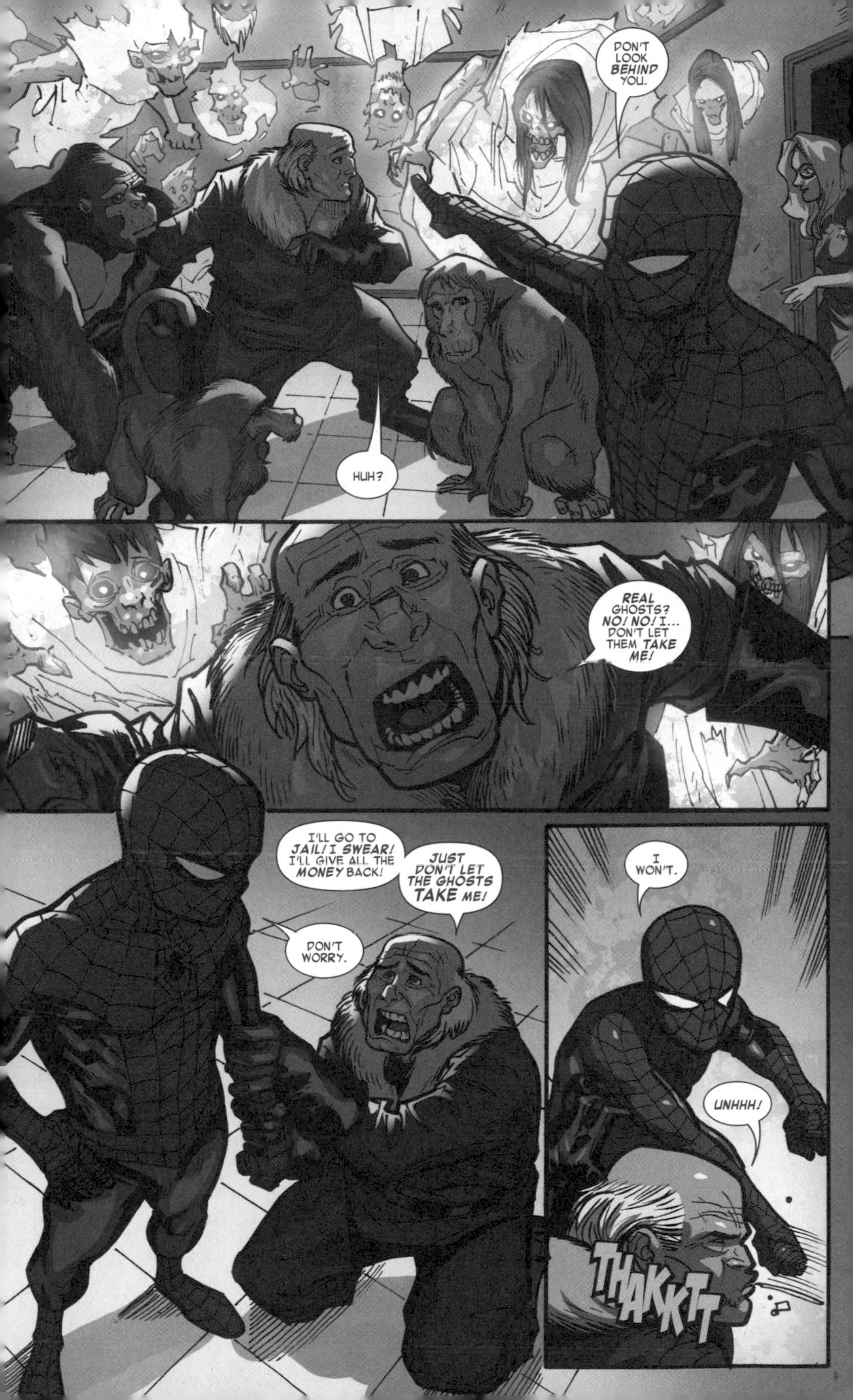
DON'T LOOK BEHIND YOU.
HUH?
REAL GHOSTS? NO! NO! I... DON'T LET THEM TAKE ME!
I'LL GO TO JAIL! I SWEAR! I'LL GIVE ALL THE MONEY BACK!
JUST DON'T LET THE GHOSTS TAKE ME!
DON'T WORRY.
I WON'T.
UNHHH!
THAKKTT

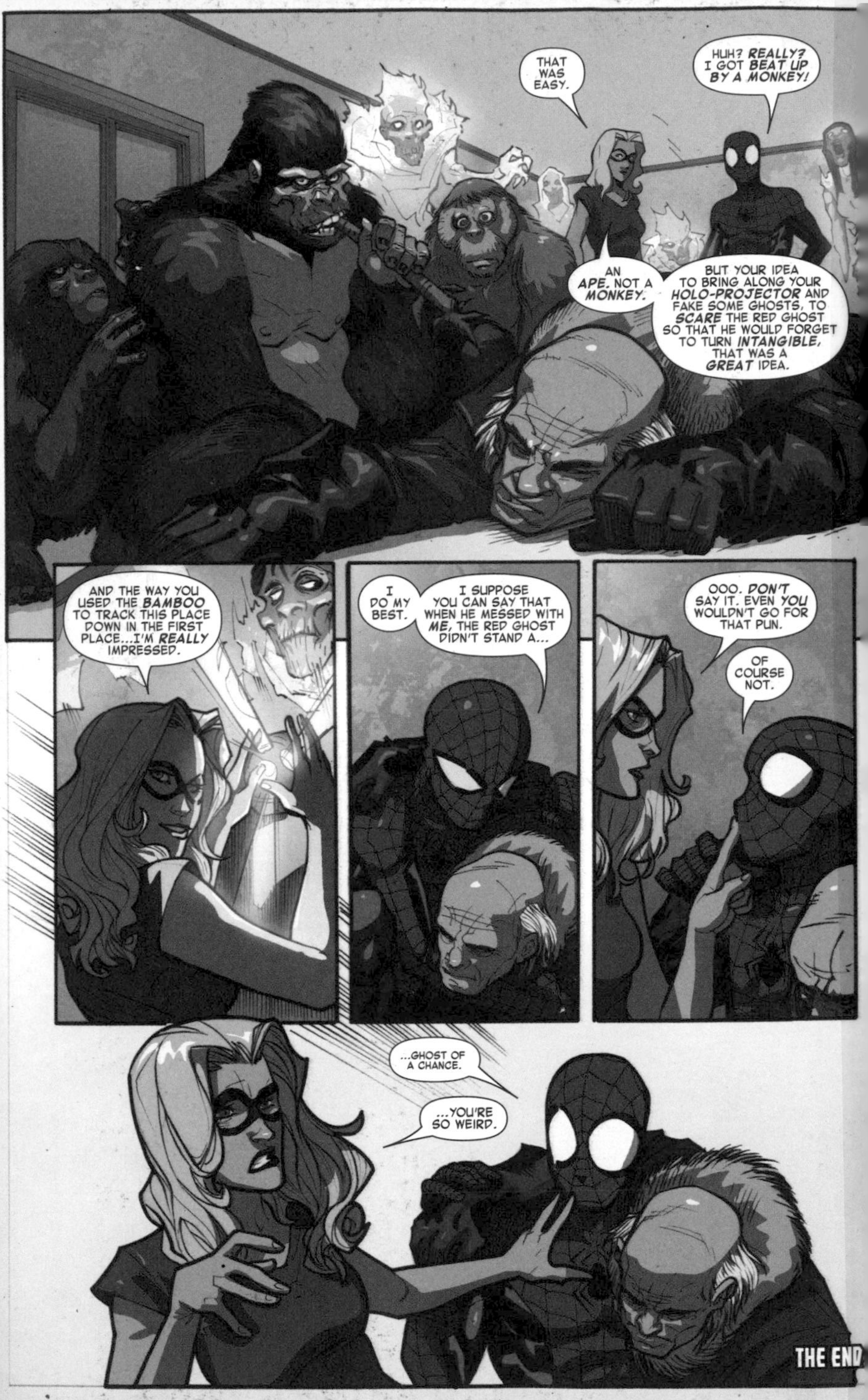
THAT WAS EASY.
HUH? REALLY? I GOT BEAT UP BY A MONKEY!
AN APE. NOT A MONKEY.
BUT YOUR IDEA TO BRING ALONG YOUR HOLO-PROJECTOR AND FAKE SOME GHOSTS, TO SCARE THE RED GHOST SO THAT HE WOULD FORGET TO TURN INTANGIBLE, THAT WAS A GREAT IDEA.
AND THE WAY YOU USED THE BAMBOO TO TRACK THIS PLACE DOWN IN THE FIRST PLACE...I'M REALLY IMPRESSED.
I DO MY BEST.
I SUPPOSE YOU CAN SAY THAT WHEN HE MESSED WITH ME, THE RED GHOST DIDN'T STAND A...
OOO. DON'T SAY IT. EVEN YOU WOULDN'T GO FOR THAT PUN.
OF COURSE NOT.
...GHOST OF A CHANCE.
...YOU'RE SO WEIRD.
THE END